Spirituality in
Young Adult Literature

Studies in Young Adult Literature
Series Editor: Patty Campbell

Studies in Young Adult Literature is intended to continue the body of critical writing established in Twayne's Young Adult Authors series and to expand it beyond single-author studies to explorations of genres, multicultural writing, and controversial issues in young adult (YA) reading. Many of the contributing authors of the series are among the leading scholars and critics of adolescent literature, and some are YA novelists themselves. The series is shaped by its editor, Patty Campbell, who is a renowned authority in the field, with a forty-year background as critic, lecturer, librarian, and teacher of YA literature. Patty Campbell was the 2001 winner of the ALAN Award, given by the Assembly on Literature for Adolescents of the National Council of Teachers of English for distinguished contribution to YA literature. In 1989 she was the winner of the American Library Association's Grolier Award for distinguished service to young adults and reading.

22. *Sharon Creech: The Words We Choose to Say*, by Mary Ann Tighe, 2006.
23. *Angela Johnson: Poetic Prose*, by KaaVonia Hinton, 2006.
24. *David Almond: Memory and Magic*, by Don Latham, 2006.
25. *Aidan Chambers: Master Literary Choreographer*, by Betty Greenway, 2006.
26. *Passions and Pleasures: Essays and Speeches about Literature and Libraries*, by Michael Cart, 2007.
27. *Names and Naming in Young Adult Literature*, by Alleen Pace Nilsen and Don L. F. Nilsen, 2007.
28. *Janet McDonald: The Original Project Girl*, by Catherine Ross-Stroud, 2008.
29. *Richard Peck: The Past Is Paramount*, by Donald R. Gallo and Wendy Glenn, 2008.
30. *Sisters, Schoolgirls, and Sleuths: Girls' Series Books in America*, by Carolyn Carpan, 2009.
31. *Sharon Draper: Embracing Literacy*, by KaaVonia Hinton, 2009.
32. *Mixed Heritage in Young Adult Literature*, by Nancy Thalia Reynolds, 2009.
33. *Russell Freedman*, by Susan P. Bloom and Cathryn M. Mercier, 2009.
34. *Animals in Young Adult Fiction*, by Walter Hogan, 2009.
35. *Learning Curves: Body Image and Female Sexuality in Young Adult Literature*, by Beth Younger, 2009.
36. *Laurie Halse Anderson: Speaking in Tongues*, by Wendy J. Glenn, 2010.
37. *Suzanne Fisher Staples: The Setting Is the Story*, by Megan Lynn Isaac, 2010.
38. *Campbell's Scoop: Reflections on Young Adult Literature*, by Patty Campbell, 2010.
39. *Donna Jo Napoli: Writing with Passion*, by Hilary S. Crew, 2010.
40. *John Marsden: Darkness, Shadow, and Light*, by John Noell Moore, 2011.
41. *Robin McKinley: Girl Reader, Woman Writer*, by Evelyn M. Perry, 2011.
42. *Immigration Narratives in Young Adult Literature: Crossing Borders*, by Joanne Brown, 2011.
43. *They Suck, They Bite, They Eat, They Kill: The Psychological Meaning of Supernatural Monsters in Young Adult Fiction*, by Joni Richards Bodart, 2012.
44. *Stephenie Meyer: In the Twilight*, by James Blasingame Jr., Kathleen Deakin, and Laura A. Walsh, 2012.
45. *Chris Crutcher: A Stotan for Young Adults*, by Bryan Gillis and Pam B. Cole, 2012.
46. *Portrait of the Artist as a Young Adult: The Arts in Young Adult Literature*, by Lois Thomas Stover and Connie S. Zitlow, 2013.
47. *Virginity in Young Adult Literature after Twilight*, by Christine Seifert, 2014.
48. *Sexual Content in Young Adult Literature: Reading between the Sheets*, by Bryan Gillis and Joanna Simpson, 2015.
49. *John Green: Teen Whisperer*, by Kathleen Deakin, Laura A. Brown, and James Blasingame Jr., 2015.
50. *Spirituality in Young Adult Literature: The Last Taboo*, by Patty Campbell with Chris Crowe, 2015.

Spirituality in Young Adult Literature

The Last Taboo

Patty Campbell
with Chris Crowe

ROWMAN & LITTLEFIELD
Lanham • Boulder • New York • London

Published by Rowman & Littlefield
A wholly owned subsidiary of The Rowman & Littlefield Publishing Group, Inc.
4501 Forbes Boulevard, Suite 200, Lanham, Maryland 20706
www.rowman.com

Unit A, Whitacre Mews, 26-34 Stannary Street, London SE11 4AB

British Library Cataloguing in Publication Information Available

Library of Congress Cataloging-in-Publication Data

NAME
INFO
p. cm. — (Studies in young adult literature ; no. 50)
Includes bibliographical references and index.
ISBNS
INFO
NUMBER
NUMBER
NUMBER

♾ ™ The paper used in this publication meets the minimum requirements of American National Standard for Information Sciences Permanence of Paper for Printed Library Materials, ANSI/NISO Z39.48-1992.

Printed in the United States of America

For David, my wise counselor, careful proofreader, and best friend.—PC

For my wife, Elizabeth, the best and most spiritual reader I know.—CC

Contents

Acknowledgments

I would like to thank Barb Dean, who took part in the early formative stages of this book. I am indebted to her broader spiritual perspective and for many enlightening moments. I would also like to thank Chris Crowe for stepping up to the plate in the last inning and for providing an interesting new dimension to this book.—PC

Many thanks to Patty Campbell for bringing the discussion of religion and spirituality to the study of YA literature years ago and for conceiving this long overdue and noteworthy project. I admire her insight and wondrous breadth of knowledge in these two fields, and I'm grateful to have played a small part in this book.—CC

Introduction

The Last Taboo[1]

In the prevailing culture, priority is given to the outward, the immediate, the visible, the quick, the superficial, and the provisional. What is real gives way to appearances.—Pope Francis[2]

Ever since Judy Blume gave us a penis named Ralph,[3] young adult (YA) authors are free to write—and have written—graphic scenes of both homo- and heterosexual love, bloody violence, cruelty to animals, and even incest, without a qualm. They can even get away with an occasional "shit" or "fuck" right there in print. Yet there is one subject that is carefully avoided by writers and publishers, a topic that is a last taboo. Young adult literature, which is distinguished by its devotion to issues of emotional, sexual, ethical, and psychological maturation, is also distinguished by its lack of devotion to issues of—devotion. Faith and belief in God seldom appear in traditional form in novels for teens.

YA author Pete Hautman commented on this situation in an interview with Joel Shoemaker in *VOYA* magazine:

> I am not a person of faith, but I think that the topic of religion is underserved in YA literature. I'll be writing at least one more book about it for teens. It's a big subject. Most writers want nothing to do with it because any mention of religion in any context is a sales killer. How many YA books have you read in which the protagonist's relig-

ion—or lack thereof—is never mentioned or even hinted at? Almost all
of them, I bet. Don't you find that rather odd?[4]

He goes on to say that the religious aspects of his novel *Godless* were a
"sales killer"—until it won the National Book Award.

Yet struggling with issues of spirituality and making one's own
peace with them is an important part of growing up. The basic teen
questions are "Who am I?" and "What am I going to do about it?"—
and a third question might be "Is anybody in charge around here?" But
the lack of spirituality in mainstream adolescent literature is a statement that can be interpreted by teens to mean that these matters are not
important or not part of other young people's thoughts.

Why are such ideas so scarce in YA literature? Why have so few
YA authors had the gumption and the theological literacy to write
about those spiritual questions that are so intensely private but so intensely troubling and important to many teens? The answer is not to be
found in blaming American culture for a lack of interest in faith. The
Gallup Poll reported in 2011 that 92 percent of Americans say they
believe in God, and 50 percent of those admit that God is very important in their lives.[5] And a survey reported in *Reuters* claimed that
"some research asserts that younger generations show greater levels of
religious adherence than the baby boomers, many of whom brought up
their children in a non-religious environment."[6]

A survey done by the Pew Research Center in 2013 found that 37
percent of Americans said that they attend church weekly, and an additional 33 percent do so at least monthly.[7] Of course, some of the re-
spondents probably lied about such a sensitive subject (a phenomenon
that polltakers call "overreporting"), but still it is impressive that when
these figures are added up, they tell us that the proportion of regular
churchgoers in America is probably around 60–70 percent.

Yet YA "realistic" fiction projects a world in which both the personal and the corporate practice of religion are absent, except for the
worst aspects of cults or fundamentalist sects. The picture of American
religious life that emerges from YA fiction is unrecognizable. First, the
stories take place in a society in which no one thinks about going to
church on an ordinary Sunday. Occasionally one of these fictional families will make a ritual visit to a church on Christmas or Easter, but as if
they are going to a performance rather than participating in worship.
Even in stories set in areas of the country where the presence of the
church is pervasive—Appalachia, the South, small towns in the Mid-

west Bible Belt—the characters are not involved in any religious institution unless a fundamentalist villain is necessary to the plot. And beyond Sunday services, where in all YA fiction are the church youth groups, the Hebrew or confirmation classes, the Bible study meetings that are so much a part of middle-class teenage American life? Where, too, is the mainstream liberal Protestant, Catholic, or Jewish practice and sensibility? And where are the good clergy or church people acting out their faith in service and love?

Parents in books of this church-negative type are usually either gullible fanatics or unbelievers who are obstacles to their child's religious interests. It seldom occurs to teens in YA fiction who are undergoing crises such as a friend's death, parents' divorce, illness, rape, or disfigurement to call on God for help. When young adults in fiction do search for God with diligence, it often turns out badly, with the loss of the young person's faith, although this is sometimes presented by the author as a step toward maturity.

"Religious doubts are part of the maturation process," observe Alleen Pace Nilsen and Kenneth Donelson in *Literature for Today's Young Adults*.[8] True, but how can teens be helped to confront and work through those doubts when the whole question of faith in God is for the large part unacknowledged in the books they trust to explain their world to them? Religious inquiry is certainly a preoccupation almost as important as sex for many young people, but it is by nature an extremely private matter, so they are not likely to share their spiritual questions with friends or—God forbid!—parents. Young adult fiction is in danger of leaving readers with the impression that they are the only ones with such questions and feelings.

Of course, there are a number of paperback fiction series published for teens by the religious press in which faith issues are addressed. Many of these publishing houses are affiliated with particular denominations, and the quality of their publications has improved enormously in recent years. However, the didactic intent of these books puts them outside the scope of this study. Here we are analyzing only the output of mainstream American publishers.

What accounts for this overwhelming secularity in even fine YA novels? The fear of transgressing the boundary between church and state has been mentioned as an underlying cause, although certainly this is a misunderstanding of constitutional principles. On this subject the Constitution says only "Congress shall make no law respecting an establishment of religion, or prohibiting the free exercise thereof"[9] —a statement that cannot possibly be interpreted to mean that religion is outside the allowed legal limits of literature.

A more realistic fear underlies the reluctance of publishers and writers to risk cutting into potential markets by offending readers with differing beliefs. However, YA fiction has dealt quite freely with the politics of abortion and the creation versus evolution controversy, the two so-called Christian issues most likely to offend certain segments of the population.

Librarians have, through bitter experience, come to associate religion with censorship attempts, and thus find the whole subject suspect. Literature that "proselytizes" has long been excluded from library collections—but how are we to decide when a book fits that definition? "Proselytize" doesn't apply to anything and everything that mentions religion.

The underlying problem, of course, is that there are so few writers who are willing to talk to teenagers about God, even indirectly, or who themselves have the religious literacy for the task. The distorted picture of the inner dialogue of young adults leaves a huge gap where God-consciousness, or at least spiritual search, might be.

However, some authors of current and past YA fiction have dealt with the spiritual struggle with honesty and integrity. We can rejoice that there are at least a few creators of YA literature who are willing to acknowledge the existence of that important reality. Among older writers Madeleine L'Engle, Chaim Potok, Sonia Levitin, and Robert Cormier come immediately to mind, and more recently Han Nolan, David Almond, Donna Freitas, Pete Hautman, Deborah Heiligman, Francisco X. Stork, and John Green are at least a few of the authors who have written YA novels that acknowledge the spiritual dimension of existence. Stork, speaking at the 2012 conference of the Assembly on Adolescent Literature, explained his commitment to writing about religion:

> I believe you should write about things you care about, and so religion and its manifestations around the world has always been something I loved. . . . I write about what I really care about—all my books have a religious element therefore. I have so many questions about this . . . there is so much mystery to this subject and it is such an important part of the important things in life . . . so I find I integrate these matters. . . .
>
> This sense of censorship authors feel when they are writing about religion. . . . They are conscious that they might be seen as preaching, so to have a character who is very human utter some real truths . . . takes

away from this sense of preachiness. . . . I try to make my books not didactic—I do this by creating characters with concerns that are rooted in the[ir] personalit[ies].[10]

On the same panel, Deborah Heiligman responded: "I believe in writing about what you want to know. I want to figure things out and it's often about religion."

The enormously popular John Green has been articulate in speeches and online about his own personal religious background and beliefs. In a blog post from September 23, 2008, that inspired—and is still inspiring—hundreds of responses from his fans he wrote:

> I don't talk about it very often, but I'm a religious person. In fact, before I became a writer, I wanted to be a minister. There is a certain branch of Christianity that has so effectively hijacked the word "Christian" that I feel uncomfortable sometimes using it to describe myself. But I am a Christian.[11]

Indeed, as Green acknowledges, in our overwhelmingly secular society any serious reference to God is regarded by many people as hopelessly outdated, delusional, or silly. Talk of God the Father Almighty or Jesus Christ outside of church services, even among alleged Christians, has become an embarrassment or a joke, and puts one in danger of being seen as simple minded, a religious nut, or at the least, politically far right. Contestants on television quiz or "reality" shows shout "Oh, my God!" at every favorable development, without the slightest intention of contacting the Deity. The invocation has even been reduced online to an acronym—OMG—in the ultimate casual use of the name of the Eternal. So is it any wonder that references to God and to Jesus Christ are so scarce in YA novels? For the large part, the spiritual dimension remains unmentionable in this literature.

Some of the ideas that try to fill this gap in the genre are pop concepts of the supernatural such as guardian angels, good and bad devils, visitors from beyond the grave—and fantasy. Fantasy literature can quite easily be interpreted as a metaphor for the spiritual search, with its dichotomy of good and evil and its heroic quest toward the possession of a miraculous object that determines the future of the world. Fantasy, at least high fantasy, is inherently spiritual, in that the movement of the plot is nearly always toward a showdown between good and evil. World-shaking happenings, vast landscapes, and unspeakable evil are negotiated by the hero with the help of an impossibly old and impossibly wise counselor. Along the way the Good Guys—our protagonists—struggle to prevail over obstacles and conflicts, each trying to become worthy of being the standard-bearer of Goodness in the final battle.

The popularity of the genre with teens is no coincidence. I would guess from the sales figures of fantasy that teens are hungry for the ineffable. Perhaps religion as it has been presented to them seems too ordinary, too "daily." Could it be that what they are seeking, what they will respond to, are the mystical dimensions of faith, the otherworldly? Are they, like the rest of us, yearning to move in thought beyond the confines of daily existence to that which is inexplicable, mind-stretching, more beautiful than earthly beauty, outside of time and space, and more real than what we call reality? Acting on that likelihood, I have examined in this study not only realistic YA fiction, but YA literature that deals with the mystical. Topics such as apocalyptical end times, mysticism, and the divine encounter have potentially high teen appeal and can lead young people to spiritual insights. So I have pointed out some areas of this kind that YA fiction might explore, as well as discussing the books that have already done so.

In addition, the divine may creep into the story as allegory or metaphor, in the shape of redeeming love or ultimate realization of a truth. In many cases writers of YA fiction have substituted other faces of the Ultimate: a profound respect for nature, or a realization of universal love, or even the redeeming nature of a loyal friendship. In the adolescent experience, there are many turning points in the form of a conversation with a friend, a teacher, or a parent, or a book, a line of poetry, a song lyric, or a moment of realization of truth or self-knowledge where the divine breaks through. These moments are inherently spiritual, and such turning points are at the heart of many YA novels. Perhaps the broadest perspective on this matter has come from Sue Tait, the former Coordinator of Young Adult Services at Seattle Public Library, a YA critic who also has a divinity degree. "The quest for the sacred," she writes, "informs much of young adult literature, although often under other names."[12]

But the reluctance of YA writers and publishers to deal with specific matters of religious faith remains and has been pointed out in articles, interviews, and reviews. Now it is time to ask what progress, if any, has been made in slaying the taboo. What authors have had the conviction and the theological literacy to struggle with those spiritual questions that are so intensely private but so intensely troubling and important to thoughtful teens?

Answering that question is the purpose of this book. I have tried to point out trends in depicting, or not depicting the spiritual, and I have tried to highlight books that I think are not only fine teen literature but have been outstanding in integrating spiritual ideas into the plot. Conversely, in the first chapter I have presented books that mostly take a negative position toward church and clergy. Throughout this study I have tried to confine my examples to twenty-first-century YA fiction, with a few exceptions, and I have made an attempt to gather in books from several different faiths. For a comprehensive list of YA books since 1967 containing ideas of spirituality, see the appendix for a bibliography I call Godsearch. My Mormon coauthor, critically esteemed YA novelist Chris Crowe, has added a chapter and a bibliography about Mormon values and Mormon YA authors and how their novels integrate those values. His words round out this study of what we hope may soon become "The Former Last Taboo."

NOTES

1. Parts of this chapter have previously appeared in Patty Campbell, "The Sand in the Oyster," *Horn Book* (September/October 1994): 619–23; Patty Campbell, "The Sand in the Oyster," *Horn Book* (May/June 2004): 353–56; Patty Campbell, "Godsearch: Issues of Faith in Young Adult Fiction," *Literature and Belief* (January 2010): 47–60.

2. Pope Francis, *The Joy of the Gospel:* Evangelii Gaudium, Publication/United States Conference of Catholic Bishops (New York: Image Books, 2013), 32.

3. Judy Blume, *Forever* (New York: Bradbury, 1975).

4. Joel Shoemaker, "Speaking the Truth to Teens," *VOYA* (June 2013): 15.

5. "Poll: 9 in 10 Americans Still Believe in God," *Huffington Post*, June 6, 2011. Accessed March 29, 2014, huffingtonpost.com/2011/06/06/belief-in-god-poll_n_872059.html.

6. Daniel Lippman, "Young Americans More Loyal to Religion Than Boomers," *Reuters*, August 6, 2010. Accessed March 29, 2014, reuters.com/article/2010/08/06/us-religion-idUSTRE67556L20100806.

7. Michael Lipka, "What Surveys Say about Worship Attendance—and Why Some Stay Home." Pew Fact Tank, September 13, 2013. Accessed March 29, 2014, www.pewresearch.org/fact-tank/2013/.

8. Alleen Pace Nilsen and Kenneth Donelson, *Literature for Today's Young Adults*, 6th ed. (New York: Longman, 2001).

9. The Constitution of the United States of America, Amendment I (New York: ACLU, n.d.), 23.

10. Panel on Spirituality, Adolescent Literature Workshop, National Conference of Teachers of English, November 20, 2012, Las Vegas, Nevada.

11. John Green, "Faith and Science," Accessed September 1, 2014, http://www.youtube.com/watch?v=Lht_JH2xi6w.

12. Private correspondence with the author, December 2, 1991.

Chapter One

Church and Clergy, Mostly Negative

A young person who is an honest spiritual seeker will have a hard time finding models for that search in YA fiction's portrayal of Christian clergymen and women or traditional church congregations. Almost half of the books that deal with spiritual matters do so by presenting Christian institutions and leaders in a negative light (see appendix). While it is tempting to dismiss these characters and situations as mere stereotypes, it is unfortunately true that in real life unholy words and actions of some church leaders and their followers appear frequently in the news—and in YA fiction. The ordinary folks who try to live their faith in kindness and good works are not news—and they don't make for exciting scenes in fiction. The ranting cult leader, the abusive priest, the hurtful words from the pulpit and the pews, the book censorship and burnings are what attract our attention and come to characterize the church in the minds of many.

Active lay members of a church, on the few occasions when they appear as such in YA novels, are often presented as despicable in direct proportion to the degree of their ecclesiastical commitment. Church congregations nearly always act as a negative force in the plots. Their members are pictured as small-minded, given to malicious gossip and meanness, homophobic, and often involved in hate-mongering and censorship attempts—which, it must be admitted, provides material for some dramatic and involving scenes.

NEGATIVE PORTRAYALS OF CHURCH CONGREGATIONS

An example might be the censorship confrontations in *The Sledding Hill* by Chris Crutcher.[1] In this semiautobiographical novel, teen Eddie Proffit resists the banning of a book, *Warren Peece*, a fictional work by a real author—Chris Crutcher. A teacher and a librarian support the book but are opposed by Reverend Tarter and his Youth for Christ. An impassioned testimony by Eddie the day before at church, a fierce plea by a Goth girl for the book at the hearing, as well as a cameo appearance by Chris himself, carry the day.

Another oft-cited example from an older YA novel is the self-righteous and malicious congregation of a small-town church in Bette Greene's *The Drowning of Stephan Jones*.[2] The outspoken homophobia of these Arkansas Baptists inspires some tough locals to beat gay newcomer Stephan and throw him in the river, where he drowns.

In *Send Me Down a Miracle* by Han Nolan,[3] Charity Pittman defends a woman who claims to have seen Jesus by confronting the congregation of her fundamentalist preacher father and the rest of the small Southern town where they live.

An extreme example of a demented cult is seen in Linda Crew's *Brides of Eden: A True Story Imagined*.[4] In 1903 in the tiny town of Corvallis, Oregon, an itinerant preacher, Franz Creffidd, gathers a group of passionate disciples, mostly women. Among them are twelve-year-old Eva Mae, her older sister Maud, and their mother. Creffidd leads them all to a summer on an island, where they wear their hair loose, go barefoot, and pray all day, rolling on the ground. Predictably, the preacher seduces Eva and the others, one by one. Their mad devotion grows, even when he is tarred and feathered by the local townspeople. Later he is jailed for adultery, and the girls and women are sent to insane asylums, where they seem to recover. But when Creffidd is released from jail, they again return to him. He deserts them, taking Eva's sister Maud with him. Word comes that he has been shot and killed, but they doggedly await his resurrection.

NEGATIVE PORTRAYALS OF PROTESTANT CLERGYMEN

If the congregations are deluded and malicious, their leaders are even worse. An early example is the charismatic but treacherous "Preacher Man" from Cynthia Rylant's *A Fine White Dust*.[5] Pete, a young teen growing up in a small town, likes church and goes to services by himself because his parents don't; they are alarmed and embarrassed by their son's attraction to church attendance. When the Preacher Man comes to preside at a Revival meeting, Pete is saved and gloriously born again. Entranced with the evangelist and convinced it is God's will, he agrees to the man's invitation to run away from home and travel with him. Pete sneaks out one night to meet the Preacher Man at the train station, but he never shows up, leaving the abandoned boy devastated and disillusioned about his faith.

Once Was Lost by Sara Zarr[6] is full of a young girl's anger at her minister father, whom she feels spends more time, energy, and perhaps love, with his congregation than with her and her mother.

Muchacho

Young Eddie Corazon, who tells us his story in *Muchacho* by LouAnne Johnson,[7] describes the effect the town's passive support of a book-burning has had on his religious attitudes.

> After that preacher burned all the books, I stopped going to church because the whole town knew he was going to do it and they didn't even stop him. He and some of his church friends went to the store and bought a bunch of Harry Potter and Shakespeare books and burned them up. They didn't even read them first. They said they didn't have to read them to know they were full of witchcraft and Satanism. And a whole bunch of other people went and stood by the book-burning preacher. (*Muchacho*, 98)

Another look at Eddie in *Muchacho* shows that he is still a spiritual seeker although he has dropped out of church. He talks about his ideas in a chapter titled "Googling God"—because that is what his smart girlfriend has done. (She tells Eddie that God "has so many hits that it will take her years to read them all" [*Muchacho*, 97].) When he thinks about the preacher who led the book-burning, he is surprised that the man wasn't arrested or kicked out of the church. "They just let him keep on going around talking about Jesus like him and Jesus were best friends or something" (*Muchacho*, 99–100). Eddie is very clear as to what being best friends with Jesus would look like.

> He should stop talking about going to hell all the time and just go around acting like he is Jesus. Not wearing a white dress and Birken-stocks all the time, but like if he had one of those families in his

neighborhood who lives in a falling-down trailer with no electricity and
all kinds of junk in the yard, he wouldn't sell his house and move to a
nicer neighborhood. He would just go down real quiet to the electric
company and apply to have that family's power turned on and he would
take them some bags of real delicious food and not just a cardboard box
full of canned beans and peas with dust on the top because people had
them in the back of their cupboard for ten years before they donated
them to the food bank. Or if he saw that crazy lady who sits outside the
library with all her stuff in a bag, he would go over and give her a
hundred dollars and say a prayer for her and hug her even if she stinks a
little bit. And he wouldn't tell anybody he did that stuff. He would just
do it nice and quiet. (*Muchacho*, 99–100)

This passage, in its quiet wisdom, might give direction to young God-
seekers who have been disillusioned with a church and are looking
elsewhere for spiritual guidance.

Long Gone Daddy

A spectacularly awful but devoted father and clergyman is drawn with
affection by Helen Hemphill in the delightful road trip novel *Long
Gone Daddy*.[8] It's 1972 and Reverend Harlan P. Stank, the father of
fifteen-year-old Harlan Quinton Stank, is the pastor of the Sunnyside
Savior Church in Bean's Creek, Texas. Paps is a dedicated Bible-
thumping preacher, and every Sunday he tells his congregation that
they are a sorry lot of sinners. Harlan Q says, "All my life, Paps had
preached to everyone about everything; he never gave it a rest" (*Gone*,
14). And he never gives praying a rest either, addressing the Lord in a
loud voice not only on ceremonial occasions and before meals, but at
every turn of events, no matter where or when. Toward his son he uses
prayer as a weapon, and Harlan Q has had enough of it. Four months
ago he told Paps that he had given up on religion, and Paps made it
clear that "if Harlan wanted to live in his house, he needed to find God
pretty darn quick" (*Gone*, 8).

   So now Harlan works and lives at the Hamilton-Johnston Funeral
Home, where nice Mr. Hamilton is teaching him the business, and his
wife Isa Faye's cooking is powerful. "Rumor had it that her coconut
cream pie could make a man bawl like a baby" (*Gone*, 10). So Harlan Q
is pretty much content, until one day the corpse of his long gone Granddaddy shows up in the prep room of the funeral business. This man had
abandoned his son when his wife—and Paps' mother—died, and he
never came back. But now he has returned—and turned up dead one

day later at the Wayfarer Motel without contacting his son and grandson.

There's nothing else for it but that Harlan Q goes to the funeral, listens to Paps preach hellfire about the father he never knew and bitterly resents, and gives in to his mother's entreaties to stay for lunch. The meal is not comfortable, especially when Harlan chokes on a bite of roll and is only rescued from asphyxiation by the coincidental arrival of the sheriff, who administers the Heimlich maneuver. Paps, with his usual obliviousness toward his son's feelings, has not even noticed that Harlan was in distress, but he's right there afterward giving loud thanks to God for saving him.

The sheriff, and a call to Grandfather's lawyer Johnny Stiletto, informs them that a $50,000 annuity and a brand new Eldorado Cadillac have been left to them, but only if they fulfill Grandfather's last wish—to be taken back to his home in Las Vegas and buried there. At first Paps refuses to take the inheritance—"That money could be the direct result of gambling or drinking or drugs. We do not have any idea what human suffering was caused to get hold of that money and that Cadillac" (*Gone*, 37). But then Harlan Q, who is dying to go to Las Vegas, has a brilliant idea. He plays it up big: "What if God's saying, 'Harlan P, take that money and do good. Save souls and serve the Lord. . . . You need your own radio show, Paps. I think God wants you to . . . start your very own radio revival right over the airwaves. God's working through me, Paps! I feel it! I feel it!" (*Gone*, 39).

Paps loves it. They fill Grandfather's now odiferous corpse with more formaldehyde, put his coffin in a wooden crate, wedge it into the church's big station wagon—and off they go on the road to Vegas, a place Paps continues to deplore. The first day out, they pick up a passenger to help with the driving—a long-haired, tattooed, Zen hippie named Warrior, or Warren. And now the fun begins. Warrior is, like Harlan Q, a PK, or preacher's kid, who is also on a rebellious spiritual journey to figure out what he believes. On the way he has picked up a smattering of exotic religions like Zen Buddhism and Native American nature worship and is busy putting together a stew of spiritual concepts and practices that suit his quest. Paps takes on his salvation with gusto. He tells Harlan privately, "The Lord has offered us up a lamb, and we need to help him find his soul" (*Gone*, 74). But Warrior can hold his own. Back and forth they spar as the miles go by, Warrior with his dimly understood Buddhist sayings, and Paps with his formulaic Bible quotes. Both are good-natured about the dialogue, but neither is willing

to give an inch. Harlan Q listens from the backseat with annoyance and
apprehension. Early in the debate, Warrior actually makes Paps smile.

> "The Bible is just a lot of nice stories to me, man. Scripture forces your
> life energy into one way of thinking. Nothing personal, but I just don't
> relate."
>   "We would just hate to see you in Hell, Warren," Paps said.
>   "I'd hate for you to see me there, too, Reverend," Warrior said. . . .
> "'Cause that would mean we both fell a little short of our plans." (*Gone*,
> 78)

Later, when they discover that Warren has a photographic memory
and can quote any New Testament Bible verse from memory, Paps has
lost his best weapon, so he changes his angle of attack. He asks Warren
directly what moved him away from God. His answer is crucial to both
Paps and Harlan in understanding their own tangled relationship—if
only they had been listening.

> "I wanted to decide on my own about God and faith, but my father
> wouldn't let me. . . . It was his way or the highway. And when he put it
> like that, the highway looked pretty good." . . .
>   Finally, Paps spoke. "Warren, do you love your father?". . .
>   "Yes, I do," Warrior said. "But it's not about love or hate, man. It's
> about acceptance. I try to accept him as he is and hope he can do the
> same for me someday."
>   Paps glanced over at Warrior. "You are wrong, Warren. It is very
> much about love. If your father accepts you as you are, you will be lost
> forever. Your soul will be damned for eternity. He cannot give up on
> you. Not if he really loves you."
>   Warrior leaned over to Paps. "Maybe my dad would do a lot better
> to just love me unconditionally." Warrior's voice was real low, and I
> had to lean forward to hear him. "You know, you can't bully someone
> into believing, Reverend." (*Gone*, 98–99)

Harlan, unaware that his father has just revealed the intensity of his
love for him, hears only that he and Warren are both on the run. He
decides to get the fifty thousand dollars somehow, and join Warren on
his flight. The journey goes on with many revelations about all three
pairs of fathers and sons. When they reach Las Vegas, they discover
that Grandfather owned a popular bar, and this is enough to once again
turn Paps away from accepting the money. Harlan decides to secretly
step into the gap and take the cash, but in the end his scheme blows up
in his face. We ache and rejoice for Harlan, applaud Warrior, and

forgive Paps, and even like him sometimes in this wise and funny story about spiritual search.

NEGATIVE PORTRAYALS OF
CATHOLIC PRIESTS AND NUNS

Following the continuing scandals about misuse of power and sexual abuse by priests in the Roman Catholic Church, several YA novels have been written that reflect this disturbing reality. The point of view is usually that of a friend of the victim, which avoids the problem of dealing with a graphic scene of abuse, and the abuser is a villain, with no attempt by the author to justify his actions.

Stained, by Jennifer Jacobson,[9] was an early attempt at using such scandals in YA fiction. As I wrote in an Amazon editorial review:

> It's 1975 and the world is in the midst of the Sexual Revolution. Except not in Weaver Falls, where seventeen-year-old Jocelyn's boyfriend Benny wrestles with guilt over their passionate lovemaking in the woods. When Benny tells her he has bargained with God to swap their relationship in exchange for his dying mother's life, and that popular Father Warren has counseled him that Jocelyn is of the devil, she feels that her soul is stained—not a new emotion for her. Although as a small child she perceived the sunlit colors of the stained glass windows in St. Mary's as God's blessing, her mother's divorce ten years ago has estranged both of them from the Catholic church and Jocelyn from the other kids at school. The relentless teasing all through her childhood by her same-age next door neighbor Gabe has left her feeling even more rejected. But now Gabe is missing and the whole town turns out to search for him day after day, as the parents grieve. . . . After a near-rape when she was twelve, Jocelyn has kept her distance from Gabe, but now she can still draw on that invisible cord that used to bind them to follow clues to his whereabouts and try to comfort his shame that he has succumbed to Father Warren's sexual demands.[10]

The next year a more complex novel by Chris Lynch turned on the same issue. *Sins of the Fathers*[11] was succinctly analyzed by Carolyn Lehman in *School Library Journal*:

> Three teens—friends since their first day in Catholic school—tease, pummel, and support one another in this story set in a working-class Boston diocese. The narrator, Drew . . . is a skeptical observer of the ways that power plays out in the classroom and church; fatherless Skitz

is one of those kids who is not going to stay in the system much longer; and Hector—well, something is really eating at Hector, the devout Altar Boy of the Year. . . . Fathers Blarney, Mullarkey, and Shenanigan, as the boys call them, have an inordinate hold over their lives, both in school and beyond. . . . As Drew's awareness of the priests' fallibility grows, so does the eerie sense that one of the priests is harming Hector in secret—and that the abuse may be sexual. This vivid, fast-paced, hard-hitting novel is no diatribe; instead it conveys with texture and conviction the damage that young people can be subjected to when adult influence goes unchecked.[12]

This Gorgeous Game[13]

While these priests, or at least one of them, are clearly pedophiles, the stalker priest in *This Gorgeous Game* is more subtle. Author Donna Freitas has done a masterful job of capturing the arrogance of his abuse of power and the growing isolation and terror of his victim.

When Olivia Peters, seventeen, wins first prize in a young writers' competition sponsored by the celebrity author-priest Father Mark Brendan, she is overjoyed at the award, and even more so by the acknowledgment and extravagant praise from the tall, strikingly handsome, and charming Father Mark. Her mother and her best friends Jada and Ashley are thrilled that he invites her to editorial consultations with him at a bar or a coffee shop nearly every day.

But soon these friends, and her new crush, beautiful Jamie, begin to feel neglected, as Father Mark takes up more and more of Olivia's time with meetings, emails, phone calls, texts, and gala writers' events. Olivia, on the other hand, is flattered and pleased with his attention, feeling that "he's becoming a true mentor with an almost Dad-like interest in my well-being and success" (*TGG*, 59). But "Dad-like" soon starts to feel like something more as Father Mark sends her expensive books, tucks letters inside her locker, slips notes under her front door. Each morning she wakes up wondering, "*What will he bring me, give me, ask me to do now?*" (*TGG*, 70). When she comes home from school one day to find him chatting with her mother in an impromptu visit, she begins to feel trapped. After he leaves, she realizes:

> I never say no to Father Mark. I go to everything he invites me to, do everything he asks of me, read everything he recommends, as if it's my new full-time occupation, becoming all mentored and improved and approved by him, so much so that lately I almost can't find time to do anything else, see anyone else. (*TGG*, 71)

Especially Jamie, who is becoming more and more important to her. So when Father Mark is rude and abrupt with the young man, she has a new insight into the priest's feelings toward her and decides to shut him out of her life for a time while she concentrates on her growing love for Jamie. Father Mark responds with a frenzy of phone calls, texts, emails, and letters, which she determinedly ignores. Finally he gives her a manuscript which he insists—and insists and insists—that she read. By this time Olivia is having trouble eating and sleeping. Her friends and family know that something is very wrong, but she has told them nothing of her fears about Father Mark, not even when it comes up at the dinner table that he has assigned some of his royalties to help reopen a church that has had to close because of accusations against an abusive priest.

Ironically, she goes to the chapel at her school to pray for help, even though she blames God for her situation. There she finds a sympathetic nun, Sister June, who gives Olivia the assurance that she will listen whenever Olivia wants to share what is troubling her so much. With this new courage, she at last gives in to Mark's pleas and reads the manuscript he has given her. She is horrified to find that he has written the story of their relationship as if they were lovers. Olivia summons the courage to write the true version. She shows both stories and the pile of letters, notes, emails, and texts to Jamie and her girlfriends, and through their support finds the strength she needs to recover her self-respect and her faith. Meanwhile, Father Mark slips out of town before Sister June can call in the church authorities.

The True Tale of the Monster Billy Dean

A priest in a different time and place, but equally malevolent, is Father Wilfred in David Almond's oddly titled *The True Tale of the Monster Billy Dean Telt by Hisself*.[14] The only cleric in the bomb-torn town of Blinkbonny, Father Wilfred casually seduces women in the confessional until one of them gets pregnant. She hides away during her pregnancy, and when Billy Dean is born, Father Wilfred demands that he be kept in a locked room so the secret won't get out. The story of his growth in confinement is written by Billy Dean in a strangely endearing phonetic script. He adores his father, and looks forward to his visits. But when the priest finally disappears, his mother allows Billy Dean to come out into the village. Eventually, in a shocking conclusion, the priest returns wearing the purple silk vest of a bishop and pays two thugs to kill the woman who keeps the secret that would damn him. When he tries to strangle his son, the boy stabs him to death.

Before we leave the subject of wicked priests, who could forget diabolical Brother Leon in Robert Cormier's classic *The Chocolate War*[15] and its sequel *Beyond the Chocolate War*?[16] Here is a man of God who is devoured by the love of power and cruelty. The elaborately decorated cross he wears—so contorted that it is hardly recognizable as a cross—becomes a symbol for his twisted soul. "The man of God who is not a man of God wears a cross that is not a cross."[17]

AND A RABBI

Intentions

Just to balance things out, here's one about a transgressing rabbi. Sixteen-year-old Rachel, in Deborah Heiligman's *Intentions*,[18] loves—no, adores—Rabbi Cohn. She describes him as:

> Middle-aged, nerdy, bushy-bearded, potbellied, Jewish Santa Claus–looking Rabbi Cohn. . . . He's . . . wise, kind, brilliant. . . . He might be the most perfect human being on the planet. (*Intentions*, 1)

Until the day she falls asleep in the rear of the temple and wakes up to hear him having sex with a woman—not his wife—by the bima, or altar. She is horrified, but she can't tell anyone—not her former best friend Alexis, who is acting more hateful and distant every day; or her almost-boyfriend Jake, whom she's growing to love; and certainly not bad-boy hottie Adam, the rabbi's son; or her mom, whom she suspects of having an affair with the rabbi herself. As the days go on, she carries her secret, and it poisons every one of the complex relationships in her life, until she betrays Jake by making out with Adam, and Alexis by setting her up for a shoplifting charge. She thinks, "What if the person you respect the most disappoints you beyond belief? What if that person is you?" (*Intentions*, 193).

At last two principles the rabbi had taught her—*tikkun olam*, "repairing the world," and *kavanah*, "intentionality"—guide her to confess her crime to the store manager and to confront the rabbi with his womanizing. These healing actions lead to a reconciliation with Jake and her parents, and even enable her to forgive the rabbi. And this heals her relationship with God, as we find out in a surprising but completely believable ending.

SYMPATHETIC PORTRAYALS OF CLERGY AND CHURCHES

It is still true that church and clergy usually get a bad rap in YA fiction, but in the last few years there has been a growing sophistication in portraying clerics. Whereas previously they were almost universally depicted as one-dimensional caricatures of pure evil, now there is a trend toward more depth in character development and more generosity in judging their motives.

Other Bells for Us to Ring[19]

Robert Cormier, who sometimes spoke of the hell he went through with nuns in parochial school, has chosen to make a nun—the ancient Sister Angela—the deliverer of spiritual truth and comfort in his most religious and least-known book, *Other Bells for Us to Ring.* Eleven-year-old Darcy is seeking some answers from God about the safety of her father, who is missing in action during World War II. Her prayers haven't helped, so she looks elsewhere. But the Catholicism of her best friend, Kathleen Mary, seems foreign and spooky to Protestant Darcy.

Here Cormier has achieved the difficult feat of stepping outside the practices of his religion to show them as they might appear to a naïve outsider. "'Everything about Kathleen Mary's Catholicism fascinated me,' Darcy thinks, 'as if Catholics were a different tribe of people who had somehow found their way to earth'" (*Bells*, 172). Kathleen Mary, always eager to put on a good show, holds her friend wide-eyed with colorful explanations of rules and rituals unfamiliar to Darcy: confession, Communion, purgatory, cardinal and venial sin—and the story of the man who ate meat on Friday and "choked to death. On the spot. Turned black and blue" (*Bells*, 172).

Through Kathleen Mary, Darcy learns about wise and elderly Sister Angela, who sits saying her rosary every afternoon in a secret courtyard garden in the convent. She is reputed to be able to work miracles, so Darcy braves the maze of hedges leading to the courtyard where Sister Angela sits, and confesses her fears and worries about Catholicism and her father's safety to the old nun. In a quiet scene suffused with afternoon sunlight and peace, Sister Angela helps Darcy to realize that loving and trusting God is all that matters, in spite of the hard truth that miracles sometimes happen and sometimes are denied.

"God comes first, you see," Sister Angela says. "Not whether you are this or that. Protestant or Catholic, young or old." Comforted, Darcy is reminded of the words she has heard from Unitarian Reverend Weems: "God takes care of us all, whether you know it or not. . . . And if you pray to him he will listen" (*Bells*, 173). And of course the father does come back safely—but somebody else dies. Cormier is too honest to ever allow a simple happy ending.

Leap of Faith[20]

Sometimes a clergyperson or a sympathetic parent can be the agent of salvation. In *Leap of Faith* by Kimberly Brubaker Bradley, Abby has stabbed a bully in self-defense, but because the boy is the principal's son, nobody—not even her parents—will believe that he has been sexually harassing her for a long time. She is expelled, and only St. Catherine's parochial school will have her. There she begins to find peace in church occasionally, although she doesn't believe in God. To annoy her parents, who are militant atheists, she decides to become a Catholic. The mother of her best friend drives her to confirmation classes and gives her wise counsel, as does the priest. Through acting in drama class she finds herself, and through wanting to believe she is finally able to take the leap of faith.

The Tent[21]

Another character who makes that leap, but without help from the church, is found in Gary Paulsen's *The Tent*. A boy, Steven, and his father, Corey, are tired of being poor. Corey gets an old tent and sets out to preach on the road, although he has no religious convictions. When two shills join them to fake healing miracles, the cash rolls in. But Corey has been reading the Gideon Bible he found in a hotel room, and eventually he realizes that they are acting a lie and stealing from believers. So he and his son decide to truly preach the word of God—but for no money.

Quaking

Once in a long while YA fiction shows the church as a force for good. The Quakers, or the American Friends, are in actuality an indigenous religious group who have acted out their commitment to peace and thereby had an effect on history. *Quaking* by Kathryn Erskine is a YA novel that features the healing power of a peace-loving Quaker community.[22] Matt has been sent to the foster home of a Quaker couple, sweet big Sam and loving Jessica, and their other foster child, retarded Rory. Matt is profoundly angry and withdrawn because she has been abused in the past, she is being bullied at school, and a militaristic teacher has made her afraid to express her antiwar convictions. But the Quakers and other churches in the town are active for peace, even though they draw attacks for their beliefs. Gradually the warmth and caring of her new family melts Matt's anger and she is able to accept and give back peace and love.

Wide Awake

Another book that shows a Christian group as a power for beneficial social change is the almost-fantasy by David Levithan *Wide Awake*.[23] In the near future, Duncan and his boyfriend Jimmy are jubilant when a gay Jew, Abraham Stein, wins the presidency. So are teenage Jesus Freaks Mandy and Janna, part of the Jesus Revolution that has made this possible. But the vote in Kansas is questioned by the governor, and a recount begins. Stein asks his supporters to come to Kansas and keep vigil at the state capitol. Although Duncan's parents are reluctant, he goes to the vigil on a bus with other friends and college kids and a teacher. At first the crowds wait peacefully, but soon the opposing groups are shouting angry slogans at each other. As tensions rise, Jesus Freak Janna offers some of their food to the hungry children of the opposition, and the parents strike back in anger. The incident is caught on TV and a flood of public opinion turns the tide—and the election—in Stein's favor.

Asylum for Nightface

An important but strange and ambiguous book, *Asylum for Nightface* by Bruce Brooks,[24] combines a wide range of these themes—cults, the charismatic leader with dubious goals, the adolescent search for authenticity in religious faith, the lack of help in that search from church or clergy, and the parents who oppose and then embrace their child's spiritual direction. The story has many complex aspects, so here we will devote ourselves only to those plot threads that relate to the subject of this chapter.

Zimmerman, a young boy named for Bob Dylan, has discovered God on his own by noticing the orderly design underlying creation, much to the discomfort of his intellectual parents. When he is praying in his room they "shuffle back and forth in the hallway" and aim "intense beams of curiosity and alarm through the green-painted wood" (*AFN*, 8). All this changes when the parents go off to Jamaica on vacation and are converted to the Faith of Faiths, a religious sect with a charming leader who calls himself Luke Mark John. They return ecstatic, but full of abject apologies and deference to their son for what they regard as his "stunning foresight in finding 'The Christ Jesus' years ago" (*AFN*, 66). Zimmerman is humiliated and furious with this awkward role reversal, but at the same time glad that they have found God. He accepts even the peculiar excesses of their new religion and their groveling adulation of Luke Mark John because he is convinced that loving any part of the design "is really loving the whole deal" (*AFN*, 39). He waits in wistful expectation for his parents to be ready to talk to him about their conversion. When his overtures meet only embarrassed avoidance, he is disappointed. Instead he tries to engage the Spiffies—his private term for the fundamentalist kids at his school—but soon finds that "they refuse to come out from behind their slogans" (*AFN*, 22). Meanwhile, Luke Mark John has been observing Zimmerman and has decided that he is a living saint, perfect to become the poster boy and leader of youth to Faith of Faiths. Zimmerman is appalled by the proposed role, but his parents are overjoyed by the prospect. When Zimmerman realizes he is sliding irresistibly toward Luke Mark John's power, he finds a way to discredit himself in a crime that ends the story in maddening ambiguity.

But beyond all this stylistic razzle-dazzle, the heart of the novel is Zimmerman's quite straightforward exposition of his faith. Brooks has given his character's beliefs a specific and coherent theological structure, in marked contrast to the fragmentary musings of the few other spiritual seekers in YA fiction. In a sense, he has become his own priest, his own church. Zimmerman sees God in the design of things and finds this revelation obvious. "Finding God is the easiest thing in the world. . . . Noticing what I call the designing is as involuntary as breathing. . . . Our natural curiosity is always sensing orderliness underneath it all, always looking for connections, always being amazed or mystified and then inquisitive" (*AFN*, 23). A love of all creation and its separate parts is a logical consequence. But much as he would like to share his faith, he does not look for a congenial church because "when it comes to my own love of God I dislike symbol, metaphor, and most of all, surrender." Nor does he try to proselytize even his own parents, because "you can't just tell someone about Creation, however loudly, and expect the devotion to spring forth" (*AFN*, 8).

Although Zimmerman, out of curiosity, explored much of the Bible when he was eight years old, it was not what initiated his interest in Creation. "If anything," he remembers "so much proclamation made me a little skittish" (*AFN*, 28). But Zimmerman thinks about Jesus a lot. Sidestepping the whole matter of the Resurrection, he feels that Jesus' importance lies not in his divinity, but in his humanity. "To me the great thing about Jesus is that he was a guy, a human. He wore shoes, he blinked, he itched. And he was able to live as the 'son of God'" (*AFN*, 18). In his room Zimmerman has a picture that shows Jesus as dark, beardless, a little annoyed and suspicious, "a man who was smart, generous, tough, compulsive, brash, almost crazy in his commitment to something hard to share, certainly intense to the point of being frightening, and definitely, definitely tired" (*AFN*, 33).

These ideas about Jesus are at odds with the portrait the Spiffies wear on their fashionable jewelry—a Jesus who radiates untroubled beauty and bliss and looks like a Swede. When Zimmerman tries to give them a more historically accurate idea of Jesus by showing them a photo of some Middle Eastern laborers, they recoil in disgust, crying "Those are Arabs!" (*AFN*, 21). Sadly, Zimmerman concludes that they "are not interested in questions. To them, religion is a list of answers" (*AFN*, 22). Nevertheless, he feels that their faith, and that of his parents, is real. He is convinced of this, he says, not because he is impressed with them, but because he is impressed with God.

Comic relief from Zimmerman's earnest theology is provided by Brooks's satirical take on the smugly self-satisfied Spiffies, and even more so by his parody of New Age cults in the Faith of Faiths. However, it is to Brooks's credit that he has resisted the easy shot of making a comic caricature out of the cult leader Luke Mark John. Instead he is, at least in Zimmerman's perception, "a pretty hip fellow, playing his role with easy humor, casual intelligence, unassuming power" (*AFN*, 38), and it is only accidental that he is the instigator of Zimmerman's crime.

This detailed analysis of a young person's discovery of spiritual meaning is unique in secular YA fiction. *Asylum for Nightface* is a major work that has been overlooked because it is strange and difficult, although finely crafted, thoughtfully conceived—and undeniably about belief in God.

These twenty-some books are representative of the treatment of church and clergy in YA literature, not only in their content, but in their numbers. Of the several hundred YA novels that appear annually, in recent years only these authors and a few more have taken up this subject. And as we have seen, they often give a picture of churches and their leaders that does not encourage teens to look for answers to their big questions from this source. However, on a brighter note, in these books the sometimes successful struggles of the protagonists to find their own ways to God may be closer to the hearts of thoughtful teens and may eventually bring them to a community of like-minded believers.

NOTES

1. Chris Crutcher, *The Sledding Hill* (New York: Greenwillow, 2005).
2. Bette Greene, *The Drowning of Stephan Jones* (New York: Delacorte, 1991).
3. Han Nolan, *Send Me Down a Miracle* (New York: Harcourt, 1996, 2003).
4. Linda Crew, *Brides of Eden: A True Story Imagined* (New York: HarperCollins, 2001).
5. Cynthia Rylant, *A Fine White Dust* (New York: Bradbury Press, 1986).
6. Sara Zarr, *Once Was Lost* (New York: Little, Brown, 2009).
7. LouAnne Johnson, *Muchacho* (New York: Knopf, 2009). Hereafter cited in the text as *Muchacho.*
8. Helen Hemphill, *Long Gone Daddy* (Honesdale, PA: Boyds Mills, 2006). Hereafter cited in the text as *Gone.*
9. Jennifer Jacobson, *Stained* (New York: Atheneum, 2005).
10. amazon.com/stained-jennifer-richard-jacobson (February 25, 2005).
11. Chris Lynch, *Sins of the Fathers* (New York: HarperTempest, 2006).
12. Carolyn Lehman, review of *Sins of the Fathers* by Chris Lynch, *School Library Journal* (October 2006).
13. Donna Freitas, *This Gorgeous Game* (New York: Farrar, Straus and Giroux, 2010). Hereafter cited in the text as *TGG.*
14. David Almond, *The True Tale of the Monster Billy Dean Telt by Hisself* (Somerville, MA: Candlewick, 2014).
15. Robert Cormier, *The Chocolate War* (New York: Pantheon, 1974).
16. Robert Cormier, *Beyond the Chocolate War* (New York: Knopf, 1985).
17. Patty Campbell, *Robert Cormier: Daring to Disturb the Universe* (New York: Delacorte, 2006), 87.
18. Deborah Heiligman, *Intentions* (New York: Knopf, 2012). Hereafter cited in the text as *Intentions.*
19. Robert Cormier, *Other Bells for Us to Ring* (New York: Delacorte, 1990). Hereafter cited in the text as *Bells.*
20. Kimberly Brubaker Bradley, *Leap of Faith* (New York: Dial, 2007).
21. Gary Paulsen, *The Tent* (New York: Harcourt, 1995).
22. Kathryn Erskine, *Quaking* (New York: Philomel, 2000).

23. David Levithan, *Wide Awake* (New York: Knopf, 2006).

24. Bruce Brooks, *Asylum for Nightface* (New York: HarperCollins, 1996). Hereafter cited in the text as *AFN.*

Chapter Two

Bible Stories in Young Adult Books

The Bible is, among other things, a treasury of great stories. These tales, their language, and their characters are part of the bedrock of our cultural literacy. As such, it is not surprising that a few authors of YA literature should use these stories as a basis for YA novels, bringing Biblical plots and people newly alive for today's teens and building on the ancient Jewish tradition of "midrash," or retelling of sacred narrative, to clothe them in the sights and sounds that make them real and meaningful as twenty-first-century coming-of-age stories. Sometimes these authors follow the Bible text closely, and at other times they deviate from the original in significant ways, and even turn the story on its head with interesting modernizations or reversals of character or plot. These are not your average Sunday school "Bible story" publications.

Although some fundamentalists may find these imaginative novels disrespectful to the Scriptures, the website of the Institute for Contemporary Midrash says:

> The Bible is one of the most important underpinnings of Western language and culture. It is an invisible glue that holds our diverse civilization together, but, sadly, a glue that is fast deteriorating through disuse. At the same time, a fundamentalist grip on the religious imagination is capitalizing on ignorance of biblical text to promote regressive agendas.
>
> The midrashic process holds the potential to re-animate biblical text for this generation, to restore ownership of religious imagination to individuals, and to provide healing and meaning in an often fragmented

society. A remarkable group of writers, artists and scholars have created
The Institute for Contemporary Midrash (ICM) to promote the development of contemporary midrash on biblical and liturgical texts." [1]

These writers and scholars include the well-known poet and feminist
Marge Piercy, the folklorist and author Howard Schwartz, and the sing-
er-songwriter Linda Hirschhorn. [2] Joining them in spirit might be the
handful of Biblically literate YA authors who have adopted the tech-
nique of midrash as their own. An early example might be Katherine
Paterson's 1980 novel, *Jacob Have I Loved*, [3] which draws on the Bible
story of Esau and Jacob as an allegory to tell a contemporary tale of a
twin sister who loses her birthright to a sibling. There have been many
examples of such use of Scripture in recent YA novels.

OLD TESTAMENT STORIES: GENESIS

The Garden [4]

> Then the Lord God formed man out of dust from the ground, and
> breathed into his nostrils the breath of life; and man became a living
> being. And the Lord God planted a garden in Eden, in the east; and there
> he put the man whom he had formed. [5]

In this rich and subtle story, first novelist and septuagenarian Elsie
Aidinoff does a retake on the Bible's account of Adam and Eve in
Eden, but with radical differences reflecting contemporary understand-
ing of issues of gender equality.

Not the least of these differences is that in Aidinoff's retelling, Eve
is the narrator—and the snake is the good guy. While God educates the
handsome but doltish young Adam in a remote part of the Garden, the
Serpent has been given the responsibility of raising the curious and
daring young Eve. He is a wise and gentle teacher, companion, and
friend. When God, eager to see if his invention of sex works, orders the
teenage Adam to rape Eve, it is the Serpent who heals her spirit afterward with compassion and love.

God, on the other hand, is not such a good guy. Drawn accurately
from the primitive understanding of the nature of the Creator that is
reflected in the early chapters of Genesis, He is almighty and awe-
inspiring, but dangerously egotistical, quick to anger, jealous of His
creation, and oblivious to the feelings of His creatures. But it should be

noted that later in the Old Testament a more developed picture of His qualities emerges, as the Jews, the chosen bearers of the idea of a monotheistic deity, grow in understanding of His nature. For instance, in Psalms we read, "The Lord is merciful and gracious, slow to anger and abounding in steadfast love."[6] However, compared to the contemporary vision of God as the infinitely loving presence beyond and within all time and space, Aidinoff's God is a cartoon.

Back to *The Garden*. Before the Fall, God is comfortably accessible to Adam and Eve as a sturdy figure wrapped in a kirtle, who lives in a house and sits on a garden bench to recite stories and poetry to His two rapt young humans. The Serpent is described as a huge snake, scales shimmering in many colors, crowned with a ruff of feathers, as he is often seen in medieval paintings.

In this novel, he alone has not been created by God. What then does he represent as an opposite but supplementary power? Not the whispering evil tempter of tradition, although he helps Adam and Eve (not just Eve) to pick the fruit from the forbidden tree. He is adamant that the pair make their own decision, but he makes sure they know what the consequences will be. Aidinoff suggests in her author's note, "Perhaps the Serpent is Wisdom, who, according to some ancient texts, was with God at the Creation" (*Garden*, 400). She explains this dualism further, in terms of her own spiritual beliefs:

> I part ways with organized religion in crucial areas. I cannot believe in an exclusive god, one who, like the old tribal gods, protects only one group of people. I cannot reconcile an omnipotent god with the suffering that exists in the world. Nor can I believe that people are inherently evil. Like the Manicheans, I view the world as a struggle between the forces of good and the forces of evil, and humans as capable both of great evil and great good. . . . My Garden is a novel, not a work of theology—a novel that departs from one of the oldest and best-known tales on earth, in which I have tried to explore questions of personal responsibility, justice and freedom. (*Garden*, 402–3)

This thought-provoking book requires an audience of older teens and young twenties who are sophisticated enough to ponder the philosophical questions it raises and to read it as literary satire or feminist commentary (although Aidinoff denies this last) rather than theology. Or perhaps the way this novel and its source work best is as a metaphor for the coming-of-age story—the deliberate loss of preadolescent innocence and the first step into the difficult world of self-determination. If

Adam and Eve had not eaten the apple, they would have remained ignorant of good and evil and not fully human, just as teens will be who bypass the hard work of making sense of the world and their place in it.

Eve and Adam[7]

Another YA novel that refers, but only superficially, to the Adam and Eve story is called just that—*Eve and Adam*—although the title and some of the letters in it are reversed. Authors Michael Grant and Katherine Applegate use the two names, computer technology, and occasional references to "playing God" to evoke the creation myth in a science fiction action thriller. As the story opens, Evening Spiker is crossing a busy boulevard when she notices a glowing red apple in a street vendor's cart, which distracts her so that she is hit by a streetcar. The accident breaks bones and severs her leg. Her mother, the powerful Terra Spiker, tough CEO of a multibillion-dollar biological research company, takes her from the hospital to heal in the infirmary of her lab complex. There Eve meets Solo, a young man who is her mother's lowly go-fer. The inevitable YA trope of mutual attraction happens, and Solo gets to narrate some of the ensuing chapters. Eve's leg heals with astonishing speed, foreshadowing the later revelation of a genetic modification her parents had long ago installed in her body.

Meanwhile, Terra has put Eve to work at using the company's secret and radical new software to simulate cloning a human being. Eve and her visiting friend Aislin have fun playing God by putting together all the parts of the ideal guy, which they, of course, name Adam. As Eve ponders the more complex software for the genetic components of the brain, she begins to realize the responsibility she will bear for her creation's life:

> I could make him reckless and bold. He might die younger. He might be a criminal. He might be a great creative mind. This is not the simple, fun art work of making a face and a body. I'm not religious, but I'm starting to have some sympathy for God. Give man a brain smart enough to name the animals, one generally useful and productive, and you have to see the whole forbidden apple thing coming down the pike. This isn't as easy as it looks. (*Eve*, 138)

Adam wakes, fully clothed, sitting in a chair, and all alone in the lab. He knows one thing for sure—he loves Eve, because she made him. But when Eve meets her creation, *she* is not so sure. His beauty stops pedestrians in the street, and Aislin is besotted with him. But Eve discovers that he doesn't kiss very well—not nearly as well as Solo.

This budding romance story is interrupted by some cinematic thriller action, as it is revealed that Terra's company has moved in illegal directions in their research. The bad guys move in; there are captures and escapes, guns are pointed, and so on and so on, to a satisfactory resolution of the several conflicts in the novel, none of which are particularly Biblical.

Storm[8]

> Noah was a righteous man, blameless in his generation. . . . And God said to Noah, "I have determined to make an end of all flesh; for the earth is filled with violence. . . . Make yourself an ark . . . make rooms in the ark, and cover it inside and out with pitch. . . . And of every living thing of all flesh, you shall bring two of every sort into the ark, to keep them alive with you; they shall be male and female.". . . The flood continued forty days upon the earth; and the waters increased, and bore up the ark, and it rose high above the earth.[9]

So the Bible, and the stories of many other cultures, tell of the flood by which God, or the gods, washed the earth clean for a fresh start. Donna Jo Napoli is known for her vivid retellings of folktales and myths and sacred stories of all kinds, and this is one of her best. But unexpectedly her protagonist is not Noah, nor Noah's wife, but a strong and resourceful young stowaway, a Canaanite girl named Sebah. When the rain begins and the waters start to rise, her parents and her three brothers are swept away in the river. She survives not only the waters, but a potential rapist, a hyena, and a boar. She escapes the tusks of the latter animal by the intervention of a young boy, Aban, who says afterward, "I protected you. . . . You're mine" (*Storm*, 32). When he tells her he has watched her all the days of her life, she gives in to his demand to be his partner. They join in the hard work of building a raft and finding food for themselves and for Sebah's pet, an independent-minded swamp kitten she calls Screamer.

So far in this novel there has been not a word about Noah—or God. Sebah prays sporadically to her own Canaanite gods:

> *Please, Ba'al, god of storms. It's enough now. Please let that be enough. Please go to sleep.* I wonder if Ba'al hears my prayers. I've been praying on and off the whole time. . . . Prayers are one thing,

thoughts are another. Gods hear only prayers. That's a relief, for I have
few good thoughts about Ba'al right now. (*Storm*, 12)

Later she thinks about another of her deities, El Elyon, and confesses that she's paid little attention to the gods all her life. "It seemed to
me that they didn't concern themselves much with the matters of humans" (*Storm*, 86).

The storms grow ever fiercer and their raft is tossed about wildly. At
last they come to something that looks like a high wooden wall, but
then realize that it is an enormous boat. A rope dangles from the deck
high above. Aban is too weak to climb it, so after a tearful farewell,
Sebah goes up hand over hand, Screamer clawing tight to her head, and
Aban is washed away to his death.

Sebah goes into the ark through a porthole and finds herself in a
cage with two kind and helpful bonobos whose primary recreation is to
mate—every few minutes. Later another stowaway appears at the porthole—a hefty and cheerful man who claims he is the king of Bashon.
The two of them—Bash and Sheba, as they decide to call each other—
make common cause to survive. Sheba hides in the straw on the floor of
the cage when Noah's sons come down from the upper deck to feed the
animals, but she eavesdrops and observes their different personalities
and secrets. Noah, she learns, has been told by the Mighty Creator to
build this ark and fill it with pairs of animals. He is single-minded and
stubborn about obeying God, much to the annoyance of his sons Ham,
Shem, and Japheth and their wives, as the days go by and tensions arise
from the confinement and hardships.

Meanwhile, Sheba gives birth to Aban's baby, and she and Bash
grow to love each other. The ingenious details of how they find food
and water and hide from the others make this part of the story an
absorbing survival-at-sea narrative. At last, after many narrow escapes,
they are discovered, but Noah's wife saves them from being thrown
overboard. In the end, of course, the ark comes to rest on Mount Ararat.
They all file out to repopulate the world, and God promises to never
again destroy life on earth with a flood:

> And God said, "This is the sign of the covenant which I make between
> me and you and every living creature that is with you, for all future
> generations. I set my bow in the cloud, and it shall be a sign of the
> covenant between me and the earth." [10]

Other Flood Stories

At least two other YA novels have been based on the story of the forty days flood. In *Not the End of the World* by Geraldine McCaughrean,[11] the story is told by Noah's daughter Timna and many other human and animal voices, and as in Napoli's retelling, the plot centers on the survival of stowaways, this time a little boy and his baby sister that Timna rescues and cares for. The book was praised for its vivid detail and evocation of the stink and claustrophobia of the ark, as well as its investigation of issues of spirit, honor, and obligation. It won the Whitbread Children's Book Award in 2005.

Anne Provoost's *In the Shadow of the Ark*[12] focuses on the human drama *before* the Deluge. Re Jana and her fisher family travel from their overflowing home marshes to the desert, where they encounter some tribal people. Among them is a madman named Noach, who is building an ark in the middle of the dry sands. Re Jana and Noach's son Ham are attracted to each other, although he marries someone else. Meanwhile, her father begins to take Noach's predictions seriously, and as the family's hopes to be chosen as passengers on the ark fade, he starts to build his own boat in secret. The book ends as they wait for the rain—but we all know how this story comes out.

Dark Sons[13]

> And I will make a nation of the son of the slave woman also, because he is your offspring. So Abraham rose early in the morning, and took bread and a skin of water, and gave it to Hagar, putting it on her shoulder, along with the child, and sent her away. And she departed, and wandered in the wilderness of Beersheba.[14]

The poet Nikki Grimes here tells a story in verse of two angry sons who feel rejected by their fathers, one the ancient "dark son" Ishmael from Genesis, and the other a contemporary "dark son," Sam. As Ishmael and his mother Hagar endure their exile in the barren desert, the boy broods over his resentment toward his father Abraham and his stepmother Sarah. In alternating sections, Sam also fumes, because his father has divorced his mother and now Sam is expected to accept a white stepmother. The book was praised for its sensitive treatment of this pair of sons betrayed by their fathers.

Robert Crumb Does *The Book of Genesis* [15]

The legendary comic artist from the sixties, Robert Crumb, has produced an astonishing graphic novel based meticulously and with great verve on the first book of the Bible. The cover screams, "Nothing left out!" Crumb has used every word of the text, relying primarily on the King James version and the translation of Robert Alter. Even the many "begats" are included, in sidebars or stacked up in small panels with faces, names, and relationships clearly laid out. Nor has Crumb left out the duplications, the breaks in continuity, and the contradictions inherent in some Biblical passages, especially in this particular book of Scripture. He provides meanings for all the Hebrew words and names in unobtrusive footnotes at the bottom of the pictures in which they occur, and his concluding commentary summarizes each chapter's story and suggests further interpretations found by scholars. But mostly this is a powerful piece of storytelling for a visual age.

The narrative emerges with clarity, its genealogical progression leaping out of the text to show a united whole, the tale of the people God picked out to carry the message of His being through all history. This is one family's story, a tale of God's relationship with Abraham and his descendants, bringing to vivid life all the drama, anguish, and joy that is sometimes muted and elusive in a text version without visuals. Crumb's style is perfectly suited to the honest earthiness of these stories. His women, especially the naked Eve, are voluptuous and sturdy; the men are bearded and turbaned, and both are pictured with strongly Semitic facial features. God has a long, long flowing white beard, as in popular imagery, and his mighty face is wonderfully expressive of love, bafflement, and anger.

The story of Genesis covers hundreds of years and dozens of characters who have made their way into our cultural memory. The first chapter, of course, deals with the creation of the world, in great swirling images that evoke the power and majesty of the mythic poetry. Next is Adam and Eve's sad story, their blank features revealing creatures newly formed and confused. Their son Cain's murder of his brother Abel and God's reaction comes after their parents eat the fruit of the tree of the knowledge of good and evil and are expelled from the Garden. Next, a bemused and terrified Noah and his family survive on the ark, and then a long interruption documents the names of his descendants. Even such passages as this last are made interesting with drawings of the characters going about their daily lives, drawings that reveal that Crumb has done his research about clothes, artifacts, and architecture of the ancient world.

One of these descendants, Abraham, is called by God, who tells him, "I will make of you a great nation."[16] But Abraham's wife Sarah is barren and ninety years old, which doesn't stop God from accomplishing His purposes. At first Sarah takes things into her own hands and calls for her maid Hagar to stand in, and soon Abraham has a son with her, Ishmael. But soon after, the long-promised child from Sarah that fulfills God's prophecy is born. They name him Isaac, and he becomes the apple of his father's eye. Nevertheless, Sarah grows jealous of Hagar's son and goads Abraham into expelling them to wander in the desert.

Next is the dreadful and inexplicable story of Abraham's sacrificial almost-murder of his son Isaac, which Crumb depicts just as it is written, not trying to answer the eternal question, "So what did Isaac think of his father after this?" The story moves on, to Abraham's nephew Lot and some turbulent and horrific drawings of the destruction of Sodom and Gomorrah by fire and brimstone. The narrative returns to Abraham's son Isaac. We see his love match with Rebekah, and their sons Jacob and Esau in competition for the land and the flocks. A comical digression is provided by the episode between Judah and his crafty daughter-in-law Tamar (a story that is never told in Sunday school). The strange episode of Jacob's night of wrestling with an angel is shown in all its metaphorical mystery. The rape of Dinah ends happily with the bloody group circumcision that paid for the crime. At last the book takes on the long story of Joseph, his fame and fortune in Egypt, his revenge on his duplicitous brothers, and their reconciliation. This pictorial feast ends with an elegiac and detailed scene of Joseph's funeral procession in Egypt, and God's assurance of return to the land He has promised this tribe of desert nomads.

Crumb's genius stands up to the challenge of this iconic and sacred text. He has provided coherence and structure to the rambling narrative and brought the overriding themes into focus. Nowhere does he descend to visual puns or impertinences with the text, and only when the words demand it is he flamboyant. His portraits are strikingly individual, even with a cast of hundreds. Their faces, often partly hidden by turbans and beards or head cloths, show subtle variations of expression and personality. Their hooded eyes peer out from their dark faces in defiance, shame, terror, supplication, and blessing, and the men grin in amusement or lust under their moustaches.

However, Crumb and his publishers are no fools. The cover carries an alarming disclaimer: "Adult supervision recommended for minors." Crumb has dared to illustrate in an appropriately direct style all the erotic episodes that are such a vital part of this honest Biblical tale of humanity and God. When the story calls for it, there is direct frontal nudity. The women's naked breasts are full and round, with protruding nipples. And there are many scenes of sexual intercourse, consensual or not.

For example, Crumb draws the enthusiastic obedience of Adam and Eve to God's command to "be fruitful and multiply"; the rapturous coupling of Isaac and his new wife Rebekah; the lustful Judah shagging his own daughter-in-law Tamar unknowingly; the rape of Dinah; Lot's daughters taking advantage of the old man's drunkenness to keep the race from dying out, the youngest having a good time as she settles her rounded bottom atop her prone and dead-drunk father. And Onan bent over in a corner of the tent spilling his seed, while his brother's widow disapproves from the bed. Thankfully, the circumcision of Abraham's sons and servants is not as graphic; we see only Ishmael's horrified face as blood spurts up from his (off-camera) member.

All of this is right there in the Bible in straightforward language, and it would be dishonest and prudish for an illustrator to tiptoe around these scenes. But what a problem for librarians. Not to mention teachers—if there are any brave enough to teach young people about the basic literary work of our civilization. And what delicious irony a censorship attempt would be! "Bible declared 'dirty book!'" "Bible is banned from X school library!" However, the American Library Association's Office for Intellectual Freedom reports no challenges in the five years that Crumb's book has been in print, although I suspect this reflects the probability that YA librarians are more likely to quietly reject this book, not because of the picture content, but because it is Scripture.

These drawings, it must be admitted, are more shocking than reading a description of the same events in words. However, to me the most shocking moment in Genesis will always be the instant when Abraham raises the sacrificial knife over Isaac.

EXODUS

Pharaoh's Daughter[17]

> Now the daughter of Pharaoh came down to bathe at the river, and her
> maidens walked beside the river; she saw the basket among the reeds
> and sent her maid to fetch it. When she opened it she saw the child, and
> lo, the babe was crying. She took pity on him and said, "This is one of
> the Hebrews' children."[18]

In his introduction to this engrossing novel of ancient Egypt, author
Julius Lester says, "It is difficult not to see Charlton Heston when one
thinks of Moses." But not in this book. Lester's Moses is a bungling
teenager, scared and confused as he tries to find the courage to decide
who he is and what he believes in. Raised as the pampered grandson of
Pharaoh, he enjoys the attentions of three mother figures: Yocheved,
his birth mother, who constantly implores him to return to his own
people; Almah, his older sister, who has left her traditions to dance
naked as a priestess of the goddess Hathor; and Batya, Pharaoh's
daughter, who saved him from death when he was a baby. But now his
anger at his unresolved split identity has goaded him into a terrible act
of violence. The Bible tells us: "The young Moses saw an Egyptian
beating a Hebrew, one of his people. He looked this way and that, and
seeing no one he killed the Egyptian and hid him in the sand."[19]

Julius Lester is a distinguished African American writer best known
for his Newbery Honor Book *To Be a Slave.* In 1981 he startled the
literary world by converting to Judaism. *Pharaoh's Daughter* follows
the time-honored Jewish tradition of midrash—as we have said, a way
of exploring a sacred text through the use of one's imagination.
"Armed with an impressive knowledge of the Hebrew language and the
history of ancient Egypt, Julius Lester jolts us out of our expectations
and brings a fresh and richly detailed perspective to the Exodus."[20]

Another book taken from Exodus is Sonia Levitin's *Escape from
Egypt.*[21] But since this tells a story that is the center of the major Jewish
holiday of Passover, it is better discussed in chapter 7, which is devoted
to Judaism.

OVERLOOKED OLD TESTAMENT STORIES

It seems puzzling that young adult Old Testament midrash should use stories from only the first two books of the Bible, Genesis and Exodus. True, some of the best tales and colorful incidents are in these two books, but there are also many other good stories in the rest of the Old Testament just waiting to be retold in YA literature. Jumping over the grim book of rules that is Leviticus; the lists of measurements and genealogies that make up Numbers; the military and judgmental excesses of Deuteronomy, we come to Joshua, who fought the battle of Jericho, a good story of a clever battle strategy that in the right author's hands would be interesting to teen boys. There are stories of empowered women like Esther, and the lovely little tale of Ruth and her mother-in-law Naomi, who won out by understanding male psychology. And the fun stories of Shadrach, Meshach, and Abednego in the fiery furnace and Daniel in the lions' den. Or the adventure of Jonah and the whale, just made for a graphic novel, and ending with one of the few comical scenes in the Bible, as a miffed Jonah, angry because God has changed his mind about destroying Nineveh, retreats to sit in the shade of a vine and fume at Jehovah, until the Almighty wilts the plant and leaves him to his temper tantrum in the blazing sun. Many more narrative gems still undiscovered by YA novelists abound in the first part of the Good Book.

NEW TESTAMENT STORIES

But for Christians the best story of all, and the most important is, of course, the story of the life and death and resurrection of Jesus of Nazareth, found in the Gospels—the first four books of the New Testament. Several YA novels have taken sections of these narratives as their basis.

Alphabet of Dreams[22]

> Now when Jesus was born in Bethlehem of Judea in the days of Herod the king, behold, wise men from the East came to Jerusalem, saying "Where is he who has been born king of the Jews? For we have seen his star in the East, and have come to worship him."[23]

In ancient Persia, Mitra, thirteen or fourteen, and her little brother Babak are keeping it together by stealing food from the marketplace, while evading the soldiers bent on avenging their father's failed plot to overthrow the local tyrant. Mitra, who is disguised as a boy, yearns for the luxurious existence they had before as royals. Everything changes when she discovers that Babak has the gift of prophetic dreams. She schemes to use his gift to improve their lot, but when he persistently has dreams of stars, angels, and a king, they draw the attention of a Magi, Melchior, who is on his way to Bethlehem to pay homage to the birth of that long-prophesied king.

Since they want to return to Palmyra anyway to rejoin their family, they go on the desert journey with Melchior's caravan, which is soon joined by two other wise men. At this point, even the dullest reader will recognize what tale is afoot. The novel was praised as richly imagined and faithful to its source in Matthew. An enlightening note from author Susan Fletcher explains her scrupulous research process and what material she chose to keep, what she left out, and why.

Song of the Magdalene[24]

[S]tanding by the cross of Jesus were his mother, and his mother's sister, and Mary the wife of Clopas, and Mary Magdalene. [25]

This book by Donna Jo Napoli is much older (1996) than *Storm*, but mentioned here because for many years it was the only YA novel to even mention Jesus, albeit as "Joshua," whom we meet in the story only once in a distant sort of way. The novel takes wild and misleading liberties with the history of the Biblical character Mary Magdalene, almost as wild and misleading as the liberties taken with her story resulting from the publication of Dan Brown's *The Da Vinci Code* and its sequels. Speculation as to whether she was the unnamed prostitute who anointed Jesus' feet with ointment, or even whether she and Jesus were lovers, had conservative Christians in an uproar. The truth is that Mary Magdalene is mentioned in all four Gospels, but only in passing, as one of the several women who hung out with the apostles, tended to their needs for food and lodging, and were strong presences at the foot of the cross.

In this book, set in first-century Palestine, a young girl named Miriam has seizures, but hides them because her people, the Jews, think cripples, idiots, and epileptics are possessed by devils. But Abraham, the crippled son of the family's servant Hannah, finds out her secret and accepts it. They grow close, and Miriam becomes pregnant with his child. But Abraham dies, and Miriam loses the baby when she is raped. Her father sends her away, and in the desert she sees John the Baptist, but goes on to live as a hermit at Qumran. A woman with a sick child passes by on her way to seek healing from a prophet named Joshua, who accepts all outcasts. Miriam joins her, finds Jesus, has a seizure at his feet, and wakes to salvation.

Lamb: The Gospel According to Biff, Christ's Childhood Pal[26]

And the Word became flesh and dwelt among us, full of grace and truth; we have beheld his glory, glory as of the only Son from the Father. [27]

The Gospels are silent about the childhood and adolescence of Christ. From the time of his birth in Bethlehem to the moment when he appears at a wedding in Cana, thirty-two years old and ready to begin his ministry, we see him as a child in only one Gospel, in one incident, when he was twelve. Christopher Moore remedies that gap with this irreverent, sometimes funny, but basically respectful story told by the Savior's best friend, Levi bar Alphaeus, also known as Biff, who was there.

So in the twenty-first century, Biff, who killed himself after the crucifixion, is resurrected by the angel Haziel and taken to St. Louis, where the angel locks the two of them in a hotel room, gives Biff a pencil and notebook, and instructs him to write what nobody else re- members about growing up with Jesus. Then Haziel flops down on the bed to watch soap operas on TV, while Biff gets to work reliving those years with the Christ.

The first encounter between the two happens when Biff finds a six- year-old Jesus with a lizard in his mouth, repeatedly resurrecting the reptile that his little brother James then squashes. "I want to do that!" cries Biff, after he's gotten over yelling "Unclean!" to impress the nearby women.

"Which part?" asks the Savior. And Biff knows he has found his best friend. He decides what to call him:

By the way, his name was Joshua. Jesus is the Greek translation of the Hebrew word *Yeshua*, which is Joshua. Christ is not a last name. It's the Greek for *messiah*, a Hebrew word meaning anointed. I have no idea

what the "H" in Jesus H. Christ stood for. It's one of the things I should
have asked him. (*Biff*, 8)

So Josh it is, although Jesus insists his real name is not Joshua bar
Joseph, but Joshua bar Jehovah (a last name that Jews are forbidden to
say). His parents are more or less comfortable with his status as the son
of God because the angels told them about that when he was born.
Mary is quiet and cautious on the subject, although not secretive, so the
neighbors think she's mad. She is sweetly devoted to her very special
child, to the annoyance of his siblings. Her husband, Joseph, on the
other hand, has the uncomfortable task of being the stepfather of God's
son. "You're not the boss of me!" Josh smarts-off to him, like every
stepkid. Nevertheless, Joseph is kind and hardworking, although a bit
bewildered by his role in this story.

The two friends are later joined by Maggie, a new girl whose family
has just moved to Nazareth from Magdala. She, too, is soon convinced
of Josh's identity when the bungling angel Haziel appears to them for
the Annunciation, ten years late. Maggie is smart and daring, and she
leads the two boys into adventures, as when they sneak out at night to
circumcise a ten-foot statue of one of the Greek gods. Graven images
are an offense to the Jews, and the three show their outrage by chiseling
away at the god's foreskin, until an unlucky blow accidentally knocks
his stone phallus completely off.

Most of their adventures end badly, and this one particularly so, as
Maggie's Zealot uncle comes out of the night to stab the Roman centurion who has been roused by the noise of stone-chipping. Maggie's
whole family is endangered, until Joshua raises the centurion from the
dead at the funeral—at least for a few minutes. He walks and talks so
that the charges are dropped, but so is the soldier, a few steps up the
road. "That raising-the-dead thing needs work," Josh mutters.

During their growing-up years Josh studies the Torah, practices
using his powers, and constantly implores God for information on how
to be the Messiah. He tells Biff, "I ask for guidance, but I get no
answer. I can feel that I am supposed to do things, but I don't know
what. And I don't know how" (*Biff*, 36). Biff, on the other hand, is
quite clear on his role as Joshua's sidekick. He is practical and pragmatic, profane to Josh's sacred, and protective but not at all respectful
of the son of God. While the adolescent Joshua spends his time praying
and learning to heal, Biff is busy in the village learning about how the
world works, and most specifically, about sex. He seems to have high

hormone levels, judging by the number of times he is troubled by erections in inappropriate circumstances. By this time, both boys are in love with Maggie, but Josh has been told by the angel that he is never to know a woman. He's resigned to this, but curious as to the sensations of this basic human pleasure he is never to experience. When Biff complains that he is getting "all wrinkly" from having to purify himself in the ritual bath so often after masturbating, Josh helpfully offers to cure his friend:

> "I could try to heal you."
> "No way, Josh. I'm having enough trouble with laying on of my own hands."
> "You don't want me to cast out your demons?"
> "I thought I'd try to exhaust him first." (*Biff*, 65)

If this is starting to sound like a stand-up routine about Jesus, let me say that the moments of humor are merely chocolate bits in the cookie, and perhaps I have given in to the temptation to share too many of them (but passed over many more) because they are so delicious. The narrative is basically respectful and sound, believable in spirit, sometimes even in event, psychologically true to the searching of these two young men who are seeking their destinies—one spiritual, one not so much. And Moore has done his historical research. His depiction of the noise and smells of crowded Jerusalem at Passover, the temperament of camels, the arrogance of Roman soldiers, the garments and food and daily life of first-century Palestine are vivid and authentic, even though he tosses in an occasional anachronism for a laugh.

Time after time we see Jesus grasp a radical new spiritual concept that will be a keystone in his adult ministry, and then fail in trying to explain it to a puzzled Biff, who, like the future apostles, just doesn't get parables. "Fishers of men," for instance, which leaves even Maggie confused. However, Biff is growing to have a sense of the tragic mission on which Christ has embarked. At Passover Biff is carrying a meek and compliant lamb to be sacrificed in the Temple in Jerusalem, when he is overcome with pity for the animal—and more.

> I couldn't breathe, and I couldn't get out of the Temple fast enough. I didn't know where I was going, but I wasn't going inside to the altar. I turned to run, but a hand caught my shirt and pulled me back. I spun around and looked into Joshua's eyes.

"It's God's will," he said. He laid his hands on my head and I was
able to breathe again.

"It's all right, Biff. God's will." He smiled.

Joshua had put the lamb he'd been carrying on the ground, but it
didn't run away. I suppose I should have known right then. (*Biff*, 93)

As the two boys approach the Bar Mitzvah age of thirteen, they are
devastated when Maggie is betrothed to Jakan, a cruel and tyrannical
man who was the bully of their childhood. They can't bear to go to the
wedding, so Joshua decides on a quest to seek wisdom from the three
Magi who sought him out at his nativity. With the scant information
Mary can give them, they set out first for Antioch, where it is rumored
that Balthasar has a palace-cave in the mountains. They find him, and
for years, while Josh learns about the Tao, Biff enjoys the company of
the eight beautiful Chinese concubines who serve Balthasar. But despite the Magi's warnings, they open a secret iron door and let loose a
demon, who destroys all of the girls except one and leaves the castle in
ruins.

Next they look for Gaspar and find him in a monastery, where they
spend six years sitting, meditating, and learning marital arts moves.
Finally, when they—and we readers—are thoroughly sick and tired of
inexplicable answers to inexplicable questions, they move on to find
Gaspar's brother Melchior in India. On the journey they become entan-
gled in a ghastly and bloody celebration for the goddess Kali and use a
clever deception to rescue the child sacrificial victims. Both young men
are sickened and horrified by this encounter.

They find Melchior "reclining in a shallow stone nook in a cliff over
the ocean" (*Biff*, 284). Joshua settles in to learn what Melchior can
teach him of Indian learning, and Biff goes off to the nearest village to
find work. There he discovers a whore who has acquired a rare copy of
the Kama Sutra and is teaching the various positions for a price. Biff
happily settles in for lessons. At last they receive a signal that it's time
to go home: a likeness of Mary's face made of condensation, mold, and
wind-blown dust appears on a wall ("Yeah, she does that," says Joshua)
(*Biff*, 298).

They head for Nazareth, but along the way they find Joshua's cousin John baptizing in the River Jordan. Joshua still feels unready to
begin his ministry as Messiah, but he steps up to be baptized anyway.
When John is holding him underwater, God's voice booms down from
the sky to say, "This is my beloved Son, in whom I am well pleased."[28]

Josh comes up out of the water, sees the crowd's astonished faces, and says, "What? What?" They tell him, and he is annoyed that he didn't get to hear this commendation himself. He and John share tips about crowd-pleasing and how to be the Messiah—although John reluctantly gives place to Joshua in this matter.

The last section of the book follows the Scriptural account closely, briefly introducing all fifteen of the disciples, including Maggie and two other women, and quickly describing Joshua's deeds and teaching and the events that led to his crucifixion and resurrection. The narrative is tender and beautiful, and all jokes are put aside for this part of the telling. *Lamb* is a delightful and rewarding book, and like all things extraordinary and exquisite, it should be held lightly.

And enjoyed. So one last chocolate bit in the cookie needs to be shared. Crossing the desert, Biff and Joshua duck into an inn to get out of a windstorm. "Shut the door!" yells the innkeeper. "Were you born in a barn?"

"Yeah," says Joshua (*Biff*, 307).

Coaltown Jesus[29]

Another, although much slighter, depiction of a contemporary and smart-talking Savior is found in Ron Koertge's verse novel *Coaltown Jesus*. However, the front cover flap gives away the best line in the book. Walker has been praying and praying for Jesus to help his mom, who can't stop grieving over her older son's death two months ago. So when Jesus appears at the foot of Walker's bed one night, he asks angrily, "What took you so long?" and Jesus answers, "I would have been here sooner, but traffic on I-55 was awful."

Needless to say, Walker does eventually get the help he needs, but not before some hard theological questions have been deliberated. Why did God take Walker's seventeen-year-old brother instead of one of the suffering old people at the nursing home where Walker's mom works? And why would he send Jesus himself to Coaltown, Illinois, to comfort their grief when there are a gazillion other people praying for help? ("That's easy," says Jesus. "I'm omnipresent"—a theologically correct but not entirely satisfactory answer.)

In addition to the fundamental story of the life and death of Jesus, there are more stories and bits of stories in the New Testament that could give rise to YA novels. The travels of St. Paul, as told by his buddy

Luke in Acts, is full of action and drama. Several of the apostles have novel-worthy backstories. And as the basis for fantasies, there are strange creatures and intriguing hints in Revelation, and also in the Apocrypha, those books and fragments that didn't make it into the Bible as we know it.

So as John writes at the end of his Gospel: "But there are also many other things which Jesus did; were every one of them to be written, I suppose that the world itself could not contain the books that would be written."[30]

NOTES

1. icmidrash.org/about/about.htm (August 15, 2014).
2. lcmidrash.org.
3. Katherine Paterson, *Jacob Have I Loved* (New York: HarperTeen, 1980).
4. Elsie Aidinoff, *The Garden* (New York: Harper, 2004). Hereafter cited in the text as *Garden*.
5. Genesis 2:7–8 RSV.
6. Psalm 103:8 RSV.
7. Michael Grant and Katherine Applegate, *Eve and Adam* (New York: Feiwel and Friends, 2012). Hereafter cited in text as *Eve*.
8. Donna Jo Napoli, *Storm* (New York: Simon & Schuster, 2014). Hereafter cited in the text as *Storm*.
9. Genesis 6:9–7:17 RSV.
10. Genesis 9:12–13 RSV.
11. Geraldine McCaughrean, *Not the End of the World* (New York: HarperTeen, 2005).
12. Anne Provoost, *In the Shadow of the Ark*, trans. John Nieuwenhuizen (New York: Scholastic, 2004).
13. Nikki Grimes, *Dark Sons* (New York: Hyperion, 2005).
14. Genesis 21:14 RSV.
15. Robert Crumb, *The Book of Genesis*, illus. R. Crumb, trans. Robert Alter (New York: W. W. Norton, 2009).
16. Deuteronomy 9:14 RSV.
17. Julius Lester, *Pharaoh's Daughter* (New York: Harcourt, 2000).
18. Exodus 2:5–7 RSV.
19. Exodus 2:12–13 RSV.
20. www.amazon.com/Pharaohs-Daughter-Novel-Ancient-Egypt/dp/product-description/0152018263/ref=dp_proddesc_b?ie=UTF8&n=283155&s=books (August 27, 2014).
21. Sonia Levitin, *Escape from Egypt* (New York: Little, Brown, 1994).
22. Susan Fletcher, *Alphabet of Dreams* (New York: Simon & Schuster, 2006).
23. Matthew 2:1–3 RSV.
24. Donna Jo Napoli, *Song of the Magdalene* (New York: Scholastic, 1996).
25. John 19:25 RSV.
26. Christopher Moore, *Lamb: The Gospel According to Biff, Christ's Childhood Pal* (New York: HarperCollins, 2002). Hereafter cited in the text as *Biff*.
27. John 1:14 RSV.

28. Matthew 3:17 RSV.
29. Ron Koertge, *Coaltown Jesus* (Somerville, MA: Candlewick, 2013).
30. John 21:25 RSV.

Chapter Three

Death and the Afterlife

The Dead walk the pages of YA novels, strolling through the literature in great numbers, contemplating their own demise, and advising and annoying the living. There have been many YA novels and short stories in which the narrator is dead or in the process of dying; other dead characters have speaking parts, or Death himself has a role. Stories in which the protagonist is grieving a dead relative or friend are so common as to be almost the standard opening situation in YA plots. Ghost stories, murder mysteries, and tales of undead zombies also abound, although these subgenres for the most part are outside the scope of this book about spirituality. But only a few YA authors have used the awareness of the inevitability of death to show their characters at prayer or wrestling with thoughts about the afterlife.

These explorations of the end of life and beyond are an appropriate response to the basic young adult question—"Who am I and what am I going to do about it?"—as thoughtful teens search for a way to discover their strengths, their talents, their joys, and how to use them to leave the world better than it was when they arrived. The broader contemplation of mortality spreads throughout YA literature in a multitude of books in which the end of life is a presence or motivating force.

Death has, to a lesser degree, been linked with YA literature from its very beginnings, starting with the 1951 early prototype YA novel, J. D. Salinger's *The Catcher in the Rye*.[1] Although this classic text is often misunderstood as a story of a rebellious teen's night on the town, a close reading shows that under his heartbreaking "suave" and sarcastic facade, Holden Caulfield is grieving for his dead brother Allie, while he searches for authenticity in a world that seems full of phoniness.

THE DEAD SPEAK

The contemporary trend, however, began with Alice Sebold's highly successful 2002 adult novel, *The Lovely Bones*,[2] which was widely read by young adults. Its then-fresh premise—a newly murdered teen speaks from heaven—led many YA authors to frame novels around deathly monologues and conversations with the deceased. Preeminent among them is *The Book Thief* by Markus Zusak,[3] narrated by the wry voice of Death himself (which didn't hinder it from becoming a major motion picture). Chris Crutcher dropped a talkative dead best friend into the plot of *The Sledding Hill*,[4] as did Pete Hautman in *Invisible*.[5] First novelist Laura Whitcomb dealt ravishingly with the fleshly difficulties of two dead lovers in *A Certain Slant of Light*[6] and its sequel, *Under the Light*.[7] Gary Soto killed his protagonist in a men's room in the first chapter of *The Afterlife*.[8] And the 2008 Printz Award for Excellence in Young Adult Literature went to a deathly fellow, as Geraldine McCaughrean's teenage Sym slogged bravely through *The White Darkness*[9] of Antarctica, teased and encouraged by her main crush, the ninety-years-dead—and extremely charming—Captain Titus Oates from Scott's South Pole expedition.

SHORT STORIES ABOUT DEATH

Not only have there been a plethora of novels about death and dying, but a number of short stories have zeroed in on the subject. *The Restless Dead*, edited by Deborah Noyes,[10] is a stunning necrobibliographic collection by some of YA's best writers, including "The Gray Boy's Work," by M. T. Anderson, in which a dead drummer boy follows a deserter home and becomes a member of the family—and a symbol of the ex-soldier's disgrace. In the same collection, Kelly Link's young poet has a surprise when he digs up "The Wrong Grave" to retrieve a sheaf of poems buried a year earlier in the arms of his girlfriend and finds a long-haired stranger taunting him from the coffin.

THE PROCESS OF DYING

Witnessing the process of dying, however, is as close as we get in this life to knowing about the experience of death. There have always been plenty of YA novels about a beloved somebody dying (Lurlene McDaniel has built an entire literary empire on the four-hankie grief-fest), but these stories are nearly always from the point of view of the survivor. It is in books where the *protagonist* is dying that we come closest to the reality of death. Several YA novels feature terminally ill narrators. Sonya Hartnett's Printz Honor book *Surrender*[11] opens with an extraordinary chapter that spares nothing in showing the small indignities and nastiness of a worn-out body dying in slow torment from natural causes—except that at the end of the passage we find with cold shock that the decrepit expiring body with which we are in bed belongs not to an old man but to a youth of twenty. Chris Crutcher's extraordinary and courageous novel *Deadline*[12] seems at first to follow the same path in its story of an eighteen-year-old about to die, but takes a more cheerful route as the young man decides to keep the diagnosis of cancer secret and to live the last year of his life as fully as possible. An inevitable comparison arises with Jenny Downham's *Before I Die*,[13] in which a girl doomed by leukemia accomplishes her endgame goal of falling in love. *Zac and Mia* by A. J. Betts,[14] gives us a pair of lovers who "meet cute" (as they say in the movie business) by knocking on the wall between room one and room two in a cancer ward. And in an unexpected twist on this basic cancer-struck lovers theme, another terminal teen, Alice, enlists the help of her best friend Harvey to help her, in various colorful ways, avenge the wrongs she feels she has been done and get even with her enemies. But then—surprise!—she goes into remission and must clean up the havoc she and Harvey have wrought.

God Is in the Pancakes[15]

> "Holy shit." That's the opening line of my prayer.
> "Holy, holy, holy shit." That's line two.
> I'm a little rusty at the prayer thing. (*Pancakes*, 1)

Here we have the startling beginning of Robin Epstein's novel *God Is in the Pancakes*, a book that deals seriously with fifteen-year-old Grace talking, or trying to talk, to God. She is facing a devastating moral dilemma, and she needs all the divine help she can get. Her favorite patient at Hanover House, where she works as a Candy Striper, has asked her to secretly help him die. Mr. Sands is a jolly old guy, not like the other elderly residents, and she has become fond of him, even as his medical condition worsens. But then he asks her to give him a final way to end his suffering. It would just be one friend helping another out with a favor he couldn't accomplish on his own, he explains. He has it all planned out—he gives her an envelope of pills, tells her to chop them up and then give them to him baked in a cake. Or pancakes.

Pancakes are special to Grace, because her father, who has now left the family, used to take her and her sister to church with him, and then to an IHOP for brunch. Otherwise her religious education has been minimal, although at least it was associated with good times. But after her father left, she began to notice that "it seemed like people were preaching and parroting one set of morals in church and then practicing another in their own homes" (*Pancakes*, 13), and this has broken her faith. Nevertheless, in the face of this dreadful choice about killing Mr. Sands, she goes down on her knees that night and asks for help:

> "Look," I say softly. "I know you haven't heard from me in a while. And you're probably mad. If you're even there at all, that is. . . . But if you are . . . and if you're listening, I really need a favor right now: I need you to cure Mr. Sands. Please just make him well again. And then just send me a little sign to let me know that this is all going to be okay. . . . Okay?" (*Pancakes*, 13)

A heartfelt prayer, even if it is naïve and a little late—why didn't she think to pray for Mr. Sands's healing until her own ethical well-being was involved? As the week goes on, her prayers take on a nagging tone, as she continues to pray that this terrible duty will be taken off her shoulders. Like Jesus, she asks that the cup should pass away—but without realizing the parallel of that ungranted prayer.

> "Hi, I'm sure you didn't forget about my request," I say, my eyes flicking to the ceiling, "but I thought I'd check back in because Mr. Sands doesn't seem to be getting better yet. And I just wanted to remind you that time is sort of 'of the essence' here. . . . I really, really want to believe you're going to help Mr. Sands. I can't help him like he wants me to, but you, you could fix it so he wouldn't even have to think about that. . . . And then I wouldn't have to think about it either. . . . So just please make him well again, okay? Please." I close my eyes as if trying to seal up the wish and send it out to the universe. (*Pancakes*, 44)

"The universe" starts to take the place of a personal God in Grace's prayers when she is disappointed that her specific request is not fulfilled; Mr. Sands's torments grow worse. But Grace fails to notice that God is answering her prayers for help in other ways—she meets Isabelle, Mr. Sands's wife, and is soon friends with this delightful lady. And one day she wanders into the chapel at Hanover House and talks with a stranger who helps her to a broader understanding of answers to prayer. Grace asks him if he thinks anybody is listening when she prays, and he answers with his own experience:

> "I've had moments of doubt. Of course I have. I don't know how anyone can live in this world where, let's face it, injustice takes place all the time, and not wonder if anyone's paying attention." He shrugs. "But what I keep coming back to is the fact that life is so fragile, someone has to be looking out for us. At least in the most basic way. So for me, prayer is not just the asking of a favor—like 'please God, let my mother be okay'—but as more of a thank you. A thank you for every minute I've had with her. I'm sure that kind of sounds corny, but it does help me appreciate the good things in my life." (*Pancakes*, 123–24)

Grace finds this "kind of interesting." Finally, when Mr. Sands goes into a coma, she knows she must act. She mashes up the pills, mixes them with water, and pours the liquid down his throat. Leaving the hospital, she is devastated by the realization that she has killed him. But later at the funeral, a hospital aide tells her that Mr. Sands's death was "a godsend." And when she confesses her crime to Mr. Sands's wife, Isabelle tells her that it was not Grace's fault but hers, because she turned off his respirator. They cry together and determine that the death could have been from either cause. After they forgive each other, Grace looks up and thinks about the new chance she's been given, and how much she has to be grateful for. "Thank you," she whispers to the universe (*Pancakes*, 248).

Irises by Francisco X. Stork[16] also shows a girl—two girls, actually—facing the huge decision about whether to pull the plug on a loved one. Kate and Mary's father has died, and their mother is in a terminal vegetative state. One girl believes it is God's will that her mother continue as she is, and the other feels that God would not want her mother to continue living with such a reduced quality of life. Kate has been accepted at Stanford, where she aspires to medical school, and her boyfriend has offered to help out by marrying her. Younger sister Mary has her own reasons for wanting to live her own life without being tied to her mother's sickbed. It would be so simple to just. . . . If they could only agree about it. Or get some advice from God.

The Fault in Our Stars

Another tale about facing death, but without the prayers, is *The Fault in Our Stars* by the charismatic John Green.[17] This story about two teens who meet at Cancer Kid Support Group and fall in love was wildly popular with young adults even before it was made into a movie. The list of the novel's many awards and honors includes being one of *Time* magazine's Best Fiction Books of the Year 2012.

Given the background of its author, it is surprising that in a novel so full of the presence of imminent death, the characters neither reach out to God nor find any consolation in the hope of an afterlife, except for one remark by Augustus. Out of nowhere, he asks Hazel, the narrator:

"Do you believe in an afterlife?"

"I think forever is an incorrect concept," I answered . . . "No," I said, and then revised. "Well, maybe I wouldn't go so far as no. You?"

"Yes," he said, his voice full of confidence. "Yes, absolutely. Not like a heaven where you . . . play harps, and live in a mansion made of clouds. But yes, I believe in Something with a capital S. Always have."

"Really?" I asked. I was surprised. I'd always associated belief in heaven with frankly, a kind of intellectual disengagement. But Gus wasn't dumb.

"Yeah," he said quietly. . . . "I don't believe we return to haunt or comfort the living or anything, but I think something becomes of us. . . . I believe humans have souls, and I believe in the conservation of souls." (*Stars*, 167–68)

The Fault in Our Stars is a book written by a self-identified Christian who grew up in the Episcopal Church, majored in religious studies at college, enrolled at Chicago Divinity School (although he never attended classes there), served as a chaplain in a children's hospital, and had aspirations to become an Episcopal priest.[18] Why then has Green backed away from the opportunity to share a faith that is evidently important to him? When a questioner on his website observed that the book was from an atheistic point of view, Green responded:

It seems to me that different characters in the book find various degrees of secular, religious, theistic, and atheistic ways to confront the reality and injustice of suffering, that the book (at least if I did it right) is more an exploration of the variety of responses to suffering than an argument in favor of one over another. . . . I do not believe the job of a novelist is to thrust his or her belief system upon a reader.[19]

However, it must be granted that John Green has acted on his belief system and his influence with teens to initiate several successful and effective worldwide philanthropic enterprises. And it is almost impossible to overestimate his current impact on YA literature. *Wall Street Journal* columnist Alexandra Alter said recently, "Some credit him with ushering in a new golden era for contemporary, realistic, literary teen fiction, following more than a decade of dominance by books about young wizards, sparkly vampires and dystopia."[20]

A Death-Struck Year[21]

In the midst of this necrophilic era for YA fiction, it was almost inevitable that a YA novel would be written about that short time in American history less than one hundred years ago when more people worldwide were killed from a flu epidemic than from the Black Death in the Middle Ages. "Between 1918 and 1920, an estimated 30 to 50 million people worldwide died from Spanish influenza—more than died in World War I. Nearly 675,000 Americans were among the dead" (*Year*, 277). The pandemic is thought to have first appeared in the United States in Kansas in 1918. It spread rapidly across the country, killing mostly healthy young adults, especially young men crowded together in military camps.

Author Makiia Lucier sets the story of *A Death-Struck Year* in Portland, Oregon. It's the fall of 1918, and Cleo Berry, seventeen, is on her own when the dreaded Spanish flu breaks out in the city. The mayor has ordered all mass activities to be shut down, including club meetings, theaters, church services, and schools. Her brother, who is much older and has been her caretaker since their parents died, is out of town with his wife. When Cleo's school is closed, she stays in the family mansion all alone, until she reads in the newspaper that the Red Cross is calling for volunteers to canvass neighborhoods, locating unattended cases of the flu and transporting them to the hospital. Cleo knows all about "unattended cases." When she was a little child, her parents were killed when their carriage veered off a cliff, and Cleo waited all night before she was rescued, an "unattended case." She can't stand the thought of another child waiting for help beside dead parents, so she drives to the temporary hospital in the new public auditorium to volunteer.

At first the staff is dubious because she is so young, but then Hannah, the strong and capable nurse in charge, says, "We do not have the luxury of turning down help when it is offered" (*Year*, 58). Cleo is given a gauze mask, a bag of pamphlets, a Red Cross armband, a list of addresses, and brisk instruction from Hannah. "Knock on doors, find those who are sick, and call for help" (*Year*, 59).

Cleo sets out knocking on doors. At first she is met with suspicion, but then she finds a house where no one answers. She peers in the kitchen window and sees a spilled box of cereal, evidence of an unsupervised child. Where is the mother? She enters the unlocked back door and finds a bedroom.

> The smell of vomit and dirty diapers filled the air. My hand flew to my mouth. It was a bedroom, dim and silent. Two bodies lay on the bed. A woman in a white nightgown was twisted in the sheets, her long dark hair matted with sweat. Dried blood crusted her nose and lips. Her face was the color of chalk. A little boy, no more than three, curled into her side. He had thrown up all over his blue pajamas. (*Year*, 66)

There is a baby, too, also unconscious with the flu. Cleo tries to telephone for the city's one ambulance, but all phones are out of service. Frantic, she hopes for someone to come and take charge, but then realizes the family's lives are solely dependent on her. She picks up the baby, scoops up the toddler, promises the unconscious mother that she will send help, and takes these "unattended cases" to the hospital.

In the days that follow, Cleo and her new partner Kate, also seventeen, have many such desperate adventures. The mortality count grows, and the makeshift hospital is more and more crowded. A young medical student, Edmund, welcomes her help, although he is uncomfortable with her neighborhood work, feeling it is unsafe for a young girl. She resents his bossiness, although she has to admit to herself that he is very good-looking. Their attraction for each other grows more serious as the pandemic rages on and helpers and workers are exhausted by the overwhelming numbers of the sick.

Most shocking to Cleo and Kate, in the midst of all this death, is the sudden demise of a young man who had been perfectly healthy when he asked directions from them on the street. A few hours later his nose begins to hemorrhage, and he falls dead on the sidewalk in a pool of blood. They are shattered by the suddenness of his death. A week later,

Kate begins to bleed and is taken away to die. Cleo is furious with God for—as she thinks—letting this happen. "I wondered how God could have made such a terrible mistake" (*Year*, 238). Yet, she has never, throughout all of her terrible experiences, thought to pray to the Almighty for help and comfort. It is Edmund who now gives her some sense of meaning and purpose in the midst of the chaos. He tells her:

> "I know what it's like to lose a friend and wonder why you're the one left behind. To think that nothing makes sense. Not one thing. . . . But when you wake up tomorrow and think there's no reason to keep going, to get out of bed and put one foot in front of the other, I hope you remember that [the children you've saved] will grow up simply because you chose to stay the course. It's no small thing." (*Year*, 241)

Finally, Cleo finds blood on her handkerchief and knows that she, too, has been infected. She recovers, of course, for an almost happy ending with Edmund, as the war ends and the pandemic is over. Lucier has brought this terrifying time in history alive with vivid details and accurate research. Although a vaccine was hastily thrown together in late 1918, it did nothing to prevent the disease, only lessening its severity. Antibiotics now give us assurance that such a pandemic will never happen again—unless a strain of flu appears that is immune to them.

SUICIDE

Suicide has always been a staple of YA lit, at least the part about how family and friends feel afterward. But there have been a few stories examining suicidal thoughts and actions from the *perpetrator's* point of view. In *Thirteen Reasons Why* by Jay Asher,[22] the dead girl becomes a technologically supported voice from the grave by having mailed a set of tapes just before her death to thirteen of her peers, explaining in excruciating detail why each one of them is guilty of an action that led her to kill herself. *Falling into Place* by Amy Zhang[23] is a fairly typical example of the suicide novel in which a girl is tormented by other girls to the point of feeling worthless and attempting to take her own life. However, this novel is atypical in that the author is still in high school, a circumstance that publishers have sought eagerly ever since Viking discovered sixteen-year-old S. E. Hinton and her groundbreaking *The Outsiders*. A different and very timely motivation for suicide appears in *Tease* by Amanda Maciel[24]: a clique of five girls suspect a new girl has stolen their boyfriends, and so at school and on Facebook they torment her to death. Literally. Two innovative and daring suicide novels have examined the motivations and mindset of a suicide bomber: *In the Name of God* by Paula Jolin,[25] in which a devout young Muslim woman is seduced by the idea of sacrificing herself, and *The Innocent's Story* by Nicky Singer,[26] which uses a dead narrator to get inside the troubled mind of the terrorist who has killed her.

The 39 Deaths of Adam Strand

A strikingly original novel that turns all the clichés about suicide upside down is *The 39 Deaths of Adam Strand* by Gregory Galloway.[27] Most people avoid death with all their might, but Adam Strand yearns for it but is frustrated by the bizarre fact that every time he kills himself, he dies, of course—but then he wakes up perfectly whole and healthy a few hours later, sometimes in the hospital, sometimes in his own bed. He has tried to kill himself "eighteen times by jumping (from bridge or building; or other high place and once from the back of a truck); five by drowning, five by asphyxiation, four by poison overdose, three by hanging, one by fire, one by gun, one by chain saw, and one by train" (*Strand*, 9). He has become a connoisseur of suicide methods, and discusses quite dispassionately the advantages and disadvantages of each. He favors jumping from a bridge.

Why does Adam want so much to die? It's a matter of simple boredom. "I'm the chairman of the bored," he tells his father, who doesn't laugh. Adam isn't unhappy, nor does he have any traumas in his life; he comes from a solid working-class family in a nice little town with parents who are loving and concerned. But everything seems bland and meaningless to him, a tormenting round of sameness over and over. "The summer dragged on for me with excruciating dullness, like a train squealing along in slow motion, derailed and scraping along the tracks with no end in sight" (*Strand*, 204).

He has friends, but their association is more a matter of habit than an affinity for each other. They spend every day of the summer at the Point, a secluded piece of land that sticks out into the river, where they drink alcohol they have filched because it's something to do. They are observed by a marble angel, a statue with outstretched arms, who is often the only spectator of the many times Adam has jumped from the bridge. The biggest thing this summer is a dead cow that floats into some branches on the river shore and stays there to decompose, a process the boys watch with fascination and much speculation. None of them have girlfriends, but Adam has Jodi, a girl who has been his confidante since kindergarten, and Maddy, a ten-year-old prodigy who adores him.

Adam's thoughts circle perpetually on death. He thinks he knows a lot about it:

> The world is perfect when you're dead. There are no problems, no grief, no distress, disgust, no disease, discomfort, or disappointment; there's no shame, sadness, betrayal, or boredom; nothing is lost or gained, nothing is wasted or wanted, nothing is said or left unsaid. . . . Nothing is nothing, and everything is quiet and calm. It's perfect. Maybe that's what heaven is, a perfect nothing, an emptying out of everything until you are as clean at the moment before your first breath, a serene absence of everything. Maybe it's not even a place, but I've been there . . . many times. I know what it's like. (*Strand*, 48–49)

His parents' reaction to his many suicide attempts is a note of humor in this somber novel. At first they are happy at his reanimations, but then with repeated occurrences they grow annoyed and petulant. But they comfort themselves by reminding each other that at least they are spared a parent's primary worry—that a child will be accidentally killed. At school Adam is regarded as a freak and often beaten up, once even stabbed. His friends are bemused at his talent and think it would make a great TV reality show where he would kill himself in front of the camera in various ways in response to contestants' suggestions. Only Don Lemley, a police dispatcher, takes his problem seriously. Don is a man of faith, and Adam comes to think of his frequent telephone calls as the Voice of God. He never once tells Adam not to kill himself, but simply listens and offers solutions, often Biblical.

Now here author Galloway has painted himself into a corner. The actors and the scenery are in place, but what can a writer do to create suspenseful and exciting developments with a protagonist that we know can't die? The book trails off, not with a bang but a whimper, as Adam finds some meaning in the love he has for Jodi and Maddy and resolves to resist the urge to jump.

THE AFTERLIFE

When the other dead fellows are not narrating or influencing the action in novels, where do they go? YA writers have imagined a wide variety of depictions of "heaven" but have almost never availed themselves of traditional Christian theology about the afterlife as a dimension outside of time and space where the soul returns peacefully to God. Certainly it is impossible for us finite beings to imagine eternity. Along these lines, Frank Wade, the Interim Dean of the National Cathedral in Washington, D.C., has said, "What lies beyond death is as darkly veiled for us as life after birth is to an unborn child. There is no way we could explain life as we know it to one whose whole existence has been in the womb. Similarly, there is no way that Jesus or anyone else can make earthly sense of heaven's ways. The key is not information . . . it is trust."[28]

"Under Hell, Over Heaven"

Nevertheless, some YA authors have been audacious enough to attempt to give us a literal picture of the afterworld. Margo Lanagan's horrifying evocation of purgatory from "Under Hell, Over Heaven," is a story in her collection *Red Spikes*.[29] Four teens have lost all ability to feel any emotion but bland resignation and hopeless doggedness as they slog back and forth between paradise and hell delivering the damned and the redeemed to their respective final destinations.

As the story opens, they are escorting a naked miscreant back to the Gates of Hell after he has visited in Heaven. The teens are not allowed in either place. They must stay in this gray, rocky plain of nothingness until they earn their eventual entrance into Heaven by accumulating credits for their escort duties. The miscreant whines and cries, but they feel no pity. "It's not as if you weren't warned," thinks Leah, one of the escort crew (*Spikes*, 108). As they draw nearer to Hell, they put on wet booties to preserve their feet from the now red-hot rocks. *Tsss, tsss, tsss, tsss* go the steaming booties; they hurry so the footgear won't dry out. Hell's Gate is attended by beings in fire suits who carry poles tipped by sharp spikes. The door to the netherworld is a big hole in the ground with a heavy rock lid. One of the fire suits slaps a switch and—

> The wheels turned. The chain tightened on the eyebolt in the ground. The circle of the lid was suddenly clear in the rock, outlined in knee-high puffs of smoke. Human screams rushed out with the smoke. . . . Something moved in the smoke like a dark sea anemone. . . . They were hands, all those movements, blood-red hands on the blood-streaked, steaming arms of the Damned. In a frenzy they waved and clutched at the outer air; they pawed the lid and the ground; they left prints; they

wet and reddened the rock with their slaps and slidings. The fire suits stood well back from the opening. Any hand that found a grip they prodded until it flinched back into the waving mass, into the high suffering howl of Hell. (*Spikes*, 109, 112)

Leah exults in the temporary return of her ability to feel, to smell, to hear even these sights and sounds. She grabs slippery white handfuls of a naked miscreant and pushes him in.

The machinery clanked; the lid shuddered and began to lower. . . . The hairless faces, all melted and remelted flesh, spat and bubbled and ran with juices. And they knew—their eyes begged and their bloodied lips pleaded in a thousand different languages. . . .

Thud. The lid closed, sealing in the Damned. (*Spikes*, 113)

"Ferryman"

A less terrifying and gentler story from Margo Lanagan is taken from Ancient Greek ideas of the transition to the afterworld. In "Ferryman," a short story in the collection *Yellowcake*,[30] we meet what seems to be a perfectly ordinary household—a mum and her teenage daughter, preparing a box lunch for the dad, which the daughter is about to take to him at his place of employment. Boring. Except that the workplace is a dock on the underground River Styx, and the dad's job is to herd the dead into a ferry and pole them across the river to the other side, where he leaves them to walk to the Blessed Place. Not without travail—they must go through fire to get there, he tells them. The trip is made bearable by the Lethe water the Ferryman makes sure they drink so that they will feel nothing—ever again.

But on this day, while the daughter watches in horror, the ferryman slips on some tears spilled on the deck and falls into the dreadful river. He is dead instantly, but still talking, still himself. His hair sloughs off in the water; his flesh becomes transparent, but he must go up to the surface to truly die. The daughter tries to persuade him to remain below, but he insists that his time has come. His wife comes down the stairs for a tearful and passionate farewell. As soon as he steps up out of the tunnel, he falls dead. Later, after he has been properly buried, the daughter goes down to the River Styx and sees him coming with all the other dead of the day. He asks her to take care of her mother for him, and then he drinks the water of forgetfulness and the light fades out of his eyes. She takes his place on the ferry and wields the pole to pump the boatload of the dead to the other side. She thinks, "I never realized, all the years my father did this, what solitary work it is" (*Yellowcake*, 174).

Other writers offer less literal versions of the afterlife, in which the afterworld resembles, for instance, either a skycam for observing the action on Earth or a waiting room in eternity where wrongs are made right. Most chilling is Philip Pullman's concept, in *The Amber Spyglass*,[31] of a place like the ancient Hades, where crowds of sad shades are condemned to mill about like human cattle in an eternal twilight world, and when they are released they dissolve into a mysterious substance called Dust. Most poetic, Sonya Hartnett evokes at least a whiff of the fragrance of the traditional idea of heaven in the last sentence of *Surrender*[32]: "Wings unfold around me and, with a mighty sweep of air, I alone am lifted skyward, from where I first arrived." And most satisfying is Harry Potter's "death," spent in a place of reconciliation, the railroad station to Hogwarts called, significantly, King's Cross.[33]

Other depictions of the afterlife are ingenious in their variety: Gabrielle Zevin imagines an afterworld where everyone gets younger all the time (*Elsewhere*)[34]; John H. Ritter depicts a homey kitchen where the InDoc cooks bacon and eggs and helps dead soldiers get in touch with their guilt for killing ("Baseball in Iraq" in *Dreams and Visions*).[35] And *Heaven Looks a Lot Like the Mall* by Wendy Mass[36] is self-explanatory.

ANGELS AND DEVILS

But what about the permanent residents of Heaven and Hell—the angels and the devils? Both kinds of otherworldly beings can be found aplenty in YA fantasy fiction, in various traditional or nontraditional guises and roles.

The idea of angels was adopted by the ancient Hebrews during the Babylonian Captivity, when they were exposed to Zoroastrianism, which posited supernatural winged beings who carried messages between God and the earth. The word "angel" comes from the Greek "angelos," and the Hebrew "mal'ak"—both words meaning "messenger." The writings of St. Thomas Aquinas in 1259 set the foundation for the Christian understanding of angels. He divided these beings into nine categories, or choirs, each with separate duties and areas of responsibility; they appear in three groups of triads, in ascending order of power: (1) seraphim, cherubim, thrones; (2) dominions, virtues, powers; and (3) principalities, angels, and archangels. Although many angels appear in the Bible, only Michael and Gabriel are named. Michael is the leader of the angels, and it was Gabriel who announced to Mary that she would give birth to the Son of God. Mohammed was said to have declared that Gabriel dictated the Koran to him. The concept of guardian angels comes from antiquity also: "The Greeks believed a familiar spirit called a daemon was assigned to each person at birth and guided that person through life." In contemporary times this has been expanded to two guardian angels per person, one good and one evil. [37]

Devils, of course, are fallen angels, who were led by Lucifer, or Satan, to challenge God for power, a concept that was developed to explain evil beings in nondualistic Judaism. This story was never incorporated into canonical Scripture, although it does exist in the apocryphal *Book of Enoch* and was used by John Milton in *Paradise Lost.* "Now they perpetually war against God by attempting to ruin the earth, God's creation." [38]

C. S. Lewis is the author of the classic devilish dialogue, *The Screwtape Letters,* a collection of instructive missives from a senior devil to a young rookie who is just learning the fine points of temptation. Because of this book Lewis was often asked if he believed in the Devil. No, he explained, not the Devil of popular imagination, a sardonic figure in red tights with horns, a pointed tail, and a pitchfork. "I believe in angels," he wrote in his author's preface, "and I believe that some of these, by the abuse of their free will, have become enemies to God and, as a corollary, to us. . . . They do not differ in nature from good angels, but their nature is depraved." [39]

It is important to remember that in Judeo-Christian theology angels and devils are separate beings from humans, a different species of creation. They are not humans transformed after death. Several YA authors of fantasy seem to be unaware of this distinction or choose to ignore it. Angels and devils appear frequently in fantasy fiction in one form or another, but are often changed to suit the story. In the great trilogy His Dark Materials by Philip Pullman, [40] each human has a daemon (not a demon) who is a lifelong companion, but in the shape of an animal that represents the essence of that person's soul. The closeness of this relationship and the pain that comes from separation are major elements in the story.

Other examples are L. A. Weatherly's Angel Burn trilogy,[41] which features some very odd angels: "Although they look like stereotypical angels, these are actually aliens who feed off human energy and are determined to take over Earth."[42] This series is also remarkable for its Killer Angels, who are opposed by human Angel Killers. Bryony Pearce's novel *Angel's Fury*[43] looks at an equally dark and grim scenario inspired by the evil and malevolent Nephilim of the Old Testament. The Demon's Lexicon trilogy by Sarah Rees Brennan[44] explores "what a demon might be like if it were brought up as a human. . . . Could an emotionless, evil creature without a voice be taught loving emotions, how to speak, how to live as a human?"[45] The angels in Scott Speer's Immortal City[46] novels are glamorous celebrities, annoyed by hordes of fans and paparazzi. Archangels Michael and Raphael are characters in *Kindred*[47] and *Spoils*[48] by Tammar Stein. And in Gina Damico's delightful trilogy, *Croak, Scorch,* and *Rogue*,[49] a misbehaving teen is sent to spend the summer with her uncle, who turns out to be a Grim Reaper and teaches her the family business. In other books there are angel academies, sexy angel lovers, angel death escorts, unwanted angel houseguests from hell, demonic armies and girl demon slayers, half-human angels and demons—most of them getting ready for a final battle between good and evil. And in fantasy fiction, who knows which is which.

Although they may be fun to read, there is very little spiritual nourishment in most of these fantastic—even grotesque—evocations of the beatific and the demonic. A fact that may be a consequence of so much angelic/demonic reading comes from YA expert Dr. Joni Bodart, who quotes a 1994 Gallup Youth Survey on "Teen Belief in the Supernatural" that found that "76 percent of more than five hundred teens ages thirteen to seventeen indicated that they believe in angels." By 2004 this figure was up to 78 percent.[50] But what bizarre shapes and purposes are these teens imagining for God's messengers?

Where Things Come Back

Almost never do angels and devils appear in contemporary realistic novels. An exception, one that hints at some of these ideas, is the 2012 Printz Award winner *Where Things Come Back* by John Corey Whaley.[51] Death, or its possibility, saturates the story. The book opens with a visit to the morgue by Cullen Witter, who is there to identify the body of his druggie cousin. The town has been revived by the discovery of a rare bird called the Lazarus woodpecker, a name drawn from the story of Jesus raising a friend from the dead. Cullen tries not to think the worst about the disappearance and probable kidnapping of his angelic little brother Gabriel. The missionary Benton Sage jumps to his death from the bell tower because "he had tried to help the world but the world wouldn't let him" (*Things*, 82), even though at the beginning of his ministry the angel Gabriel had appeared to him in the form of a boy, saying Benton had found favor in God's sight. Cullen's brother Gabriel is evidently named for the angel, and his absence and presence in the story seems to be significant, although in the last chapter, when he does return, it is ambiguous whether he has actually escaped his kidnapper or whether Cullen, who seems to be prone to hallucinations, is having another such episode. The Book of Enoch, too, and its description of the origin of the Nephilim is dropped with no discernable purpose into this death-filled and puzzling story.

WHY HAS DEATH BECOME SO UBIQUITOUS IN YA FICTION?

A troubling aspect of this deathly trend is that so rarely do we find spiritual questioning on the part of the dying or any consolation of faith. The characters seldom ask in prayer for release from suffering, for peace, for comfort for themselves and their grieving relatives and friends. Church ladies are not there to bring casseroles, the clergy are not called in to help the transition of the soul, and God is almost never blamed or invoked in any way—except by the suicide bombers who call on Allah. There is only a bleak sense of ending, of an imminent black nothingness.

So if spiritual exploration is not the point, what *is* behind all this interest in death on the part of YA authors and readers? Has the subject surfaced so intensely as a reflection of our perilous times? Is it because suburban teens are bored with their seemingly safe existence and want to contemplate scary extremes? Teens, as the cliché goes, think they are immortal. Is it more comfortable for them than for adults to read close-up accounts of death, since they are theoretically further away from having to accept their own mortality?

Or is it simply a literary trope? YA critic Jonathan Hunt suggested to me in an email that "the dead narrator gives the narrative a sense of immediacy that is so characteristic of YA fiction, but at the same time allows for a degree of reflection and self-awareness that would probably otherwise seem jarring for a young adult narrator."[52] Or perhaps it is a by-product of the craze for fantasy, a taste for extreme and bloody fiction of the supernatural. Or maybe vice versa—so much fantasy reading has led to a desire on the part of teen readers for more intense reality in even the most realistic novels. In any case, death has become a fact of life for YA literature.

NOTES

1. J. D. Salinger, *The Catcher in the Rye* (New York: Little, Brown, 1951).
2. Alice Sebold, *The Lovely Bones* (New York: Little, Brown, 2002).
3. Markus Zusak, *The Book Thief* (New York: Knopf, 2006).
4. Chris Crutcher, *The Sledding Hill* (New York: Greenwillow, 2005).
5. Pete Hautman, *Invisible* (New York: Simon & Schuster, 2005).
6. Laura Whitcomb, *A Certain Slant of Light* (New York: Graphia/Houghton Mifflin, 2005).
7. Laura Whitcomb, *Under the Light* (New York: Houghton Mifflin, 2013).
8. Gary Soto, *The Afterlife* (New York: Harcourt, 2003).
9. Geraldine McCaughrean, *The White Darkness* (New York: HarperTeen, 2005).
10. Deborah Noyes, ed. *The Restless Dead: Ten Original Stories of the Supernatural* (Somerville, MA: Candlewick, 2007).
11. Sonya Hartnett, *Surrender* (Cambridge, MA: Candlewick, 2005).
12. Chris Crutcher, *Deadline* (New York: Greenwillow, 2007).
13. Jenny Downham, *Before I Die* (New York: David Fickling Books, 2007).
14. A. J. Betts, *Zac and Mia* (New York: Houghton Mifflin, 2014).
15. Robin Epstein, *God Is in the Pancakes* (New York: Dial, 2010). Hereafter cited in the text as *Pancakes*.
16. Francisco X. Stork, *Irises* (New York: Scholastic, 2012).
17. John Green, *The Fault in Our Stars* (New York: Dutton, 2012). Hereafter cited in the text as *Stars*.
18. Marc McEvoy, "Interview John Green," *Sydney Morning Herald*, July 12, 2009. Accessed July 31, 2014, www.smh.com.au/entertainment/book/interview-john-green-20120119-1q71w.html.
19. Accessed July 19, 2014, johngreenbooks.com/questions-about-the-fault-in-our-stars-spoilers/#beliefs.
20. Alexandra Alter, "John Green and His Nerdfighters Are Upending the Summer Blockbuster Model," *Wall Street Journal*, May 14, 2014. Accessed July 25, 2014, http://online.WSJ.com/articles/john-green-1270230443110457955217306616 9420.html.
21. Makiia Lucier, *A Death-Struck Year* (New York: Houghton Mifflin, 2014). Hereafter cited in the text as *Year*.
22. Jay Asher, *Thirteen Reasons Why* (New York: Penguin, 2007).
23. Amy Zhang, *Falling into Place* (New York: HarperCollins, 2014).
24. Amanda Maciel, *Tease* (New York: Balzer & Bray/HarperCollins, 2014).
25. Paula Jolin, *In the Name of God* (New York: MacMillan, 2007).
26. Nicky Singer, *The Innocent's Story* (New York: Holiday House, 2007).
27. Gregory Galloway, *The 39 Deaths of Adam Strand* (New York: Dutton, 2013). Hereafter cited in text as *Strand*.

28. Frank Wade, *Forward Day by Day* (Cincinnati, OH: Forward Movement, 2014), 68.

29. Margo Lanagan, *Red Spikes* (New York: Knopf, 2007). Hereafter cited in text as *Spikes*.

30. Margo Lanagan, *Yellowcake* (New York: Knopf, 2013). Hereafter cited in text as *Yellowcake*.

31. Philip Pullman, *The Amber Spyglass* (His Dark Materials, Book III) (New York: Knopf, 2000).

32. Sonya Hartnett, *Surrender* (Cambridge, MA: Candlewick, 2005).

33. J. K. Rowling, *Harry Potter and the Deathly Hallows* (New York: Scholastic, 2007).

34. Gabrielle Zevin, *Elsewhere* (New York: Square Fish, 2007).

35. M. Jerry Weiss and Helen Weiss, eds. *Dreams and Visions: Fourteen Flights of Fantasy* (New York: Starscape/Tom Dougherty Associates, 2006).

36. Wendy Mass, *Heaven Looks a Lot Like the Mall* (New York: Little, Brown, 2007).

37. Evelyn Dorothy Oliver and James R. Lewis, *Angels A to Z* (Detroit, MI: Visible Ink, 1996).

38. Oliver and Lewis, *Angels*.

39. C. S. Lewis, *The Screwtape Letters* (London: Geoffrey Blos, 1942).

40. Philip Pullman (His Dark Materials, I–III) (New York: Knopf, 1995–2000).

41. L. A. Weatherly, *Angel Burn* (Somerville, MA: Candlewick, 2011).

42. Joni Bodart, *They Suck, They Bite, They Eat, They Kill: The Psychological Meaning of Supernatural Monsters in Young Adult Fiction*. Scarecrow Studies in Young Adult Literature, No. 43 (Lanham, MD: Scarecrow, 2012), 198.

43. Bryony Pearce, *Angel's Fury* (London: Egmont, 2011).

44. Sarah Rees Brennan, *The Demon's Lexicon* (Demon's Lexicon Trilogy) (New York: Simon & Schuster/Margaret McElderry Books, 2009).

45. Bodart, *Suck*, 201. www.gallup.com/poll/11770/eternal-destinations-americans-believe-heaven-hell.aspx.

46. Scott Speer, Immortal City series (New York: Penguin/Razorbill, 2012–2014).

47. Tammar Stein, *Kindred* (New York: Knopf, 2011).

48. Tammar Stein, *Spoils* (New York: Knopf, 2013).

49. Gina Damico, *Croak, Scorch, Rogue* (New York: Houghton Mifflin Harcourt, 2012–2013).

50. Bodart, *Suck*, 231.

51. John Corey Whaley, *Where Things Come Back* (New York: Atheneum, 2011). Hereafter cited in the text as *Things*.

52. Jonathan Hunt, email to the author, June 12, 2011.

Chapter Four

End Times and the Apocalypse

Apocalyptic themes began to appear in young adult literature as the millennium approached and have continued to do so in the postmillennium age. The growing visibility of human evil and suffering as brought to us every evening by the TV news, the ever more desperate need to find a way to change society for the sake of the environment, "wars and rumors of wars" and the specter of nuclear war, our cold materialistic culture—all this makes people expect, or even long for, the imminent end of the world. Such thinking shows up in YA fiction, in realistic novels in which a young person's spiritual search is shaped by a family's expectation of the apocalypse, and also in novels set in past times when the end seemed near.

One of the first of these end-times stories was published four years before the millennium, and reflected the widespread uneasiness that was beginning to emerge about that impending date. *The Rapture of Canaan* by Sheri Reynolds[1] takes place in a rural religious commune called the Church of Fire and Brimstone and God's Almighty Baptizing Wind. The founder keeps his flock in line with constant reminders of the coming return of Jesus and the end of the world, while his granddaughter makes the best of her time on earth by getting pregnant with her prayer partner.

Three years later, *Armaggedon Summer*[2] was written collaboratively by Jane Yolen and Bruce Coville in two voices. Marina (written by Yolen) and Jed (written by Coville) have been taken unwillingly by their parents to the top of a mountain, where the members of a cult are waiting for the end of the world on July 27, 2000. On the appointed day, violence erupts, but not in the shape they had anticipated. Outsiders attempt to force their way into what they think will be salvation in the mountain camp, and Jed's father dies in the crossfire. Later the two young people find their own separate spiritual paths leading away from the hilltop: hers, a restored belief in God, but still with doubt, and his, only a conviction that something bigger exists that we're part of.

THE RAPTURE

Belief in the end-times scenario called "The Rapture" is embraced by many American fundamentalist sects. They base their ideas on several Bible passages. First, in the Gospel of Luke, Jesus describes "the day when the Son of man is revealed":

> On that day, let him who is on the housetop, with his goods in the house, not come down to take them away, and likewise let him who is in the field not turn back. . . . I tell you, in that night there will be two men in one bed; one will be taken and the other left. There will be two women grinding together; one will be taken and the other left. [3]

And in the Gospel of Matthew Jesus talks in a similar vein of "the coming of the Son of man":

> Then two men will be in the field; one is taken and one is left. Two women will be grinding at the mill; one is taken and one is left. Watch therefore, for you do not know on what day your Lord is coming. [4]
>
> Immediately after the tribulation of those days the sun will be darkened, and the moon will not give its light, and the stars will fall from heaven, and the powers of the heavens will be shaken; then will appear the sign of the Son of man in heaven, and then all the tribes of the earth will mourn, and they will see the Son of man coming on the clouds of heaven with power and great glory; and he will send out his angels with a loud trumpet call, and they will gather his elect from the four winds, from one end of heaven to the other. [5]

The book of Revelation also has much to say about the end of the world, often in spooky metaphors about strange creatures. And a passage from First Thessalonians, taken in its entirety, seems to have been meant to comfort, with assurance of resurrection, those who were grieving their recent dead:

But we would not have you ignorant, brethren, concerning those who are asleep, that you may not grieve as others do who have no hope. For since we believe that Jesus died and rose again, even so, through Jesus, God will bring with him those who have fallen asleep. . . . For the Lord himself will descend from heaven with a cry of command, with the archangel's call, and with the sound of the trumpet of God. And the dead in Christ will rise first, then we who are alive, who are left, shall be caught up together with them in the clouds to meet the Lord in the air; and so we shall always be with the Lord. Therefore comfort one another with these words.[6]

However, the interpretation given these passages by fundamentalists is far from comforting. A central part of Rapture belief is that only a few faithful Christians will be "taken up," and the rest of us will remain behind to endure a terrible time of fire and brimstone and plagues called the Tribulation. These ideas, preached today in scary detail by popular evangelists, were originally developed in the Scofield Bible.[7] First printed in 1909, and then in 1917, it used the standard King James Version for a basis, but added the innovation of an extensive—and wildly creative—commentary which appeared alongside the text, rather than as a separate volume. (Among the legacies of this commentary is the confident declaration that the world was created in 4004 BCE, an assertion that has fueled the evolution controversy.) Both editions were extremely popular, but it was the 1967 reprinting that captured the imaginations of American fundamentalists in a turbulent Cold War era. Since then many churches have adopted their own versions of these ideas, although most mainstream denominations accept the idea of the Rapture only in the sense of a general final resurrection.

A tendency to predict an imminent date for the end-times has led to embarrassment for a number of religious leaders when that date comes and goes. A recent failed prediction by radio personality Harold Camping in 2011 gave great *schadenfreude* to the media, and financial collapse to the radio station that had spent millions publicizing the non-event.[8]

But as Scofield told it, the Rapture is a good story, and many televangelists and other popular Christian leaders like Jimmy Swaggart and Hal Lindsey have seized on it to add theatrics to their preaching and writing. Most successful among these adaptations is the Left Behind book series, authored by Tim LaHaye and Jerry Jenkins, which generated forty adult titles and many spin-offs such as CDs, three action thriller films, graphic novels, musical albums, an audio play, and several computer games.

However, it is LaHaye's series for young adults, Left Behind: The Kids,[9] that is most relevant here. Published between 1997 and 2005, the slim plots of these little books derived from incidents in the adult series. They trace the harrowing lives of some teenagers who are eponymously left behind and become the Young Tribulation Force to confront and battle with the Global Community and its leader, the Antichrist. Many action scenes result. Although the Left Behind series was enormously popular both in its adult and juvenile versions, it is not to be taken seriously, either as theology or literature.

This Side of Salvation

A YA novel that rings the bell on both qualities is *This Side of Salvation.*[10] The author, Jeri Smith-Ready, is utterly successful in conveying the creepiness and the appalling unfairness of the idea of the Rapture *and* its appeal for troubled souls, while at the same time succeeding on the level of a suspenseful mystery novel, a sensual romance, a baseball story, a gender-identity novel, and a spiritual-search narrative. Along the way she even tosses in some YA tropes like the Big Game, the Losing of the Virginity scene, the Gay Best Friend, and a writerly fancy dance in the form of shuffling the time frame of the novel. But it is the theme of the Rapture and subsequent disappearance that holds this rich mix together.

David, his parents, and his sister are grieving the death of the family's eldest son from a random shooting. Each of them reacts to the loss in his or her own way—the parents by withdrawing, and David and his sister by rebelling. David is mad at everything and everybody, especially God. He emblazons his rage on the walls of the town in midnight graffiti asking "Why God why?" When he defaces the big blank highway sidewall of Stony Hill megachurch on a Saturday night, he is shocked when his father drives the family there for Sunday services the next morning. Their accustomed house of worship is St. Mark's Episcopal Church where, as the congregation often reassures newcomers, "You don't need to check your brains at the door." But there is only coincidence and no hidden agenda this Sunday in the change of church, as becomes apparent when David confesses the graffiti to the pastor and is warmly forgiven.

The shift in denominational allegiance seems to make David's parents happier, and so it is moderately okay with David and Mara, in spite of the megachurch's evangelical slant. Stony Hill's congregation debunks climate change—David's homeschooling mom writes a big red "LIES" on an article he writes on the subject, although she doesn't read it. And this church accepts the inevitability of the Rapture, although they decline to put a date on it. After all, David thinks, there are times when the Rapture seems like the ideal solution. "This planet is so screwed up, how could God *not* want to hit the universal delete key and start over?" (*TSS*, 8). (A sentiment that may shed light on why the apocalyptic theme is so common in YA fantasy fiction.)

Meanwhile, David's spiritual search takes a leap forward when he discovers Bible research.

> It had happened accidentally. Last year, I'd fallen behind in Bible-study class, so I'd looked up the lessons' Scripture passages on Wikipedia. The entry not only summed up stories for easy memorizing, it also put them in historical context. That's when I got curious and started doing real research in books and articles. For the first time, I saw the Bible as a human creation. Rather than making Scripture seem like BS, this discovery made it even more fascinating. Because what people are *trying* to say is even more interesting than what they actually say. (*TSS*, 121)

This research tool serves him well when his gay best friend Kane, who has newly come out, is invited to David's birthday dinner at IHOP by his disapproving parents. At the restaurant table the pair harass Kane with quotations from Scripture. David's father, who has recently decided to speak only in Bible verses, weighs in with the dreaded Leviticus 18:22: "You shall not lie with a man as with a woman. That is an abomination."[11] But David is prepared and able to explain the passage in historical context. His mother is not impressed. "The Bible is not some dusty old history book. . . . It is the living Word, which means every word in it applies to us today" (*TSS*, 121–22), she says, biting off each syllable with curled lips. And then, when David tries to change the subject by reminding them that Kane is going to be confirmed next month, she asks, "Does the bishop know that our friend here is a deviant?" Kane stays cool and turns the tables by assuring them that he doesn't know if the bishop is aware of his orientation, but his pastor knows, "and he's fine with it. Everyone is welcome at St. Mark's. . . .

Including you guys, whenever you're ready to come back." David feels like applauding (*TSS*, 119).

The opening of the presents is a welcome change of focus. David has been hinting for a certain sports video game, and he's sure that's what his parents have given him. But, no. Inside the wrappings is the latest Left Behind video game—Tribulation Squad 6. David has been repelled since his brother's death by all weapons and shooting, and he protests, but his mother says, "It's intended to be a nonviolent game. In fact, the reviews say that your spirit points drop if you kill your enemies. Except in self-defense, of course" (*TSS*, 117). Also you get points whenever you pause to pray, she explains. David hides his disappointment, but cheers up when he finds that Kane's gift is the video game he has wanted.

Soon the still-grieving parents are caught up in a cult that isn't afraid to name the date of the end of the world—and it is to be less than six months from the present. The ministry is led by the charismatic and beautiful Sophia Visser, who doesn't ask for money or weekly attendance and conducts her church as a one-on-one affair online. When his father goes away on weeklong "fishing trips" and comes back glowing, David asks no questions, but when his parents, as preparation for the Last Day, require that he "voluntarily" give up all his worldly attachments—his friends, his newly blooming romance with the lovely Bailey, the baseball team, his special school—he is bitter and resentful.

The loss of his closeness with God is a catastrophe of this emotion, and he yearns for it back:

> Part of me wishes I'd never lost that all-consuming hunger [for the divine embrace]. My soul still craves the unseen, unflinching love that was there for me in my darkest hours. Sometimes my lungs still need it to breathe. But even the sweetest faith can taste sour when it's used as poison. (*TSS*, 2)

At last the evening of the Rapture arrives. As a final gesture of rebellion, David and his sister, Mara, sneak out to a prom after-party, planning to be home by two-thirty, in time to comfort their parents when the scheduled time of 3:00 a.m. comes and goes with no Rapture. But it's a great party; they are drunk; the police come; everyone runs, and the upshot is that they don't get home until three-thirty. Cringing in the expectation of their father's anger, they enter the dark house and call. No answer. They go upstairs to the parents' bedroom, and find a horror. Smith-Ready has given us an unforgettable image that will dominate and haunt the rest of the book, and ultimately provide salvation for David and Mara:

> Half under the sheet and comforter, where my mother and father should be, lie their clothes: my dad's blue-striped pajamas, a white undershirt peeking above the top of the V-neck; my mom's pale-pink nightgown, magenta roses embroidered on the wide shoulder straps.
> Matching gold crosses dangle off their pillows, in place of their absent necks. (*TSS*, 14)

When David and Mara recover a bit from the shock, they draw in Bailey and Kane, and search the house for clues, especially their parents' computers and cell phones. Then the four sit down to focus on an explanation for the disappearance. Option one: they've been raptured is immediately discarded as "plain crazy." Option two: they've been kidnapped, and option three: they ran away, seem almost as unlikely, but eventually, when David discovers the coordinates for the location of his father's "fishing trips," he and his sister set out on an eventful rescue mission that leads to a surprising conclusion.

Along the way this journey parallels David's spiritual journey, with another satisfying conclusion. He has come through anger at God, confession of his crime, forgiveness for his parents, discovery of a new way of understanding Scripture, sorting out and speaking up for what he believes, and now he regains that closeness with God that he thought he had lost, as the peace and beauty of the wilderness night leads him to a prayer as intimate as just talking with God about what is on his mind. Facing his apocalyptic concerns, he prays:

> If I really love you, I should want you to show up now. Nothing personal, God, but . . . you've made something good here. I think you should see it through to the end. The natural end, not the one humans have written. (*TSS*, 304)

A story that begins with grief and anger and ends with joy and reconciliation, *This Side of Salvation* is a complex and honest novel. The *VOYA* reviewer, Kristi Sadowski, gave it a rousing five for popularity, and four for quality. She described it as "a frighteningly realistic story that delicately handles the issues of religion and family—an emotional mystery sure to be popular and perfect for discussion."[12]

At least two other YA novels have used the search for Raptured parents as a framework for the plot. *Shift* by Charlotte Agell[13] takes place in a future world that is being taken over by hypocritical religious fundamentalists after an accidental nuclear bomb has made the far northern United States a dead zone. When their mom disappears, Adrian, Shriek, and his friend Lenora flee the HomeState forces to look for her. They find their dad in the family's Maine mountain cabin, and take part in a Resistance attack on the headquarters of HomeState, but not in time to prevent an end-of-the-world holographic fake Rapture in the sky. They rescue mom, who has been a counteragent, and set out for further north, although the sequel that would have told the rest of the story evidently was never published. Christianity itself, albeit an exaggerated version, is the villain in this book.

Vivian Apple at the End of the World

The same is true of Katie Coyle's *Vivian Apple at the End of the World*.[14] The Rapture has come and gone, but only a few thousand believers are missing, among them Vivian Apple's parents, who seem to have gone up to heaven through two holes in their bedroom ceiling. The world is divided between Believers, who are dangerously angry at being left behind, and Non-Believers, who just want to get on with their lives before the predicted second and final apocalypse. But the Believers make this difficult, as they have been taught by the founder of the Church of America, Pastor Beaton Frick. He is not only the religious leader, but the CEO of the accompanying multimillion-dollar corporation that publishes the church's magazines, runs their television networks, and sells end-of-the-world food supplies.

At the almost deserted high school, one brave but clueless teacher is speaking to a gathering of kids who are desperate for truth:

> "Listen," she says. . . . "There is nobody on this earth whose life is not of value. And that includes those of us who have been left behind. I don't know where all those people went. Maybe they did go to some Christian heaven. But what I'm saying is, we're good people too. . . . I don't want you to write off the rest of your lives, just because someone else's God didn't try to save you. Because you know what? The fact that he didn't means he's a bad God." (*Apple*, 35)

She goes on to lead them in a list of things they can do to start remaking the world—recycle, carpool, support unions. The whole scene is a bit pathetic as the teacher settles for comfort in yesterday's platitudes, although author Coyle's intention seems to be to present her as a wise mentor.

Vivian's audacious friend Harp persuades her to go to a Rapture party, where she tries to make conversation with a cute boy. Unexpectedly, he asks her, "What do you believe?" She disappoints him—and herself—by not being able to answer the question. Later in the story, she and Harp, Harp's boyfriend Raj, *and* the cute boy, whose name is Peter, set out to find Vivian's parents and Peter's father. Throughout many adventures in a world where those who believe in God have become the enemy, she continues to look for belief, but not very hard. Eventually, when they corner Frick in his hideout and discover that he has become decrepit and senile, Peter asks her again:

> "Tell me. Do you believe in heaven?"
> I shake my head.
> "Do you believe in God?"
> I hesitate, then shake my head.
> "What *do* you believe, Vivian?"
> I've been asked this question so many times at this point—and asked it of myself even more—that I should have for him an articulate answer, one that encompasses everything I think is important about the world I inhabit, the world I think Frick has made significantly worse. I believe, like Peter said, that we should love each other. I believe . . . . that we are all people before we are groups. But what I'm feeling at this moment is something deeper than these platitudes. It's something huge and primordial and completely beyond my understanding. I believe in Peter. I believe in Harp. I believe in me. (*Apple*, 223)

And maybe she believes in God without knowing it.

Rapture Practice

But if these pictures of parental commitment to an apocalyptic expectation seem extreme and unrealistic to some readers, I recommend a YA nonfiction book that is a memoir of just such an experience. Aaron Hartzler wrote his debut autobiographical novel *Rapture Practice*[15] to show his personal and spiritual struggles with the beliefs of his fundamentalist parents—the limitations they imposed on his young life as a teen, and the agonizing fight to become his true self instead of a lying facade to please his father. He begins with the basics:

> Something you should know up front about my family.

We believe that Jesus is coming back. . . .

I don't mean metaphorically, like someday in the distant future when the lion lies down with the lamb and there is peace on earth. I mean literally, like glance out the car window and, "Oh, hey, there's Jesus in the sky." There will be a trumpet blast, an archangel will shout, and Jesus Christ will appear in the clouds. We believe that people all over the world who have been born again by accepting Jesus as their personal savior from sin will float up into the air to meet him. . . .

It could happen today.

It could happen tomorrow.

It could happen before you finish reading this sentence.

It's only a matter of time. (*RP*, 3–4)

This expectation shapes their daily lives. The father, a lay preacher, teaches at a Bible college and speaks to church groups, often to draw more souls to Jesus before it is too late. The mother leads the neighborhood kids in a weekly Good News Club, where she makes the idea of the Rapture fun for little ones. Both are decent, good, and even charming people, but, as Aaron says, "My parents believe right and wrong are absolute, and I will never convince them otherwise" (*RP*, 56). On the "wrong" side of behavior is listening to rock music, so Aaron takes his clock radio to bed, turns the volume way down, presses his ear to the receiver, and enjoys the local rock station secretly under the sheets. He has never seen a movie because his mother long ago decided that films were not pleasing to the Lord.

But the summer he is a counselor at a Christian camp, his new, very cool friend Jason and some of the other counselors decide to top off their free evening in town with a movie, and Aaron must make an embarrassing decision—whether to sit on the curb waiting for them for two hours, or break one of his parents' strictest rules by going in. He chooses the movie, and later drinking and many other transgressions. But not without guilt, and fear that eventually he will be found out.

The choice that gnaws at my stomach isn't between heaven and hell. I have a hunch that God isn't disappointed with me, but my parents are a different story. I know in my head that Mom and Dad love me, but I can sense in my heart that I'm going to have to choose between their approval and making my own decisions—doing the things that feel right to me. (*RP*, 73)

The day of reckoning comes inevitably when Aaron's parents find out that he bought a rock music CD for a girl he likes. When his father questions him, he at first tries to lie his way out of it, but this makes the situation much worse. The parents are devastated. His father cries tears of disappointment, accuses him of rebellion, and then tells him that he will not be allowed to act in the school play. This is the worst punishment Aaron's parents could have devised. His leading role in the play, and his plans to become an actor, are central to his life. Ironically, it is his talent in performance that has formed a bond between him and his father and has always earned him praise and approval from his parents. He is hurt and angry and loses control, shouting "I HATE YOU!" over and over, loud enough for all the neighbors to hear.

But love of family and Jesus heals the break, and there are many scenes of warm celebration and togetherness and family fun before another, and even worse, confrontation. When Aaron is eighteen, it comes to light that he has answered the door at a party with a rum and coke in his hand. Again he tries to lie his way out, and again in the end he has to tell the truth, in an epiphany of self-revelation:

> I decide to be exactly who I am, and to let Mom and Dad catch a glimpse of who that is. I take a deep breath and look Dad in the eye. "Yes, I drank at the party."
>
> Saying what is actually true about this situation instead of what I wish were true causes something to break free inside me. . . . I steel myself for their response, something big and loud and dramatic. Instead, Dad only nods, then reaches across the table and places his hand on mine. "Thank you for telling me the truth."
>
> . . . In a flash, the version of myself so carefully constructed for Mom's and Dad's eyes crumbles all around me. I have let them see . . . not the son I pretend to be, or the son they thought I was, but the son I really am." (*RP*, 360)

Again the punishment is hard and humbling. Aaron is not allowed to graduate with his class, and he must apologize in front of the whole student body. But he has finally made peace with his real self and with God, on his own terms.

But a much more difficult revelation lies outside the boundaries of this story. Just under the surface of the narrative are many hints that Aaron may be gay, but hasn't yet realized it. The jacket flap of the book confirms how this worked out by telling us that Aaron now lives "with his boyfriend Nathan, and their two dogs" (*RP*, back flap). We can only hope for a second book as honest as this one, about what must have been for Aaron's family a coming-out as earth shaking as the Rapture itself.

NUCLEAR HOLOCAUST

While the Rapture may have an effect on the lives of those who believe in it, and fantasy writers have used the theme so often in dystopias that references to "the zombie apocalypse" have become a staple for political satirists, actual historical events have brought many to a confrontation with the very real possibility of the imminent end of the world. *Fallout* by Todd Strasser[16] is a novel that portrays the ultimate apocalyptic expectation of our times in chilling detail. It's late October 1962, and the Russians have dropped the nuclear bomb. Scott's family is the only one in the neighborhood with an underground shelter. People hysterical with fear try to force their way in; Scott's father fights them off, but when the battle ends, not four, but ten occupants have crowded into the shelter. There isn't enough room, enough water or food. The radio doesn't work. They are generally miserable, and their condition is worsened by the adults' verbal attacks on Scott's father for keeping people out. In the sweaty pressure cooker of the shelter, there is no room for kindness, mutual support, or prayer. At last, when the radiation count has gone down and they have run out of food, they try to open the trap door, but something heavy is holding it down. After repeated attempts, they finally get it open and find that the heavy objects are the dead bodies of their neighbors and friends who had been trying to get into the shelter. When they emerge to a scene of devastation, Strasser gives his readers one tiny ray of hope. A little boy expresses his joy at coming back into the world by spinning on his toes around and around, his arms spread out, and laughing.

The Fire-Eaters

A very different reaction to the prospect of the end of the world is movingly shown by David Almond in *The Fire-Eaters*.[17] Set in the autumn of 1962 in the shabby little town of Keely Bay, on the English coast near Newcastle, the novel captures the lower-class life and language of this venue in realistic detail, while at the same time it often rises into mysticism (which we will discuss in the next chapter). Bobby Burns is growing up here, aware of his parents' love for him and the beauty of the coal-filled sea and the coaly shore. Through his eyes we

are immersed in the rich life of this tiny place—his friends and enemies, the strange arrival of mad McNulty the fire-eater, his father's
mysterious illness, the miracle of healing a baby fawn, his hard life at a
school where he is scorned as lower class, the outsider family who
come to live at Keely Bay to take photographs, his expulsion from
school.

But all this seems irrelevant when a day arrives that makes the
whole world hold its breath in fear of complete annihilation. Bobby's
family follows the news on the TV, and the next day on the school bus
his friend Daniel tries to explain the danger to a couple of unimpressed
boys, who respond in the local slang of contempt:

> "America's told Russia to get the missiles out of Cuba," said Daniel.
> "And Russia's said hadaway and shite," said Diggy.
> "And now," said Daniel, "there's Russian ships taking more mis-
> siles there, and America's told Russia to turn the ships back. . . . "
> "And Russia's said hadaway and shite," said Diggy." (*Fire*, 164)

Bobby writes a desperate prayer, laying out all the creatures, people,
and things that he loves and asking God to save them and take him
instead. The next day the villagers prepare a huge bonfire on the beach.
Joseph, Bobby's older friend, tells him:

> "At least you can yell and scream and stamp your feet and build a fire
> high as bloody heaven and you can yell out, No bloody no, I won't put
> up with it."
> "No!" he yelled, and I clenched my fists and joined in with him.
> "No! No! Bloody no!"
> "Aye!" he said. "At least make a noise. At least say, 'I'm me! I'm
> Bobby Burns!' At least if the worst comes to the worst you can say I
> been here, I existed!" (*Fire*, 182–83)

The news on the television is worse and worse, as the American
secretary of state Dean Rusk reveals that the Russian ships have not
turned back, and America is ready to sink them. "We're in as grave a
crisis as mankind has ever been in," he says. (*Fire*, 190)

Everyone goes down to the beach to sit together by the bonfire and
share memories and food. Even Daniel's father, the outsider upper-
class photographer, is welcomed. They communicate their dread in
companionable silence and in jokes and warm remembering of scenes
from their past, interrupted by sudden pauses to scan the sky and listen.

Bobby gives the paper with his prayer to the fire and asks God again to take him instead of the others.

> Mam asked us to pray.
> "Even if you don't believe," she said. "Even if you think there's nothing but nothing."
> So we knelt there, all of us, beside the fire and the water and we sent our voices upward with the flames.
> "Don't let it happen.... Please. Please." (*Fire*, 211)

And it doesn't happen. The Russian ships turn back; both sides relent, and life at Keely Bay can go on again. But later Bobby muses:

> If. If Kennedy or Khrushchev had given the order to launch the missiles that night. . . . If some general in some bunker under the earth, or some commander of a submarine deep down in the sea, or some pilot of some plane, had gone mad with the pressure of it all and stabbed the launch button all alone. . . . If some primitive computer had simply gone wrong. . . . If the ship heading for Cuba had continued heading for Cuba. If . . . If . . . Maybe there'd be nothing, no world at all, just a charred and blasted ball of poisoned earth and poisoned air and poisoned seas, spinning through the darkness and the emptiness of space. (*Fire*, 213)

Every one of us who was alive at that time remembers the day we faced the end of the world. This is a moment that we need to share with young people, as David Almond has done with such beauty.

CULTS AND THE APOCALYPSE

Eden West

One of the very best novels about expecting the apocaplypse, and a superb exploration of the cult mentality, is Pete Hautman's *Eden West*.[18] Set in the wilds of Montana, it describes a religious sect that has built itself a self-sufficient little town fenced away from the evils of the world. Jacob, soon to be eighteen, has been brought here to Nodd by his parents when he was just a toddler, so he remembers no other way of life. In an earnest and naïve voice he tells of the group's rules and rituals, their separation from the gadgetry and conceits of modern life, their simple sustenance from the land, their devotion to the sacred Tree at the center of the village. The group call themselves the Grace and their prophet and leader is Father Grace, a large and enormously charismatic man who has lost an eye in a lightning strike. "His blasted eye remains fixed upon the Heavens, waiting for Zerachiel," explains Jacob (*Eden*, 48). Brother Jacob has laid out the tenets of the faith in exact detail, and Jacob explains them to his new friend Lynna:

> "The Lord has given us a second chance. Years ago, when Father Grace discovered the Tree, he bought this land. The Tree now grows at the Sacred Heart of Nodd." I am speaking more quickly now, I want to get it out, to share the Good News with her. "It lives that we might create a new Eden around it, a Garden as beautiful as Eden, and only then will the fruit of the Tree grow large and sweet, but still we must not eat of it, and the Tree will die, and the Ark will come with the Archangel Zerachiel at its helm to carry the Grace to the arms of the Lord while all else withers and dies."
> "*All* else? You mean like me?'
> "Unless you join us," I say.
> Lynna's eyes are enormous; she is staring at me as if I am the only thing in all of creation.
> Then she laughs. (*Eden*, 117)

Jacob first encounters Lynna when he is on fence patrol, walking the thirteen miles of chain link and barbed wire that separates Nodd from the adjacent Circle K Ranch. She tempts him to do what he has never done before—to leave Nodd by climbing under the barricade. She is amused by his naïveté, and he is fascinated by her worldliness and is sexually attracted to her, emotions that fill him with guilt.

To punish himself for his sin, he goes back to his cell in the men's dormitory and beats himself bloody with sharp, prickly red-cedar boughs. He says, "Shirtless, I flail my back until the stinging becomes burning, the burning an exquisite throbbing, the throbbing a soul-searing agony. I do not stop until that which lies below my waist feels as far away and insignificant as the faintest star in the blackest sky." But still atonement eludes him: "Can I yet redeem myself by confessing? Or have my sins hurled me beyond the boundaries of redemption? Even now . . . images of . . . the Worldly girl dance about the tattered edges of my soul . . . and once again the Beast attacks me through my groin" (*Eden*, 23–24).

Jacob has very little practice in speaking to girls. The only time when conversation between the sexes is encouraged is at the Babel Hour in the evenings, when the single adults of the community compete, males against females, in shouting out Bible verses; then the women and girls spread out the treats they have made, and the men and boys sample them and praise the cooks, while exchanging secret smiles with the girl of their choice. After many Babel Hours Jacob has set his heart on Sister Ruth. He has known her ever since they were children, and he has always expected that they would be married—until Father Grace adds her to his harem of three other wives. And until Lynna appears.

Jacob's preoccupation with his nether regions is somewhat diverted when three new converts join the Grace—an older woman, her pregnant daughter, and her seventeen-year-old son, Tobias. Brother Grace assigns Jacob to show Tobias the ways of the community, but the street-hardened kid has only contemptuous scorn for everything Jacob tries to teach him. Finally, in a last effort, Jacob takes Tobias on a hike to a place of awe, a high boulder above the River Pison far below.

> Together we look down into the gorge. He gasps.
> It is said there are men and women who believe the Almighty does not exist. I would bring them here, to this place. . . . One can look straight down past layer after layer of ancient rock to the roiling, rocky silver ribbon that is the Pison. Here the hand of the Lord sliced through stone like a knife through ripened cheese, tearing a slot for the river to pass through the ridge. Below us, the Pison bellows and thunders, using the walls of the chasm as its megaphone. Who could stand here and deny the magnificence and truth and power of the Lord?
> Tobias is struck nearly, though not entirely, speechless.
> He says, "Holy shit." (*Eden*, 52–53)

Later, when Tobias is locked into the Pit for his obstreperousness, Jacob sins again by cautioning him to say he repents, even if he doesn't. Jacob is afraid that if Tobias remains recalcitrant, he will be lobotomized, as Jacob suspects was done to Father Grace's mentally ill son.

In spite of all these dreadful consequences imposed on the erring members of Grace, this community Hautman has created is oddly attractive in its simplicity, its ordered relationships, its certainty of beliefs. While they wait for the imminent end of the world, they give each other loving support in their mutual assurance that they will be saved. Even Father Grace, who in the end is revealed as mad, has his moments as a mentor who is comforting to his people in his strength of leadership. And as Jacob showed Tobias, the grandeur of the Montana landscape (and Hautman's poetic skill in evoking it) casts a majestic light over the scene—for example, this description of an approaching thunderstorm: "The thunderheads are great gray towers a mile high, boiling and frothing above a base as black as the bottom of a cast iron pan, walking on claws of lightning from the mountains to the plains. The air is effervescent; I detect the sharp scent of ozone even though the storm is still twenty miles distant. Is this what the End Days look like?" (*Eden*, 304–5).

In spite of the fact that this is a book about the peculiar beliefs of a cult, there are moments of authentic spiritual search. Lynna takes Jacob to a forested place where she says she comes to think. "What do you think about?" he asks.

> She says, "I think about nothing."
> I know what she means. I have spent many hours kneeling before the Tree, thinking of nothing as my mouth speaks the words of the Arbor Prayer. The repetitive movements of my lips free me to have no thoughts, to embrace the peace that comes with that blankness of the mind.
> "Do you feel the presence of the Lord?" I ask.
> "I feel the presence of something," she says. "But I think it's more like when I'm here, I know that my life is only a small part of something huge. I don't know if it's God or what." (*Eden*, 221–22)

Eden West could have been a simple action adventure about some weird people with peculiar ideas. But in Hautman's hands, it is a literary feast. Nodd is palpable as a society; one could arrive there and fit right in, with the guidance Hautman has given. We know the people, their history and their individual personalities, and we understand why they have come to Nodd. And over all the engrossing events of this story is the elusive presence of the mystical lone wolf who savages their sheep and in his eventual death becomes a shimmering symbol of Jacob's spiritual journey.

The apocalypse in these end-of-the-world tales, whether Biblical or secular, imaginary or real, provides a dramatic background for stories of teens searching, in the face of death and destruction, for meaning and evidence of a loving God.

NOTES

1. Sheri Reynolds, *The Rapture of Canaan* (New York: Putnam, 1996).

2. Jane Yolen and Bruce Coville, *Armageddon Summer* (New York: Harcourt, 1999).

3. Luke 17:30–36 RSV.

4. Matthew 24:39–42 RSV.

5. Matthew 24:29–31 RSV.

6. 1 Thessalonians 4:13–18 RSV.

7. R. Todd Mangum and Mark S. Sweetnam, *The Scofield Bible: Its History and Impact on the Evangelical Church* (Downers Grove, IL: InterVarsity Press, 2009), 188–95, 218.

8. "A Conversation with Harold Camping, Prophesier of Judgment Day," *New York Magazine*, May 11, 2011.

9. Tim LaHaye and Jerry Jenkins, Left Behind: The Kids Series (Carol Stream, IL: Tyndale House, 1995–2007).

10. Jeri Smith-Ready, *This Side of Salvation* (New York: Simon Pulse, 2014). Hereafter cited in the text as *TSS*.

11. Leviticus 18:22 RSV.

12. Kristi Sadowski, *VOYA* , April 2014, 74.

13. Charlotte Agell, *Shift* (New York: Henry Holt, 2008).

14. Katie Coyle, *Vivian Apple at the End of the World* (New York: Houghton Mifflin, 2015). Hereafter cited in the text as *Apple*.

15. Aaron Hartzler, *Rapture Practice* (New York: Little, Brown, 2013). Hereafter cited in the text as *RP*.

16. Todd Strasser, *Fallout* (Somerville, MA: Candlewick, 2013).

17. David Almond, *The Fire-Eaters* (New York: Delacorte, 2003). Hereafter cited in the text as *Fire*.

18. Pete Hautman, *Eden West* (Somerville, MA: Candlewick, 2015). Hereafter cited in the text as *Eden*.

Chapter Five

Mysticism

In contrast to the dark visions evoked by the millennial apocalypse and the Rapture, a new, and perhaps consequent hunger for hope through authentic spiritual search has led to at least a few YA books where fictional depictions of the mystical are attempted. Although such things are by definition "ineffable," or impossible to describe, there is no lack of scholarly writers who have given it a shot, starting, of course, with dictionaries. The *American Heritage Dictionary* in 2009 said that mysticism is:

> 1a. Immediate consciousness of the transcendent or ultimate reality of God. 1b. The experience of such communion as described by mystics. 2b. A belief in the existence of realities beyond perceptual or intellectual apprehension that are central to being and directly accessible by subjective experience. [1]

However, the editors hedged their bets with a third option. They sneered, "Obscure or confused belief or thought." [2]

The great Christian writer C. S. Lewis, speaking from a more theological perspective, referred to mysticism as "the wonderful foretastes of the fruition of God vouchsafed to some in their earthly life." [3] Finally, William James, whose *The Varieties of Religious Experience* is the classic study on the subject, offered a broader view: "The feelings, acts, and experiences of individual men [*sic*] in their solitude, so far as they apprehend themselves to stand in relation to whatever they may consider the divine." [4] This is the form in which mysticism most often appears in YA literature, usually in a Christian or Jewish context, although scholars point out that mystic phenomena are not limited to those religions.

Fantasy may look like mysticism, but there is a crucial difference. Fantasy projects an imaginary world, and mystics claim to be experiencing the ultimate reality. Again we turn to the *American Heritage Dictionary* for a definition of the ineffable, and find "Fantasy—The visionary world, the product of the imagination given free rein, esp. to elaborate mental imagination having little similarity to the real world; [i.e.] make-believe."[5] So the two terms are opposites, although in literature the boundaries may seem to blur.

However, fantasy has been useful in expanding our minds, perhaps to reach the unreachable. Kevin Johnson, in *Apparitions*, explains this idea (although he confuses fantasy and science fiction)[6]:

> Ironically enough, science fiction has made the idea [of mysticism] clear to most Americans. We're used to stories about portals between dimensions, between worlds that are normally invisible or insensible to the other. And we're used to tales of superior beings coming through those portals to interact with Earthlings. . . . Think of that other dimension as Heaven.[7]

MYSTICAL SYMBOLS OR PERSONS

A mystic element sometimes appears in YA fiction as an unexplained person, animal, plant, or object. For example, in Yann Martel's extraordinary story *Life of Pi*,[8] a young boy tries to survive a shipwreck that has swept his father's zoo into the sea. He is joined in his lifeboat by a hyena, a zebra, an orangutan, and a 450-pound Bengal tiger—a tiger named Richard Parker. Although the tiger mostly behaves like an animal, dispatching the other creatures, Pi manages to keep the feline at the other end of the boat, even when both of them get very hungry. Over many days and nights at sea Richard Parker's majestic presence becomes more than that of a large carnivore. By the time Pi finally comes to an island and the tiger slips away into the jungle, he has become a figure of awe and mystery.

The Fire-Eaters

A similar transformation takes place in *The Fire-Eaters* by David Almond,[9] a book we have discussed in another context in the previous chapter. Early in the story Bobby Burns and his mother encounter a small, wild-eyed, bare-chested man who performs masochistic tricks on the street for coins. When he looks into the man's eyes, Bobby feels connected to a mystic importance. "It was as if my heart stopped beating and the world stopped turning. That was when it started. That moment, that Sunday, late summer, 1962." The man chooses Bobby to be his assistant, to pass a bag on a stick for coins. "Pay!" the busker yells and snarls. "You'll not get nowt till you pay" (*Fire*, 2). Much to the shock and disgust of the onlookers, he pushes a skewer through his cheek and out the other side, to make a bloody metal bridge in his mouth. Bobby's mother whisks him away before the man does his tricks with fire.

Later, Bobby is startled to find out that his father knew the man, whose name is McNulty, when they were in World War II together.

> "He was on the same boat as me, coming back from Burma. He was one of them that'd seen too much, suffered too much. It was like his brain'd been boiled. . . . The man was such a mess. . . . His mind was all gone. Chants and spells and curses and dances. Them things he did with ropes and swords and fire. There was them that said he was a proper magic man." (*Fire*, 15)

McNulty inexplicably comes to Keely Bay one night while Bobby and his friend Ailsa are on the beach. They see:

> A dark hunched figure, the shape of a man. A shadow, a moving silhouette. It moved toward us from the south, through the night, skimming the water's edge. It moved quickly, legs striding forward. A sack bounced at its back. It kept its head down. No eyes glittered. (*Fire*, 120)

When he huddles in an abandoned house, McNulty becomes not a mystic figure, but a pathetic madman as the children try to care for him.

When the Cuban Missile Crisis overtakes the village and the world's last night seems imminent, all the villagers go down to the beach to a bonfire where they share memories and food. Bobby and Ailsa go to McNulty's hiding place to try to persuade him to join them. He does, but keeps his distance after he performs a chain escape and the cheek skewer trick in exchange for their welcome. Later, as Bobby lies drowsing with his friends and neighbors all around him, he opens his eyes and sees "the fire-eater far beyond them in the darkness, all alone, breathing his flag of flame into the air. . . . We saw how marvelous McNulty was and how his face blazed like his fire and how when he ate his fire we couldn't tell where the fire ended and the man began" (*Fire*, 212).

At last when the international crisis is eased and the terrible night is ending, McNulty breathes the fire into his lungs and kills himself. The mysterious madman has come to represent the madness of the situation, a symbol that is explained only through the words David Almond chooses to describe him. And he leaves another mystery for us to ponder—why is the title in the plural?

Skellig

Another book that uses the symbol of a mysterious person to evoke the ineffable is *Skellig*, also by David Almond.[10] In this wondrous telling, two children discover a strange white-faced man lying against the back wall of a tumbledown garage, a man who is covered with spider webs and dead flies, who eats mice but loves take-out Chinese, and who—as they discover when they lift him up to move him to a safer hiding place—has crumpled wings under his shabby jacket. Who is this being? A madman, an owl-creature, the angel of death? As they secretly befriend him over several days, he becomes stronger and more holy, and at last lifts them up in a circle dance of light before he flies away on his great wings. This strange and luminous tale is firmly set in reality at the same time that it brilliantly conveys a sense of the sacred, the Other. As the great Robert Cormier said, "I read this luminous novel with a sense of wonder, and it's left an imprint on my mind—and yes, my heart—that will not easily, if ever, fade. In fact, I think *Skellig* deserves that risky adjective—unforgettable" (*Skellig*, back jacket).

Godless

In Pete Hautman's strikingly original tale *Godless*,[11] an object becomes a mystical deity—but only until it isn't fun anymore. Jason Bock has just been beat up by the bully Henry Stagg, and as he lies on the ground under the water tower, he has a religious experience:

> I was flat on my back looking up past Henry at the silver, dripping bottom of the water tower tank, my head still scrambled, when it hit me

just how important that tower was to St. Andrew Valley. It was the biggest thing in town. Water from that tower was piped to every home and business for miles around. The water connected all of us. It kept us alive.

That was when I came up with the idea of the water tower being God. (*Godless*, 8)

Jason is only half-serious about this idea, but he enjoys shocking adults and his church youth group with it. "Why mess around with Catholicism," he thinks, "when you can have your own customized religion. All you need is a disciple or two. And a god" (*Godless*, 18). So he convinces his friends, pragmatic Dan, timid Shinn, and even bully Henry Stagg, to become the congregation of the Chutengodian Church of the Ten-Legged One—that is, the water tower. They come up with sacraments—the Sacred Washing of the Hands, the Giving Thanks to the Tower, the Flushing of the Toilet. . . . They assign offices: Jason is Founder and Head Kahuna; Dan is First Acolyte Exaltus. Shinn is appointed First Keeper of the Sacred Text. He immediately sets about writing the scriptural history of the tower in Biblical language, a project he takes very seriously, to Jason's rising concern. Next they acquire a High Priestess—cute-as-a-button Magda, whose first question is "Do they let women be priests in the Ten-Legged church?" Jason tells her that the Ten-Legged One has yet to address that issue.

The game gets riskier when Henry challenges them to climb the tower. Despite the difficulties, they make it all the way to the rounded top—all except Shinn, who goes home because he is terrified of heights. The adventure grows even wilder when Henry saws open the lock on the trap door to the interior and they all climb down inside and go for a swim in the tank of the Ten-Legged One. But Jason is worried about Shinn, who seems to be taking the invented religion too much to heart. Sure enough, in the next few days Shinn tries again to climb the tower and freezes halfway up, in a lightning storm. Jason rescues him, but in a later climb Henry rolls off the rounded top and is almost killed. The authorities step in with jail, lectures, and penalties.

They are all heavily punished by their respective parents. Jason feels that "it's persecution is what it is. Religious intolerance. A violation of the separation of church and Jason" (*Godless*, 145). He sneaks out to check on Shinn, and finds he has filled his sketchbook not only with Chutengodian scripture, but with drawings of water towers as people they know. He tells Jason that the towers are extraterrestrials and walk at night, a fact he knows because, he explains, he has been talking with them. In an interchange that lays bare the contradictions of blind faith, Jason asks:

> "Shinn, are you crazy?"
> "I don't know," he says. "Do you think I am?"
> "Well, this water tower stuff . . . it seems like you're, you know, so *into* it. You don't really think the water tower is God, do you?"
> His eyebrows crumple. "Don't you?"
> "As a joke, sure. But . . . no, I don't."
> "You said you did," he says.
> "Yeah, but I was—"
> "How do you know it's not true if you don't believe in it?"
> "I . . . huh?" (*Godless*, 192)

The day comes when Jason and his father have a talk about the situation, and Jason admits that he doesn't believe in God. His father unexpectedly gives him a level look of recognition and understanding. He says,

> "You're sixteen, old enough to make your own choices. I'm not going to force anything on you. If you don't want to go to church anymore, that's up to you. . . . Worship water towers, trees, frogs, whatever."
> "What's the catch?"
> He laughed, shaking his head. "There are a lot of perfectly good religions out there. You're a smart kid, Jason. I know you'll find what you're looking for." (*Godless*, 194)

At the end of the book, he is still looking. He thinks, "Maybe one day I'll find a deity I can believe in. Until then, my god is made of steel and rust." (*Godless*, 198)

I Am the Messenger

Markus Zusak used Death as a narrator in *The Book Thief*,[12] as we have seen, but in *I Am the Messenger*,[13] an invisible and even more mystical somebody initiates the action. Ed Kennedy, nineteen, is a deadbeat cabdriver whose life is going nowhere. He lives with his old dog, the Doorman, and plays cards with his friends Marv, the miserly owner of a terrible old car; Ritchie, who is far too laid-back; and Audrey, whom Ed yearns for.

One day Ed gets an envelope in the mail that contains an ace of diamonds. Three addresses are written on the card, with dates and times. Curious, he follows up and goes to one of the addresses at the appointed time, watches, and comes to understand, after a cheerful beating by two unlikely hit men, that he must do something about each situation. So he visits with a lonely old lady, gives a girl who runs belief in herself, and beats up an abusing husband. More cards come, and he delivers more messages of hope and begins to grow and change from it. Finally the last card, the ace of hearts, has the names of his three friends on it. He bullies Ritchie into beginning to take charge of his life, helps Marv reunite with his child and girlfriend, and at last is able to free Audrey to love him—and to grow into being worthy of her love. But who sent the cards? The author? Or God?

Send Me Down a Miracle

A chair takes on mystical properties in Han Nolan's *Send Me Down a Miracle*.[14] Charity, the preacher's daughter in a small, very quiet rural village, is delighted when a bohemian New York artist, Adrienne Dabney, comes to town and announces that she intends to initiate a sensory-deprivation project to benefit her art. She plans to stay locked in the dark, boarded-up old house she has rented, meditating and surviving for a month only on fruit juice. Charity's pastor father is horrified. "Only evil can be contemplated in such a circumstance," he says. "The devil is in our midst" (*Miracle*, 14). He does admit that perhaps it might be a good prayer time, but then he is scandalized when Adrienne tells him she doesn't believe in prayer. Or God.

Nevertheless, Adrienne proceeds with her plan for isolation and renewal. At the end of thirty days when she emerges, the good-hearted townsfolk welcome her back with a coming-out picnic. Young Charity sees that the artist is all smiley, and she senses that Adrienne is about to share something special with the crowd around her.

> "One time I had been sitting in my spot who knows how long and I noticed this glow in front of me. . . . I stared at it for a long time and I could see it was my chair, my little wooden chair with the rush seat, and it was all lit up. . . . Then the light changed. It started circling around the chair, moving and growing until the light took form. I can't believe what I saw." Adrienne opened her eyes wider, looked around at all of us with her mouth open and her shoulders shrugged up around her ears.

"He was in my chair," she said. "He was sitting in my chair! Jesus
Christ was sitting in my chair!" (*Miracle*, 55)

She goes on to explain that Jesus came to her two more times, and
the third time he told her that there was something she was supposed to
say, something she was supposed to do. But she doesn't know what it
is.

The townsfolk are stunned into silence, but then bedlam breaks
loose as they all try to crowd into the house to see the chair. Charity's
daddy tries to restore order, but it is Mad Joe, the crazy town drunk,
who calms them. By the next day people have begun to expect the
Rapture, and Mad Joe tells Charity he believes that his two sickly
daughters will be healed by the chair. Unexpectedly Adrienne shows up
at church just in time to hear the preacher denounce her as a false
prophet and the Antichrist. She marches up the aisle in her bare feet and
demands a hearing. She has come to understand that what Jesus wants
her to do is to tell her tale about the third vision.

"I saw this place, this town, and as before, it was covered in the light
and love of God. . . . But then I noticed this black spot in one corner . . .
and it began to spread . . . until it covered the whole view . . . and I knew
this darkness was like a blackened soul, cold and evil. . . . Then . . . the
ground was splitting open and this light coming from below was burning away the edges of darkness. . . . Only it wasn't God's light . . . fiery
fingers caught hold of someone's leg and pulled that someone under.
. . . Then the ground closed up." (*Miracle*, 100–101)

The church erupts into a tumult of confessions, each person claiming to be the sinner that brought the darkness. Later Charity gets to
spend some private prayer time with the chair and feels forgiven and
comforted. The next day there is a long line of people outside
Adrienne's house waiting to have a turn at the chair, while the preacher
loudly denounces idol worship with many quotes from Scripture.

Mad Joe, who had believed that his daughters would be healed by a
chair miracle, is wild with grief and alcohol when one of them dies. He
blames the preacher, who has taken the chair to hide it in the church,
and forces him, at the point of a shotgun, to return it. Meanwhile, Mad
Joe's other daughter dies, and when he is alone with the chair, he
shoots himself dead. Later, in an agonized confession before his daughter, the preacher blames himself for bringing Mad Joe to the point of
suicide. Charity is able to help him find forgiveness. Adrienne has left

town, but they find that she has left Charity a painting titled *The Holy*, which she has "dedicated to Charity Pittman, who always looks for the best in people" (*Miracle*, 247).

Asylum for Nightface

Yet another mystical figure appears on the trading card that culminates the action of *Asylum for Nightface* by Bruce Brooks,[15] a novel discussed at some length in chapter 1. The genius trading-card designer Drake Jones has drawn a strange person standing in the darkness on a tilted rock, wearing a cowl, and under it, where his face should be, is only the night sky itself. The narrator Zimmerman thinks:

> Questions occur. One wants to ask them directly of this partial person, who, despite his oddity, seems somehow a figure of sadness, and, therefore, a figure one can meet. One wants to ask: What happened to you? What can you do, with the night for your face? What power has been given, or taken away?
> Are you good? . . .
> Are you alone? (*Asylum*, 98)

On the back of the card is an enigmatic comment that may or may not link this strange symbol with Zimmerman's spiritual search: "Nightface seeks asylum in the highest of places" (*Asylum*, 99).

A Monster Calls

A last and most startling mystic figure is a tree, a yew tree, that appears to thirteen-year-old Conor one night outside his bedroom window, in the haunting and elegant story *A Monster Calls* by Patrick Ness.[16] One night, a monster shows up "just after midnight. As they do" (*Monster*, 1).

> As Conor watched, the uppermost branches of the tree gathered themselves into a great and terrible face, shimmering into a mouth and nose and even eyes, peering back at him. Other branches twisted around one another, always creaking, always groaning, until they formed two long arms and a second leg to set down beside the main trunk. The rest of the tree gathered itself into a spine and then a torso, the thin, needle-like leaves weaving together to make a green, furry skin that moved and breathed as if there were muscles and lungs underneath. . . .
> *I have come to get you, Conor O'Malley*, the monster said, pushing against the house. . . .

But Conor didn't run. . . . "So come and get me then," he said.
(*Monster*, 6–7)

In the morning he convinces himself the apparition was a night-mare—until he sees that the floor of his bedroom is covered with short, spiky yew tree leaves. The next night the monster comes again. He tells Conor that he will be telling him three stories, and then Conor will tell a fourth, a story that is his truth. Conor indignantly denies the whole thing, but the monster continues to appear, even sometimes in the daytime.

Meanwhile, his mother is ill with what seems to be cancer. The treatments make her sicker, and Conor's grandmother, whom he dislikes, comes to stay with them. Conor is having a secret recurrent nightmare, in which he is clinging to the hands of someone who is falling off a cliff. When his mother goes to a hospital to stay, Conor must move into his despised grandmother's elegant house. The monster visits him there at night and tells his three stories. Finally it is time for Conor to tell the fourth by accepting the terrible truth of his nightmare: he doesn't want his mother to die, and yet he does, so it will be over. At his mother's bedside, they confess their mutual lies to each other. "Conor held tightly onto his mother. And by doing so he could finally let her go" (*Monster*, 225).

The first hardcover edition of this achingly beautiful story was illustrated with dark images by Jim Kay interwoven throughout the text, evoking not only the spiky tree monster, but the themes of death, loss, and redemption. The book won the Carnegie Medal and a broad spectrum of other awards, but regrettably was overlooked for ALA's Printz Prize.

OTHER MYSTIC PHENOMENA

A whole range of odd and astonishing events and talents are connected to mysticism. An occasional YA novel draws on one of these rich possibilities to enliven a fantasy, but only a few writers have embedded these phenomena in a realistic setting in a way that qualifies them as spiritual. Examples are found in many of the brilliant and strange short stories by the Australian author Margo Lanagan. For instance, in the collection *Yellowcake*,[17] a story titled "Into the Clouds on High" features a quite ordinary mum who once in a while has spells in which she levitates without warning, to the distress of her husband and son Marcus. For her, however, this is a blissful event. She is lifted up by happiness and lies floating in the air. Each time she goes higher, and afterward feels disappointed that she was not yet taken to the next plane of existence toward which she yearns. Anticipating that she will soon have to leave her family behind, she teaches her young son to do all the daily things, like cooking and taking care of his little sister. At last there comes a day when she goes off to the city to do some shopping and doesn't come back. A phone call summons Marcus, his father, and his sister to a department store, where his mum has levitated from a cubicle in the lady's restroom. There she floats, emanating joy, and no matter how much her husband pleads with her to stay, she finally falls, or flows, or melts into the blackness and is gone.

> He and Dad held a rag-Mum between them; he had her skirt end and stocking legs, from which the shoes had clattered to the floor, while Dad held her collapsed upper dress. The handbag teetered where it had *donked* onto the toilet lid, and then it tipped and fell to join the shoes. ("Clouds," 108)

They gather up her things—clothes, shoes, shopping bags—and Marcus is comforted by the joy that had poured down from her floating body, and by knowing that "if he were to need her badly, she might summon something of herself from its dispersal" ("Clouds," 109).

The Drowned Forest

Yet another book whose plot is driven by the protagonist's need to contact a dead person is *The Drowned Forest* by Kristopher Reisz.[18] Before the story starts, Jane's dearest friend Holly has drowned in the river, probably caught in the branches of the trees the water has engulfed. Now Jane talks to Holly in a long monologue that makes up the narrative, telling her everything that is going on in their small Alabama town and in their church, where her father is the pastor. The book opens with a baptism, neatly setting the stage with the metaphor of going under the water into death, and then rising up to new life, which is what Jane wants to help Holly do. At the picnic that follows the baptism, Jane and Tyler, the boy who was Holly's boyfriend, encounter a giant catfish on the river bank. It spits out a ring that Tyler had given Holly, and on it is engraved one word: "Help!" They are sure that this is a message from Holly, but when they tell the story to the pastor, he denies that the ring has any significance. Only Holly's Pa-paw believes them. The three go out on the river in a boat and play music to attract the spirit of the dead girl. It works. They hear her voice calling for help, and her father pulls her into the boat, not noticing that she has become a hideous mud-thing of sludge and water weeds. He holds her in his arms, and vines and leaves grow on his body wherever her hands touch until he is strangled and drowns. Tyler and Jane escape the river-monster, just barely. With the help of a band called Stratofortress, they set out on a quest to find peace for Holly's soul so she can go on "to the other side." Finally, with the help of the band, they entice the mud-creature Holly to play the music that always brought her closer to God, and her soul is freed to leave.

Because Jane has been raised in the church, she often thinks in Bible phrases and analogies. When she tries to tell her mother about the catfish and the ring, she says, "Listen, listen, in Matthew 17, the apostles find a coin inside a fish's mouth, just like we found Holly's ring. See? And in that same chapter, Jesus tells them they—" (*Forest*, 48). Her mother's answer is to call the mental health counselor. Pondering how ancient the river is, Jane compares it to "when Nephilim walked the land and men were like grasshoppers at their feet."[19] She tells Holly she won't be afraid, because "perfect love casteth out fear."[20] And when she loses heart about the quest and feels abandoned by God, she thinks of Jesus in the Garden of Gethsemane and prays desperately, like Him, "I beg God to let this cup pass from me."[21]

This religious perspective bothered *School Library Journal*'s reviewer. Instead of finding Jane's faith and that of her family an enrichment to the narrative, the reviewer said, "The abundance of Biblical verse is appropriate for Jane's character, but it bogs down the story and may alienate some readers."[22] Sadly, such a timid and narrow-minded judgment is fairly typical of the attitude that prevails in the publishing community toward any specific expression of religion.

However, in the publishing phenomenon of the Harry Potter series there is evidently no such worry about "offending" readers. J. K. Rowling has slipped in a striking mystical appearance at the very end of the last volume. In a pause during the terrible final battle with the evil Voldemort and his forces, Harry's friends Sirius, James, Lupin, and Lilly, who have been killed, come back to support and accompany him to his death. He has just realized that he must give up his own life to end that of Voldemort. He allows himself to be killed by the arch-fiend's hand, but wakes in a place he recognizes as the railway station King's Cross (which Rowling also uses, significantly, as the name of the chapter). There he meets his dead mentor Dumbledore, who gives him some final words of explanation and guidance. Harry, like Christ, is resurrected to fulfill his mission of saving the world for goodness. These metaphors of Christian belief are ironic, considering that the Harry Potter series has been vigorously attacked by evangelicals for supposed witchcraft and Satanism.

FAITH HEALING

Another manifestation of mysticism granted to an occasional person is the power to heal those who are sick. A very few YA novels have explored the implications of this gift for the healer. Corinne, in Gina Linko's novel *Indigo*,[23] discovers she has this power when she tries to save her little sister Sophie from drowning. But there is an indigo blue flash, and when Corinne wakes, Sophie is dead. She blames herself, but then she meets Rennick, a boy who sees auras, and he helps her come to terms with her fear of using her gift, and to learn in the end that lightning was what killed Sophie.

The True Tale of the Monster Billy Dean

The gift of healing and other mystic phenomena appear in yet another book by David Almond, *The True Tale of the Monster Billy Dean Telt by Hisself*,[24] which was mentioned in chapter 1 for its portrayal of a fallen priest. Like all of Almond's tales, it is suffused with a shimmering mysticism laid over the grim world of working-class England. In the bombed-out village of Blinkbonny, Billy Dean has been hidden away in one room all his young life. When his father disappears, his mother at last lets him emerge into the ruined village, where he is befriended by the medium Mrs. Malone. She grooms him to participate in séances as the Anjel Childe, who can speak with the dead. At first it is a hoax, but then at one session Billy Dean is possessed; he feels ripped apart and thrown into the dark, and the dead begin to speak through him. He writes about this and other experiences in the third person, using the primitive phonetic spelling he has taught himself:

> He gros to dred it for it brings such pane. He gros to love it for it leevs such peese in its wake. The voyses of the dead posess his throte & tongue & lips. They gossip & natter & wisper & grone. They are as deep as the voys of an old man & sweet & hiy as a childes. They tell

tales that seem so real. . . . The voyses come like memories from insyd himself. (*Billy Dean*, 184)

The bereaved are overjoyed to hear from their loved ones, and Billy Dean's fame spreads. Soon he also finds he has the power to heal the sick. Word spreads of his healing touch, and more and more people come to be healed.

They come with canser or with heart disees or with funguses or sores or rashes or spots. They limp acros the rubbl on crutches or are weeld bumpily acros it in chares. They cum with depreshon & distress. They tremble & qwayk. They wisper ther feres and sadness and broaken dremes to me. They bring ther sikly children & ther weke & pityus baybys. Plees help, they say. Plees tuch. . . . O thank you Aynjel. Thank you Billy Dean. The payn is gon. . . . You wer sent by God. You ar a saynt. . . .
And another. And mor and mor of them. (*Billy Dean*, 209–10)

Soon he is overwhelmed, cast into visions of the horrors and brokenness of the world at the same time that he becomes an unwilling Christ figure. He takes no pleasure in the adulation, nor finds any comfort from God. Indeed, although he feels the wonder and beauty of creation all around him, he thinks that God has become disgusted with people and has gone away.

Mebbe this is how things became for God. Mebbe once there really was a God who loved his world when it was lovabl and new but he did not want his world to be insyd him when it turnd to war & agony & death. He came to hate & fear the world that he had made but ther was no way for him to stop it just as ther is no way for me. . . . He abandond it. . . . So he wons was here in this world but now hes not. And without a God the worlds just left to its own devises. And it gets wors & wors & wors & bluddy wors. (*Billy Dean*, 219–20)

He yearns for peace and his absent father, as his monologue becomes more and more strange, to the point where no summary can do justice to the unexpected savage violence and subsequent peace of the last chapters. David Almond has again proven that he is a master in writing about the spiritual in a nontraditional way.

THE IMPOSTER GOD

Few writers have had the audacity to try to picture the ultimate mystic symbol, God himself. When they do so, it is sometimes considered sentimental or, at the other end of the scale, blasphemous. But Philip Pullman has had no hesitation about plunging into this delicate task. In *The Amber Spyglass*, the third book of the His Dark Materials series,[25] he has produced a horrifying portrait of a weak and dying God. The passage brought on a storm of controversy, and Pullman was widely criticized for it, and for his supposed atheism.

Throughout the trilogy, the universes have been managed by a malevolent entity called the Authority, who heads the Church and has absolute power. As society deteriorates, in *The Amber Spyglass* Lyra and Will are pursued by evil creatures. On a wild mountain slope they discover a whimpering being enclosed in a crystal bubble. Lyra is struck with pity:

> "Oh, Will, he's still alive! But—the poor thing. . . ."
> Will saw her hands pressing against the crystal, trying to reach in to the angel and comfort him; because he was so old, and he was terrified, crying like a baby and cowering away into the lowest corner.
> ". . . Oh, Will, can't we let him out?"
> Will cut through the crystal in one movement and reached in to help. . . . Demented and powerless, the aged being could only weep and mumble in fear and pain and misery, and he shrank away from what seemed like yet another threat.
> "It's all right," Will said, "we can help you hide, at least. Come on, we won't hurt you."
> The shaking hand held his . . . feebly. . . . The old one was uttering a wordless groaning whimper that went on and on, and grinding his teeth, and compulsively plucking at himself with his free hand, but as Lyra reached in, too, to help him out, he tried to smile, and to bow, and his ancient eyes deep in their wrinkles blinked at her with innocent wonder.
> Between them they helped the ancient of days out of his crystal cell; it wasn't hard, for he was as light as paper. . . . But in the open air there was nothing to stop the wind from damaging him, and to their dismay his form began to loosen and dissolve. Only a few moments later he had vanished completely, and their last impression was of those eyes, blinking in wonder, and a sigh of the most profound and exhausted relief. (*Spyglass*, 210–11)

Freitas (*This Gorgeous Game*) and King, in a scholarly book titled *Killing the Imposter God*,[26] argue that this whimpering person is not meant by Pullman to be the true God. Instead, he is an imposter, the first angel to be created. Taking advantage of his first-born status, he convinced the angels who appeared later that he was the Creator. Ever since, for eons, he has maintained the deception, and now the long-sustained effort has worn him down to the sniveling fearful creature found by Lyra and Will.

So if this is a false god, where and what is the true God, the Creator of Heaven and Earth? Or does he even exist? Is it Dust, that strange golden stuff that fills the air? Is Dust sentient, then? And there is also the question about whether the daemon that is paired with each human is meant to represent the soul. Pullman has denied this last, but he has not proven to be an accurate interpreter of his own intentions. However, he *has* said several times that his underlying theological position is Gnosticism, that ancient heresy that valued intellectual inquiry over faith. Other sources of this mighty trilogy are Milton's *Paradise Lost*, the mystic poetry of William Blake, Virgil's *Aenid*, the philosophy of Nietzsche, and even the findings of quantum physics. Donna Freitas and Jason King have praised the trilogy as "offering readers a narrative endlessly erupting in possibilities, not only for general readers but also to scientists, psychologists, literary critics, political theorists, philosophers, and theologians."[27]

There have been floods of articles, essays, interviews, and at least three books written about His Dark Materials that explore and puzzle over these and many other aspects of the story, so I will not attempt to add to that body of critical work except to ask just one more theological question that has not been asked, as far as I know, by any other critic. In the series title, His Dark Materials, just whom does "His" refer to? Some writers have equated dark materials, or dark matter, as it is called in quantum physics, with Pullman's Dust.[28] In *The Amber Spyglass*, he seems to be suggesting that Dust is intelligent, or even divine. If so, why did he not call his vision simply "Dark Materials?" Is this a clue to a huge joke in this seemingly atheistic work? Could it be that the creator of Dust, the hidden personage referred to in the word "His," is God himself?

NOTES

1. William Morris, ed. *American Heritage Dictionary of the English Language*. 4th ed. (New York: Houghton Mifflin, 2009).

2. Morris, *American Heritage Dictionary*, 2009.

3. C. S. Lewis, *The Joyful Christian* (New York: Simon & Schuster, 1996), 195–96.

4. William James, *The Varieties of Religious Experience* (New York: Penguin Classics, 1982).

5. William Morris, ed. *American Heritage Dictionary of the English Language* (New York: Houghton Mifflin, 1975).

6. Science fiction projects the knowledge and/or things of the real world into the future in a new form that could possibly come to exist. Fantasy takes place in a world created in the mind of the author with no limitations except that it must be internally consistent.

7. Kevin Orlin Johnson, *Apparitions: Mystic Phenomena and What They Mean* (Dallas, TX: Pangaeus Press, 1998), 123.

8. Yann Martel, *Life of Pi* (New York: Houghton Mifflin, 2002).

9. David Almond, *The Fire-Eaters* (New York: Delacorte, 2003). Hereafter cited in the text as *Fire*.

10. David Almond, S*kellig* (New York: Delacorte, 1999).

11. Pete Hautman, *Godless* (New York: Simon & Schuster, 2004). Hereafter cited in the text as *Godless*.

12. Markus Zusak, *The Book Thief* (New York: Knopf, 2006).

13. Markus Zusak, *I Am the Messenger* (New York: Knopf, 2005).

14. Han Nolan, *Send Me Down a Miracle* (New York: Harcourt, 1996). Hereafter cited in text as *Miracle*.

15. Bruce Brooks, *Asylum for Nightface* (New York: HarperCollins, 1996). Hereafter cited in text as *Asylum*.

16. Patrick Ness, *A Monster Calls* (Somerville, MA: Candlewick, 2011). Hereafter cited in text as *Monster*.

17. Margo Lanagan, "Into the Clouds on High." In *Yellowcake* (New York: Knopf, 2013). Hereafter cited in the text as "Clouds."

18. Kristopher Reisz, *The Drowned Forest* (Woodbury, MN: Flux/Llewellyn, 2014). Hereafter cited in text as *Forest*.

19. Not an exact quotation, but probably derived from Numbers 13:33.

20. 1 John 4:18 RSV.

21. Matthew 26:39 RSV, Mark 14:36 RSV, Luke 22:42 RSV.

22. Leigh Collazo, review of *The Drowned Forest, School Library Journal*, 2014. www.amazon.com/Drowned-Forest-Kristopher-Reisz, Accessed January 11, 2015.

23. Gina Linko, *Indigo* (New York: Random House, 2013).

24. David Almond, *The True Tale of the Monster Billy Dean Telt by Hisself* (Somerville, MA: Candlewick, 2014). Hereafter cited in the text as *Billy Dean*.

25. Philip Pullman, *The Amber Spyglass* (His Dark Materials, Book III) (New York: Knopf, 2000). Hereafter cited in the text as *Spyglass*.

26. Donna Freitas and Jason King, *Killing the Imposter God* (San Francisco: Jossey-Bass, 2007).

27. Freitas and King, *Imposter God*, 2007.

28. Mary Gribbin and John Gribbin, *The Science of Philip Pullman's His Dark Materials* (New York: Knopf, 2003).

Chapter Six

The Divine Encounter

The ultimate mystical experience, one that has been equated with a meeting with God Himself, is the Divine Encounter. Many of the great mystics, from Thomas Aquinas to Thomas Merton, have had such an experience and have tried to describe it, but—as we have seen—the ineffable defies description. However, the analytical mind of William James has managed to reduce the mystical experience of the Divine Encounter to four characteristics:

1. Ineffability—No adequate report of its content can be given in words [but nevertheless, William James goes right on talking]
2. Noetic quality—Can be apprehended by the intellect
3. Transciency—Of short duration, but the effect persists
4. Passivity—Mystics come to their peak experience not as active seekers, but as passive Recipients[1]

A century later, at the Sixth Annual Hawaii International Conference on Arts and Humanities (2008), Professor Douglas Shrader, quoting H. C. Happold, added three more characteristics. He also redefined "noetic quality" as "the notion that mystical experiences reveal an otherwise hidden or inaccessible knowledge." His additions were:

1. Unity of opposites (a sense of wholeness, a consciousness of the oneness of everything)
2. Timelessness

3. Encounter with "the true self"[2]

The three instances of the Divine Encounter that I have been able to find in YA novels are all remarkably faithful to these seven criteria, as well as remarkably beautiful.

This theophany has a long history. "The best way to get a frame of reference on apparitions and other mystic phenomena," says Dr. K. O. Johnson in his book *Apparitions*, "is to look at the writings of three of the greatest mystics who ever lived: St. Teresa of Avila, St. Ignatius of Loyola, and St. John of the Cross. . . . All three were born about the same time and in the same region of Spain, and each of them described with unequalled clarity some distinct areas of the continuum of mystic experience."[3]

But there have been many serious instances of the Divine Encounter even in the twenty-first century. In a 2014 interview with Peter Matthiessen for *Smithsonian Magazine*, interviewer Ron Rosenbaum[4] asked a provocative question and got more than he anticipated from the famous mountain climber and explorer. In answer to being asked, "What about spirituality?" Matthiessen said, "I've had many experiences with it. Certain circumstances bring it out, which all the mystics know. . . . It's called an 'opening.'"

"An opening," explained Rosenbaum, "through what he calls a kind of 'gauzy' veil that separates us from the spiritual realm."

Matthiessen continued, "For a second, you see what the world is. It is a whole other way of seeing, which is horrible, terrifying, and extraordinary and a great blessing to have."

The Divine Encounter, like many mystic occurrences, is reflected in some YA novels in a nonexplicit way. But, as I have said, only three YA novels have consciously depicted the Divine Encounter. I have quoted these scenes from each of the three almost in their entirety, to give a sense of their quality, to show them in context, and also to demonstrate their startling similarity in spite of being embedded in three very different stories.

THREE ENCOUNTERS WITH THE DIVINE

Not Exactly Normal

Not Exactly Normal by Devon Brown[5] is on the surface a light-hearted little book that is dead serious in its depiction of the mystical experience. It is written for younger young adults, which is appropriate for its status as a beginner's guide to the Divine Encounter.

Todd Farrell is a nice, ordinary sixth grader at St. Ann's Episcopal upper-school. His best friend, Nitro, is a Jewish intellectual, and his other friend, Leda, is a bizarre intellectual. Between the two of them, Todd gets some not-exactly-normal ideas, and the strangest by far is his determination to write his social studies final report on mystic experiences after Leda claims to have had one. His parents are amused, but don't discourage him. His mother tries to help by describing the phenomenon in a simplistic way:

> Well, you could say a mystical experience is when a person experiences something strange or out of the ordinary, something that he or she can't explain. . . . Some people who have had a mystical experience tell about a vision they had. . . . They might see God, or an angel. They might suddenly understand something they never understood before. They might see a person far away, or even dead people sometimes. (*Normal*, 35–36)

This isn't enough for Todd. He goes to the public library for some serious research, and takes notes about Joan of Arc and St. Francis and Meister Eckhart and Julian of Norwich. He finds a sentence he likes a lot: "A mystical experience wipes away the film of the familiar from the glass of the world" (*Normal*, 68). Still, he isn't satisfied, and on the way home he has an epiphany:

> Every account I read about said that a mystical experience is a very personal thing and difficult to put into words. You can't fully understand it by reading a book. I am going to have to have my own mystical experience—not just read about other people's. (*Normal*, 70)

In the next few days, he prays for a mystical experience and watches carefully, but nothing happens except that he notices things more. The day for the final report is coming up too soon, when he and Nitro go out on the expanse of the newly frozen river to play soccer. The ball rolls into an open water hole; they reach way out for it, and Nitro falls in and is swept under the ice and into the rushing spillway, where he disappears. Todd hesitates only a second, but then jumps into the freezing water to rescue his best friend in a hair-raising scene. They survive, and Todd, much to his embarrassment, is a hero. As he is recovering emotionally, the next morning he goes for a walk at dawn, and at last a mystical experience overtakes him:

> I looked up into the morning sky, and it was vast and endless.
>   . . . As the world turned, I could feel the darkness falling away. I was riding on a huge ball, turning to face a round fire. I listened, and far away I thought I could hear the crackling, steady roar of the sun like a million blazing furnaces. And everywhere I looked, the world seemed full of goodness. . . .
>   Then I heard a quiet, constant crackling around me. Next spring's grass buried beneath the snow was burning, so were the roots of the bare trees, deep below the ground, burning, alive, and growing.
>   *I am burning too,* I thought. *I am like a furnace of life.*
>   I listened more intensely, and deep down I heard, or maybe felt, something like a slow, steady heartbeat, like the endless repetition of day and night or the eternal cycle of the seasons. A sound filled with sadness, but more full of joy. Definitely more joy.
>   . . . And then I felt the surge of something wonderful. Something just beyond my reach. Something that Leda might call, well, a gloriousness.
>   And not just a gloriousness but a love.
>   One that went on and on forever. (*Normal,* 205–8)

When We Were Saints

A novel in which a Divine Encounter motivates the action, and that goes on to explore the highest levels of spirituality and mystic experience, is Han Nolan's *When We Were Saints.*[6] Archie Caswell's parents are dead, and he lives on a farm with his grandparents. He has fought for most of his fourteen years with his granddaddy over the pranks his friend Armory leads him into, so when the old man on his deathbed tells him, "Young man, you are a saint!" Archie isn't sure whether his grandfather's last words have blessed him or cursed him. Days later, pondering this question, he climbs the mountain behind the farmhouse, and is suddenly overwhelmed by something he has never felt before:

> Archie stood up and experienced a strange sensation of weightlessness. He could not feel himself. . . . His whole body had no beginning and no end. The sky, the air, the sun, the earth, and the trees belonged as much to his body as his skin and bones. He walked toward the trees. He felt light and transparent. The pines swayed and bent, speaking with the creaking of their branches, the bristling of their needles, the thump of their cones as they fell to the ground. Archie listened, but it was like the

speech of his grandfather when he spoke in tongues—foreign, and powerful. He felt the power and the energy of the trees course through his body. They were alive as he was alive, full of spirit and consciousness. He dropped to his knees and cried. Tears of joy and of worship flowed from his eyes. His heart, his whole being, filled with joy. (*Saints*, 25–26)

Afterward he longs to have this experience again, and again, maybe to feel that joy all the time. And he wants to become a saint, to make his grandfather's prophecy true. Both of his goals take shape and direction when he meets Clare, a beautiful girl of his own age who feels that she is destined to be a modern version of St. Clare. They immediately bond, and she calls him Francis, after the saint who was the medieval Clare's companion.

Clare is intensely spiritual. She tells Archie that to become saints they must pray for hours, repeating the words "Be still and know that I am God" over and over thousands of times. They must eat and sleep only enough to stay alive, and they must get rid of all their earthly possessions. Archie thinks of his computer and his new dirt bike, and he's not so sure anymore that he's cut out to be a saint. But he tries, praying long hours for forgiveness from his grandfather and God.

When a broken hip puts his grandmother in the hospital, he worries that she might die, and then where would he live? His anxiety grows so much that he can no longer bear to visit her in the hospital, so when Clare announces they are going on a pilgrimage, the plan fits with his feelings. They take the neighbor's truck and set out on the highway. Archie asks, "Where are we going?" and is surprised when Clare tells him they are going to New York City, to the Cloisters, a medieval museum where she grew up. He wonders for a moment if maybe she is using him to get to a place she wants to go, but when he sees how everyone they meet loves her, how sure she is about everything, and how beautiful she is, he can only follow her directions blindly. People are drawn to Clare instantly because she honestly cares for them and asks them questions about themselves and their deepest desires and fears. But Archie doesn't understand this. To him this ability of hers seems mystical, a gift from God. On the trip Clare tells him that her mother was so alarmed by her daughter's spiritual devotions that she put her in a mental hospital, where they gave her drugs that blurred her mind. She has terrible memories from that time and a horror of hospitals.

They have only enough money for gas, but Clare is calmly certain that God will take care of them. Sure enough, strangers give them food as they go, but Archie is still hungry all the time. Clare insists that they drive without ever stopping to sleep, so he is desperately tired by the night they finally arrive at the Cloisters. There in the park Clare makes friends with a bedraggled old man, who takes them to dinner and invites them to stay with him in his apartment. They do, and the old man is transformed by Clare's loving acceptance. The next day Clare is overjoyed to be in the Cloisters. She shows Archie the medieval spiritual treasures that shaped her when she was a child. She is determined they will sneak up the stairs after hours to sleep in the tower room of the museum.

She is not eating or sleeping at all now and has become bone thin and fragile, with great dark circles under her eyes. Finally, as she is kneeling in prayer, she is seized by a convulsion, and blood begins to drip from her palms, her side, and her feet. It is the stigmata, the imitation of the wounds of Christ, a mark given only to the holiest of saints. But it scares Archie into betraying Clare by phoning her parents, and they come and get her. Archie makes peace with himself and his grandmother and goes home. Months later he visits Clare in the mental hospital where her parents have installed her and finds that the drugs have zombified her keen spirit, but she is still finding ways to say the prayers they have forbidden her.

"Is Clare insane?" asks the reader. She is kind and loving and perceptive with others, and her elevated aspirations seem holy and admirable. But when she tells Archie she talks with Jesus, and when she punishes her frail body by not eating or sleeping, we begin to suspect there is an explanation for her behavior other than saintliness. In the end the stigmata, for us as well as for Archie, is a sign that a diagnosis of mental illness does not explain everything. Or maybe anything.

The Neddiad[7]

Daniel Pinkwater is a quirky comic genius, far more inventive than anyone else who currently answers to that description. Fantasy author Neil Gaiman has said, "While all writers are unique, Pinkwater is the uniquest. And so are his books . . . *The Neddiad* is funny and tender and strange and impossible to describe."[8]

But I'm going to try. In *The Neddiad*, Pinkwater has given his grateful fans a fanciful semiautobiographical tale of his adolescent years in Hollywood. For me this story is especially poignant because I, too, grew up in the Hollywood of the forties. Pinkwater knows the secret places, the mysterious corners, the beloved icons of that town, and he works them into his story with names that are sly disguises for the Hollywood cognoscenti to pounce on. A restaurant called the Hat, a haunted hotel called the Hermione, a school called Brown Sparrow Military Academy—where Pinkwater himself was enrolled, and also *The Neddiad*'s protagonist Neddie Wentworthstein. All are fictional names for the Brown Derby, which was too expensive for my family; the Chateau Marmont, which *did* have ghosts; and Black-Foxe Military Institute, where my brother was enrolled.

Pinkwater is equally sly in the wildly improbable names for his characters: a Native American shaman called Melvin (when he's not pretending to be Sheldon or Irving); a swashbuckling movie star named Aaron Finn (a rhyming reference to Errol Flynn, a swashbuckling movie star of the forties); the Marsh Brothers—Gaucho, Harpy, Chicklet, and Gumball—the villain Sholmos Bunyip; Neddie's spunky girl sidekick Yggdrasil Birnbaum ("Don't call me Iggy!"); and many more.

Neddie Wentworthstein, his snotty big sister Eloise, his mother, and his unpredictable and eccentric father have left Chicago and are crossing the United States on the Super Chief to live in Los Angeles. They are traveling in a deluxe double drawing room because Mr. Wentworthstein is the shoelace king of America and very rich. Neddie finds the trip full of interesting events, but the best times are when Colonel Ken Krenwinkle joins them in the dining car and tells stories that are mostly true of his early years in the Old Wild West—tales of Wyatt Earp, Bat Masterson, Sitting Bull, gunfights, vast buffalo herds, and the fascinating fact that his Native American Osage name means "Only shoots when absolutely necessary" (*Neddiad*, 27).

The journey takes on new meaning when the colonel puts his hand on Neddie's shoulder and tells him, "If you should meet a Navajo shaman named Melvin, you'll be in luck, so keep your eyes open" (*Neddiad*, 24). He pays close attention, and sure enough, in Albuquerque the family gets off the train to stretch their legs, and as Neddie is browsing in an Indian museum of odd artifacts he *does* meet a Navajo shaman named Melvin, who gives him a little turtle carved out of stone. "Don't let anybody get it away from you," he warns (*Neddiad*, 36).

As the story goes on, the little turtle takes on more and more significance. On a plane trip later to catch up with his family after he has missed the train, Neddie is accosted by a man named Sandor Eucalyptus, who steals the turtle at gunpoint and jumps out to parachute into the Grand Canyon, taking the artifact with him. Or he would have, except that Neddie's friend Seamus, Aaron Finn's son, has pulled a trick and substituted a jelly bean for the turtle when he handed it to Eucalyptus. Later in the flight, the pilot shows them a natural rock formation called Turtle Rock and tells them it is considered very important by the Hopi people. "Has some kind of ritual meaning—something to do with preserving the world, or protecting the world, or something" (*Neddiad*, 72).

More details about the turtle accumulate when they get to L.A. and settle in at the haunted Hermione Hotel. Aaron Finn tells them some facts he has learned from the encyclopedia he keeps in his dressing room to read during long delays on the movie set:

> "In many Indian creation myths the world is said to have been created when certain animals . . . brought mud from the bottom of the Great Water and piled it on the back of Big Turtle—then trees grew, and so forth, and the world is carried on the back of Big Turtle. In fact, to this day, most indigenous peoples refer to North America, or the world in general, as Turtle Island." (*Neddiad*, 85)

Neddie enrolls at Brown Sparrow Military Academy to join his new friend Seamus Finn. And at the Hermione Hotel Neddie meets the spunky girl Yggdrysil, who also lives there and knows all the resident ghosts. The three of them make common cause to solve the mystery of the turtle's power. But Neddie worries, since he is not sure what he, as the bearer of the sacred turtle, is supposed to do to prevent the destruction of the world as we know it. Steve Kraft, the owner of a curiosities shop called Stuffed Stuff 'n' Stuff where Neddie and Seamus find an exact replica of the turtle, adds to his anxiety. "Very sacred thing," he says. "Only a hero can possess the sacred turtle, and he has to defeat powerful forces of evil, or the world will cease to exist" (*Neddiad*, 143). To hide the turtle safely, they secretly exchange it for the replica in the shop's showcase, but their strategy backfires when Kraft sells it to an agent for the evil Sholmos Bunyip. Later they get it back from a surprising source and are told its colorful history, from the fifth century BCE in ancient Greece to its present identity with Native Americans.

Then, in the middle of this preposterous but delicious story, Neddie has an authentic Divine Encounter, in a scene that shimmers with transcendence and reverent beauty. One night he wakes up around three a.m. and, for no reason that he can explain, he goes down in the elevator in his pajamas and around to the overgrown and neglected swimming pool behind the hotel. He gets into the water amid the soggy leaves and swims to the middle of the pool. He feels strangely content and very, very happy.

> Then I realized . . . I wasn't the only one swimming. It came up slowly, a dark shape in the darkness. Round. Huge. It rose up out of the water. I knew right away what it was.
>
> I wasn't scared for a second. Just the opposite—I felt this tremendous . . . warmth. No, not warmth . . . joy. Oh, it was more than joy. It was . . . just the biggest kind of love. . . . This gigantic turtle, as big as a car, and so impossibly old, and I was brimming over with love for it. And it loved me. I could see its old turtle head now, and its old turtle eye, could hear it breathing and feel it moving in the water right in front of me—and it was just radiating the purest kind of love. And it was wise. It knew everything, had seen everything—and it was telling me things . . . things that couldn't be told in words. . . . The best way I can translate what the great turtle told me—is to say that this is a beautiful world, and it wants to take care of us. I'm pretty sure I was crying. We just floated there, the great turtle and me. (*Neddiad*, 252–53)

After about a half an hour, the turtle sinks back down into the dark water; Neddie gets out of the pool, wrings out his pajamas, and goes back into the hotel. He feels quite peaceful about his role in saving the world, trusting that he will know what to do when the time comes.

In the end, he does. In a fake coliseum movie set filled with prehistoric carnivores, he faces down the evil Kkhkktonos and saves the world. The conclusion is extravagantly absurd, even without mentioning Billy the Phantom Bellboy or reverse evolution or the bowling team of shamans from West Covina. But if the story is peculiar, it is also tender and completely satisfying, full of wonderful things from the mind and heart of Daniel Pinkwater, comic genius.

NOTES

1. William James, *The Varieties of Religious Experience* (New York: Penguin Classics, 1902/1982). As quoted in William Harmless, *Mystics* (Oxford University Press, 2007), 13.

2. oneonta.edu/academics/philosophy/Shrader/mysticalexperiences.pdf, Accessed June 6, 2014.

3. Kevin Orlin Johnson, *Apparitions: Mystic Phenomena and What They Mean* (Dallas, TX: Pangaeus Press, 1998).

4. Ron Rosenbaum, "The White Veil," *Smithsonian Magazine* (May 2014), 28.

5. Devin Brown, *Not Exactly Normal* (Grand Rapids, MI: Eerdmans, 2006). Hereafter cited in text as *Normal*.

6. Han Nolan, *When We Were Saints* (New York: Harcourt, 2003). Hereafter cited in text as *Saints*.

7. Daniel Pinkwater, *The Neddiad: How Neddie Took the Train, Went to Hollywood, and Saved Civilization* (New York: Houghton Mifflin, 2007). Hereafter cited in text as *Neddiad*.

8. Pinkwater, *Neddiad*, back cover.

Chapter Seven

Other Faiths and Spiritual Practices: Judaism

The religious orientation of the YA books examined so far, with only a few exceptions, has been mainstream Protestant Christian. Most YA novels in the United States with any spiritual content have this general perspective. But now it is appropriate to look at some YA books that come from other religious viewpoints. This chapter and the one following will attempt to show how the beliefs and practices of other faiths appear in YA literature, and how these differences shape the search for spiritual meaning by young people of those religious identities.

So what are these other faiths? There are commonly said to be five major world religions: Christianity, Judaism, Islam, Hinduism, and Buddhism. All of these belief systems appear, and in that order of frequency, in YA fiction. But their degree of literary visibility does not reflect the numbers of their population and practice in the United States. The four major online sources of statistics about religion list the rank of these faiths by numbers of adherents in the United States as Christianity, Judaism, Buddhism, Islam, and Hinduism. [1]

The order differs once more when looked worldwide through the research of these same major online sources. From this broader perspective, Christianity is again at the top, but Islam is second. After that comes Hinduism, and then Buddhism. Judaism is far down the list, lower than the numbers of even such exotic sects as spiritism and Juche. In addition, several of those online statistical sources include a sixth category—nonbelievers/agnostics/atheists—which shows up third or fourth in numerical order.[2] However, the Pew Forum says that "roughly half" of these so-called nonbelievers are deists; that is, when asked "Do you believe in God?" they answer in the affirmative.[3]

JEWISH CULTURAL CONTRIBUTIONS

But in YA literature, there are more novels and short stories drawn from the Jewish tradition than any other except Christianity. What accounts for this visibility, not only in YA literature but in American society at large, of Jews and Jewish culture, in spite of their low numbers? The Jewish presence in the United States is enormously enriching. Jews are prominent in cinema, art, music, and literature, as well as science, mathematics, and medicine. Many words from Yiddish have been adopted into our daily speech because English has no equivalent: schlep, glitch, maven, klutz, nosh, chuzpah, spiel, bupkes . . . We love Jewish humor and comedians like Mel Brooks, Billy Crystal, George Burns, Gilda Radner, Woody Allen, the Marx Brothers—and yes, Jon Stewart. As Mark Twain said:

> [The Jewish people] are peculiarly and conspicuously the world's intellectual aristocracy. The Jew's contribution to the . . . list of great names in literature, science, art, music, finance, medicine, and abstruse learning are way out of proportion to the weakness of his numbers. He has made a marvelous fight in this world . . . and has done it with his hands tied behind him.[4]

Judaic history goes back four thousand years. According to the Scriptures, the Jews were chosen by God to bring the message of His nature to the world—at a high price.[5] Many of the world's powers have tried to wipe them out, but they survive. So stories drawn from the rich storehouse of Jewish history and the evocative rituals of contemporary Jewish practice and belief are a fertile source of novels, short stories, and poetry for young Jews who are finding out who they are and what that might mean.

A much earlier book, a YA novel that has become a classic, is *The Chosen*, by Chaim Potok.[6] Published in 1967 at the beginning of the genre's identity, it establishes the YA trope of father–son struggles, but goes much further with this theme to portray two fathers and their two sons, clashing and finally resolving differences of political and religious convictions. Warm and wise, this book and its sequel *The Prom-*

ise[7] were ground breaking in their early treatment of Jewish themes in YA literature.

HOLOCAUST STORIES

Maus I and II: A Survivor's Tale[8]

Any discussion of Jewish history and literature for our times must begin with an invocation of the horrors of the Holocaust. A superb example is Art Spiegelman's great pair of graphic novels, *Maus I and II: A Survivor's Tale*.[9] These autobiographical "comics" tell the story of the suffering of the artist's father under Nazi persecution in Poland. On the publication of the first volume in 1986, there had been nothing previously in the graphic novel genre that approached the unity and coherence, the sustained narrative power of *Maus*. It was, in essence, the first of a new kind of literature. It garnered impressive reviews from the literary world—and the Pulitzer Prize in 1992 on the publication of the second volume.

Although Spiegelman has here a subject for which the most detailed depiction of violence might be morally justified, his drawings have classic restraint. There is no gore, no close-ups of shootings and beatings, no screams of "Aieee!" The few scenes of mass carnage are seen from an emotional distance and have the silent rhythm of Greek friezes. In the forefront is the simple story of a very human man trying to survive with dignity in a world full of terror and menace in which he and his kind must hide in the walls like rodents. The horror is pervasive and inherent, and the artist needs no cheap tricks.

The structure of *Maus* is intriguing. The first volume is subtitled *My Father Bleeds History*. A second volume, *Maus: And Here My Troubles Began*, was published in 1992. As the story begins, Artie, a cartoonist in his mid-thirties, goes to visit his aging father to talk to him about a project he has in mind, a comic book based on the old man's memories of the Holocaust. The father, Vladek Spiegelman, agrees to tell his story to his son, although he protests. "Better you should spend your time to make drawings what will bring you some money" (*Maus I*, 12). As Vladek's tale proceeds chronologically, each episode is framed by a visit from Artie in which he struggles with his tortured relationship with his father. At the same time, the Holocaust story he is researching and plans to draw is the very story we are reading.

These three narrative levels intersect at several points with intricate reverberations. Artie shows his father the work in progress (which the reader has previously seen). "I've already started to sketch out some parts," he says. "I'll show you. See, here are the black market Jews they hanged in Sosnowiec" (an episode from the Holocaust story). "And, here's *you* saying, 'Ach, when I think of them, it still makes me cry!'" (an incident from the relationship story). And in the present Vladek looks at the picture of himself and says, "Ach, still it makes me cry" (*Maus I*, 133). Add to this a fourth level, the fact that we know that this story is true and it is likely that all three of these scenes really happened singly and together.

The structural centerpiece is entirely different in both style and subject—a short piece, first published in 1973, titled "Prisoner on the Hell Planet." It shows Artie's pain at the suicide of his mother, Anja, and it bursts off the page like a shriek of anguish. It is a relief to get back to the more universal emotions of the cool, meticulously detailed story of the tightening Nazi noose.

Spiegelman's mastery of structure is equaled by his skill at character. The portrait of his father is a rich, detailed likeness of a complex and contradictory personality. Vladek's actions and words reveal him. The drawings show only a rudimentary mouse-face—a single line of pointed nose and two dots for eyes—with which the artist does manage nevertheless to convey some surprisingly subtle nuances of expression. The reader sees Vladek simultaneously as both an old and a young man, as he tells his story and as he appears in it. The elder Vladek is obsessive and miserly, a man who quarrels constantly with his second wife and who loves his son but shows it in paranoid, intrusive ways. He speaks with a clumsy accent. The young Vladek is elegant and articulate in his native Polish, a tender husband and father, a resourceful quick thinker with an iron will to survive. The connection between the two is in the events that changed the one into the other.

As Vladek begins his story in 1935, we see him a dapper young man courting Artie's mother, Anja, and marrying into her wealthy family. Soon after the birth of their first child, Richieu, Anja has a nervous breakdown, a first indication of the neuroticism that would later lead to her suicide. Vladek is drafted into the Polish army and captured by the Germans. As a prisoner of war he barely escapes a mass execution of Jewish soldiers. Back home he is shocked to discover that the Nazis have confiscated all his in-law's textile factories and they are reduced to living on their savings.

As the Nazis close in, the family hide in secret compartments in the coal cellar and in the ceiling, foraging for food at night. At last they are betrayed and taken to a depot to await transport to Auschwitz. Vladek bribes a way out for himself and his wife, but is unable to save his father- and mother-in-law. Vladek and Anja wander about, paying one person and then another to conceal them, squeaking by in breathless hairbreadth escapes. They survive on Vladek's hoarded money, on his wits and sheer force of personality. When Anja wants to give up he exhorts her, "To die, it's easy. . . . But you have to struggle for life!" (*Maus I*, 122). At last they make a desperate break for Hungary and are caught on the train. This first volume of the story ends as they arrive at the dreadful gates and are separated. "And we came here to the concentration camp Auschwitz, and we knew that from here we will not come out any more," says the old Vladek, staring into the past (*Maus I*, 157).

But they did—both of them. In the concentration camp Vladek bluffs his way through by working as a tinsmith and a shoemaker, and with bribes and bartering. Later they are sent to Dachau, but eventually survive, and end up in the Catskills, where Artie's interview visits take place. The last section of *Maus II* shows Artie struggling with complex guilt and grief, anger and love brought to him by his father's death.

The matter of the animal metaphor in *Maus* bears some examination, both for its own interest and because naïve critics have found it trivializing to the subject. "Maus," of course, is German for "mouse." The Jews in Spiegelman's drawings are mice. Other nationalities also have animal identities: the Poles are pigs, the Germans cats, the Americans dogs. Yet this is no barnyard world like *Animal Farm*. Except for their pointed, whiskered faces, the characters are completely anthropomorphized. After a few pages we think of them as people, so much so that it is a surprise to glimpse a long tail under Anja's skirts, or to see them don pig masks to go undetected among the Poles.

Spiegelman plays with these metaphors in literary ways, beginning with the pun in the subtitle. Obviously, the idea of "cat-and-mouse games" is appropriate in the way the Jews must hide by day in bunkers and tunnels and attics. When Anja and Vladek crouch in one particularly damp cellar, she sees a scurrying shape and is terrified that it may be a rat. "They're just mice," Vladek comforts her. Less amusing is the opening quotation from Adolf Hitler: "The Jews are undoubtedly a race, but they are not human" (*Maus I*, 4).

But what is the real function of these animal identities? There is a long literary tradition, going back before Aesop to the folktale, of

masking our everyday human selves in story with the features of birds
and beasts. When the drama is more serious, these animal tragedy
masks have an elevating, distancing effect. Internal evidence for this
point can be found in *Maus*. The characters in "Prisoner on the Hell
Planet," the story of the suicide of Artie's mother, are drawn as humans, and the emotions are unbearably personal and intense. When the
Spiegelmans resume their mouse-faces and return to the Holocaust narrative, the serenity of classical pity and terror returns. The story becomes larger, more significant—less particular and more universal.

   Maus has been analyzed and praised by some of the best critics in
the business. To their voices I can add only one new thought: This is a
book that is supremely important and appropriate for young adults. Not
only because teenagers have always found the comic strip congenial,
not only because it is a story of the pain of parent–child conflict, not
only because it is a superbly original piece of literature, but also because it is a stunning evocation of the terror of the Holocaust—and we
dare not let the new generation forget.

   Twenty-two years later Sonia Levitin began to write YA novels
drawn from Jewish identity and history, although she does not limit her
fiction writing to these subjects or to this age level. Levitin is herself a
Holocaust survivor, so the four novels that she has set in the time of the
Nazi persecution are intense with remembrance.

Journey to America trilogy

Journey to America[10] opens in Berlin, 1938, where the Platt family is
agonizing over whether to escape the growing Nazi threat by fleeing to
neutral Switzerland. This would mean leaving their country, their
friends, and most of their money and possessions. They decide that
Papa will go ahead to America, where he will try to get them all visas
to emigrate. Mama and the three girls will wait in Switzerland, although they have no place to stay and little means to survive. After a
grueling year made bearable only because a Swiss family finally takes
them in, the visas arrive and they leave to begin a new life. In the
sequel, *Silver Days*,[11] teenage Lisa Platt learns a new language and new
ways with her family in New York. And in the final volume of the
trilogy, *Annie's Promise*,[12] the youngest daughter copes with anti-Semitism and builds an identity for herself in California after the family has
moved west.

Room in the Heart

In another Holocaust-centered novel, *Room in the Heart*,[13] Levitin tells the story of the role of ordinary people in the heroic rescue of the eight thousand Danish Jews. She employs multiple viewpoints: a young Jewish girl, a boy who is attracted by Nazi power, another boy who is appalled at the misuse of that power and so joins the Danish Resistance, and a young Nazi soldier writing home to his "liebe Mutti."

SONIA LEVITIN STORIES FROM OTHER JEWISH HISTORY

The Cure

Levitin has also drawn on other times in Jewish history for her stories. *The Cure*[14] uses a time-travel fantasy to frame a dramatic tale of the maltreatment of Jews in the Middle Ages. It is 2407, when everyone wears a mask to emphasize conformity, and tranquility has been implemented via genetics, drugs, and therapy. It is also the year 1348, the time of the Black Death in Strasbourg, France, where sixteen-year-old Gemm has been sent back from the future to cure his nonconformist forbidden desire to create music. In this past time he is the son of a wealthy moneylender in a small Jewish community that finds comfort and strength in the daily rituals of their Judaic faith. But as the plague sweeps the land, terrified people in city after city scapegoat the Jews as the cause of their problems. Officials find it convenient to have someone to blame, and soon realize that they can wipe out their debts by torturing and burning the Jewish moneylenders and their families. But they play music all the while to make the execution scenes less horrible. Sonia Levitin draws on historical fact for this story's powerful emotional impact. As I said in the Amazon editorial review, "The vivid details of ghetto life in the Middle Ages . . . make [this story] overwhelmingly real, with layers of meaning for our own times."[15]

Escape from Egypt

The same is true for Levitin's Passover novel, *Escape from Egypt*.[16] The stirring tale of how Moses led his people out of Egypt is remembered in the rituals and symbols of this holiday. The commemorative narrative read at the Passover seder table reminds Jews every year of the mighty deeds of God in freeing them from Egyptian slavery. Levitin's novel relates these events from the alternating points of view of two teenagers: Jesse, a Hebrew slave, and Jennat, a half-Syrian, half-Egyptian girl. The double perspective provides an opportunity for exploration of spiritual ideas, as the two young people caught up in this vast Biblical panorama struggle with the big questions: Why is there evil? What is God's will? What do I believe? What am I willing to risk? *Booklist* said, "Levitin is certainly courageous. At a time when authors are steered away from writing controversial books and when stories are pre-sifted to make them palatable to the lowest common denominator, she has written a book that is troubling, moving, and sensual—and that forces its readers to think."[17]

CONTEMPORARY JEWISH RELIGIOUS DIVISIONS

Levitin has explored not only the relationship of Jews to the world, but the differences and tensions among the three divisions within Judaism: Reform, Conservative, and Orthodox. To the left of Reform are nonobservant Jews, or secular Judaism, and to the right of Orthodox Judaism is Hasidism.

Strange Relations

This last is the focus of Levitin's most recent YA novel, *Strange Relations*.[18] Marne, fifteen, is being sent to Hawaii to spend the summer with Aunt Carole. She looks forward to long lazy days at the beach, but what she finds is a different world. Her Aunt Carole has become Aunt Chaya and has married a Hasidic rabbi. They run their crowded household by strict Hasidic rules and are part of a Jewish community of the same tradition. At first Marne, who has been raised as a secular Jew, is bewildered and resentful. But gradually she accepts the sense of peace and happiness in this ordered society. When her friend Kim comes to visit, Marne finds her shallow and silly and realizes that her altered perceptions are because she herself has changed. *School Library Journal* praised the book: "It's rare to find such well-developed characters, empathetic and sensitive religious treatment, and carefully crafted plotlines in one novel."[19]

The Singing Mountain

The Singing Mountain[20] also presents a spiritual dialogue between two divisions of Judaism. Carlie, fifteen, has lived with her aunt and uncle and her cousin Mitch ever since her parents were killed in an accident. The summer before he is to enroll at UCLA, Mitch, who has never been very religious, travels to Israel with his temple's youth group and is attracted to Orthodox Judaism. When he sends word to his Reform parents that he is going to stay on in Israel and study at a yeshiva, they are worried that he has been brainwashed. At Christmas, Carlie and her aunt go to Israel to try to bring Mitch back, but find him ready to argue knowledgeably for his choice. He and Carlie grapple with big issues of faith and politics and spiritual growth, and eventually Carlie comes to terms with her feelings about her parents' death, and Mitch's mother accepts his right to make his own decisions.

Like No Other

In her YA novel *Like No Other*, author Una LaMarche[21] uses the rituals and rules of Hasidic Judaism to shape a tender love story. Devorah is sixteen; Jaxon is sixteen. Devorah is the middle child of seven with hardworking and loving parents; Jaxon is the oldest child of five, with loving and hardworking parents. Devorah is well-behaved and smart at school; Jaxon is well-behaved and smart at school. They live on the same street in Brooklyn, but they might just as well be universes apart. Jaxon is a black kid from the West Indies, Devorah is a Hasidic Jew, and each lives in a tight community of their own kind.

They would never have met if not for an unlikely accident. Both are at the hospital—Jaxon to watch out for his best friend Ryan, who has been hurt on his skateboard, and Devorah to watch out for her older sister Rose, who has just given birth to a premature baby. The two teens are alone in the elevator when it shudders and screeches to a stop, trapping them between floors. Jaxon is awkward with girls, but Devorah is more than awkward with boys—she has never spoken to, or been alone with, a male outside her immediate family because this is forbidden by *yichud*, the strict Hasidic code for women under which she lives. Clothes, as well as behavior, are dictated by *yichud*. In the summer heat she is wearing "black shoes, opaque black tights, black skirt to mid-calf, white long-sleeved T-shirt with a purple cardigan" (*LNO*, 30). But what Jaxon sees is her long dark hair and beautiful face.

She crouches in a corner of the dim elevator, speaking only to tell her name, while Jaxon thinks, "I need to make her feel comfortable" (*LNO*, 34). He manages to kick open the trapdoor in the ceiling and climb up, but this doesn't help. Devorah, however, is impressed. "That was really brave," she says, in spite of *yichud* (*LNO*, 38). Jaxon gazes at her wide gray eyes and knows he is in trouble.

And so is Devorah. As they make tentative conversation (she has decided that it doesn't count if she limits herself to answering his questions), she has a thought that touches something that she has kept hidden from herself—a fierce desire to be her own person.

> I've never had a private conversation like this with an outsider. I've never had to explain anything, because in my world everything just *is*. For a second, I consider lying and just pretending I'm someone else. After all, I'll never speak to Jaxon again once the power comes back on. This might as well be a dream. A very lucid and as it turns out very enjoyable dream. But then I decide that this opportunity is too valuable. Where else will I find someone to listen without judgment? This might be the only chance I ever get to be completely honest without worrying about being proper. (*LNO*, 45)

And so they talk, easily after a while. Jaxon is astonished to learn that Devorah is not allowed TV or cheeseburgers, and she is surprised to hear that he helps around the house. They describe their families, share secrets, even tease and flirt a little. They each know that something important is growing between them. But when the elevator finally begins to move, Devorah thinks, "It's over. It's over before it had a chance to begin" (*LNO*, 54). And Jaxon thinks, "That felt real. And suddenly I'm filled with dread that I'll never feel it again. . . . I was more myself in that elevator than I think I've ever been anywhere else" (*LNO*, 60).

They go home to their respective families. Devorah has to take charge of the preparations for the Sabbath dinner, since her mother is at the hospital arranging to bring Rose home. LaMarche gives readers an evocative chapter that shows the meaning of the Sabbath, or Shabbos, in Jewish life. She describes in detail the preparations and the rush to get everything ready before sundown (when the Shabbos rule against using electricity will take effect), the gathering of the family members around the table, and the ceremonies that precede the meal. However, Devorah can't participate with her usual enjoyment because she is pre-occupied with thoughts of her encounter with Jaxon. She is further worried to find that her stern, cold brother-in-law Jacob has shared the news with her family that she was alone in an elevator with a black man.

Over the next few days, their yearning to see each other again takes over, and they manage a few secret moments. As their connection grows, Devorah is terrified that they will be found out and she will be ostracized and shunned by her family and community. But their need will not be denied. They sneak a Shabbos afternoon date, and Jaxon takes her to the basement of his apartment house, where he has arranged rugs and pillows in a romantic nest. There Devorah introduces Jaxon to the ritual of the Shabbos meal with the grapes and strawberry Twizzlers he has provided for refreshments, in an amusing and touching scene. Finally they scheme to go away for a weekend, hoping the act of rebellion will shock their families into acknowledging their need to be together. But the plan backfires. Jacob and the shomrim, or religious patrol, apprehend them and beat Jaxon mercilessly. Devorah is sent to stay at a Hasidic correction facility, to be counseled into returning to the rule of her faith by a kindly and understanding rabbi. Meanwhile, her parents hire a matchmaker to get her hooked into an arranged marriage, but her straight talk puts off the first prospective suitor.

Jaxon finds her, and they have one last moment before the inevitable ending of their impossible love. Una LaMarche has made the bittersweet tension between this unlikely pair palpable. Rather than settle for the easy explanation of teenage lust, she has justified the intensity of their attraction by showing how it fulfills a psychological need for each in the search for identity. Although the details of the strict Hasidic life are fascinating, the spiritual content of this book lies in the nature of the bond that links these doomed lovers. Devorah tells Jaxon, at the last, "Meeting you has changed my whole world around, and I feel like I owe the rest of my life, whatever it ends up being, to you" (*LNO*, 322).

YA NOVELS OF JEWISH SPIRITUAL SEARCH

Another story set in the Hasidic tradition is not so warmhearted. In *Hush*, a YA novel by Eishes Chajil and Judy Brown,[22] Gittel, seventeen, has grown up deeply immersed in that religious sect. When she witnesses her best friend being forced into incest by her brother, and when guilt and shame lead the girl to commit suicide, Gittel's repressive relatives and neighbors refuse to acknowledge the crime. They maintain that such things do not happen in their community, leaving Gittel to struggle to reconcile this secret with her faith.

In a pair of recent novels by Elana Arnold, *Sacred*[23] and *Splendor*,[24] a girl looks for solutions to her problems of life and love by delving into the Kabbalah, the ancient Jewish book of esoteric mysteries. An even more outré plot device is found in Matthue Roth's *Never Mind the Goldbergs*,[25] in which a punk rock Orthodox teen goes to Hollywood to find her place in the world. Another girl who hopes to find her destiny by a change of geography is Sarah, the protagonist of *The Weight of the Sky* by Lisa Ann Sandell.[26] She jumps at a chance to spend the summer on a kibbutz in Israel to escape her hometown life, where she is a band nerd and the only Jew in her school, but the idyllic life she has imagined falls short of her expectations. And Simone, in Dana Reinhardt's charming *A Brief Chapter in My Impossible Life*,[27] has always known she is adopted. She's quite okay with that, until her Hasidic birth mother Rivka shows up, dying of ovarian cancer. Simone must learn to accept her Judaic heritage and deal with some big questions about life, as Rivka teaches her about Jewish beliefs and customs.

MORE JEWISH HISTORY

A second YA author who, like Levitin, has made good use of Jewish history is Gloria Miklowitz. Two of her many novels are based on dramatic times in that history.

Masada[28] tells the story of the siege and eventual fall of the last fortress during the First Jewish–Roman War. Herod the Great had built this fortified palace on a rocky plateau as a place to make a last stand if it became necessary. Ironically, it was the Sicarii, an extremist Zealot group, who retreated there in 66 CE. A Roman legion led by the governor of Judea, Lucius Flavius Silva, laid siege to the fortification in 73 CE. After several months, they were able to breach the walls by building a ramp to the plateau. There they found that the 960 inhabitants had killed each other in an elaborately choreographed mass suicide.[29] Miklowitz tells this tragic tale in the alternating voices of the Roman general and a seventeen-year-old Jewish youth, Simon ben Eleazar.

Secrets in the House of Delgado[30] takes place in 1492 CE, at the time of the Spanish Inquisition. Maria, fourteen, is an orphaned Catholic girl, who has been sent by her priest to work (and spy) in the household of a family of "Conversos," Jews who had converted to Catholicism under duress. She is to watch for any sign that they are secretly practicing their original religion. At first she is horrified at the idea of working for former Jews, but she gradually comes to love the warm-hearted family. However, when she reports to the priest on their activities, the father is taken away to be questioned and possibly tortured. She agonizes over her part in this disaster and tries to undo her betrayal in a story from history that makes a breathless page-turner.

Canadian author Eva Wiseman uses traditional and also recent Jewish history in her middle-grade and YA novels. Several of these books have won prizes in Canada for their literary quality, but unfortunately this author's work is only available from Canadian reprint publishers and is not well known in the United States.

CONTEMPORARY JEWISH STORIES

My Basmati Bat Mitzvah

Tara Feinstein says she is suffering from "multiple ethnicity disorder," in this delightful YA novel by Paula J. Freedman.[31] Tara's father's folks are New York City Jews, and her mother's family is from India and so they are—at least nominally—Hindu. But many years ago her mother converted to Judaism, so that makes Tara Jewish, by that faith's rules. When all her relatives get together, it's what her Yiddish-speaking Gran calls a *mesuggeneh mishpacha*, or crazy mixed-up family.

To add to Tara's identity crisis, she goes to Hebrew school and is studying for her bat mitzvah, which is coming up soon when she turns thirteen. But that doesn't keep her from rubbing ashes on the elephant head of the little statue of Ganesha that she keeps in her bedroom in memory of Nanaji, her beloved Hindu grandfather. Other problems swirl around her head: Does she want to be more than best friends with her best friend, Catholic Ben-O? Does her other best friend, Jewish Rebecca, like Sheila Rosenberg better than Tara? And what is she going to tell her mother about the big hole she and Rebecca have accidentally burned in a precious family heirloom sari? The one she wanted to wear for her bat mitzvah?

But the real problem that dwarfs and underlies all the others is that she isn't sure she believes in God. And she's sure that a bat mitzvah is a commitment to that belief.

Whether or not *I* believed in God—that was the main question. I had
thought about it all summer, and I still didn't know the answer. There
wasn't even anyone I could talk to about it. I mean—it wasn't exactly
something you wanted to ask your rabbi. Rabbi Aron is probably the
coolest rabbi in the world, but still. My heart did a flip just thinking
about that conversation. (*Basmati*, 8)

Eventually she does have that conversation, but not before the
whole family gets together for a double celebration of Duwali, the
Hindu festival of lights, and Hannukah, the Jewish festival of lights.
For the party Tara's father makes potato latkes with tamarind chutney
and yogurt sauce. Gran brings a big pot of matzoh ball soup, and on the
sly the Indian relatives spice it up by sneaking in some cayenne pepper
and green chiles. "Auntie Meena brought out two trays of her famous
potato-pea samosas, which she only makes once or twice a year since
they are such a pain in the *tuchis* (a word she learned from Gran)"
(*Basmati*, 132).

All of this intercultural celebrating leads Tara to wonder what her
grandparents would have thought about her having a bat mitzvah. She
tentatively broaches the subject with her mother.

"Mum, I just wanted to know. . . . Were Nani and Nanaji . . . Were
they—religious?"
Mum studied my face for a long moment before she answered me.
"Yes, but maybe not in the way you think," she said finally. "I
would say Papa was a very spiritual person—he thought . . . that everyday things were holy." (*Basmati*, 134)

Tara ponders this and decides:

It was a comforting thought, and I kind of liked the sound of it. If
spiritual meant being kind to animals, and being adventurous, and loving flowers and trees and every kind of food, and having an open heart
and mind—then maybe I was spiritual, too. (*Basmati*, 137)

Meanwhile, Tara is working out her relationship problems with
Ben-O and Rebecca. Her Gran helps her confess to her mother about
the damage to the sari, and then rescues the heirloom by having it made
into a beautiful dress that Tara will wear for her bat mitzvah. And
Rabbi Aron guides her to realize that her doubts are all right with God.

"Find comfort in your doubts, Tara," he said. "Only the weak are absolutely sure of everything." . . .

So it was okay to have questions, even about something so important. That was reassuring, I guess. It didn't make me any less good, or strong. It didn't make me any less Jewish. I didn't have to know everything. I just had to keep my heart and mind open. I could do that. Maybe I did believe—or could. I wanted to. I could try. And maybe that was good enough. For a while. (*Basmati*, 159)

At the bat mitzvah, Tara's *parashah*, or Torah reading, is the story of Joseph and his coat of many colors. In her remarks, she tells the story of the ruined sari and makes a comparison to draw the lesson. Afterward the Rabbi gives her a two-edged compliment:

"Thank you, Tara, for that—very original interpretation of scripture," he said. He went on to tell the congregation how impressed he had been by my many thought-provoking questions these last few months and said that not everyone my age is mature enough to know what they don't know. Which was a nice way of putting it. (*Basmati*, 229)

While this novel may seem on the surface to be a multicultural romp, it takes Tara's spiritual search seriously and has much wisdom and comfort to offer teens of all faiths.

As does our next piece, a short story that beautifully describes an episode of the complexities of searching for God.

With All My Heart, With All My Mind

This short-story collection, edited by Sandy Asher,[32] showcases thirteen well-known YA authors, such as Sonia Levitin, Gloria Miklowitz, and Susan Beth Pfeffer, in stories about growing up Jewish, followed by brief interviews in which the authors talk about how they define and relate to their own Jewishness and how it has influenced their writing. Not all of these writers are religiously observant Jews, and for several, the important thing is cultural identity and the link to the past through tradition. But most of them speak of how their writing grew through increasing connection with their spiritual roots, and their stories invoke predictable but appropriate themes like Holocaust remembrance, resistance to anti-Semitism, continuity with the past through ritual and tradition, and (of course) coming-of-age at the bar or bat mitzvah.

But near the end of the book is a story that sheds a sudden brilliant flash of light on the adolescent search for God. Carol Matas, in "Wrestling with Angels," uses as her metaphor that mysterious story from Genesis 32 in which Jacob wrestles all night long with a stranger—perhaps an angel, perhaps God himself—and although Jacob has been wounded in the encounter, he prevails and demands the blessing that will give him his name, identity, and purpose. In Matas's story, a young girl, Jaci, dreams that she is the one who struggles with the angel, and wakes confused and troubled. She carries the dream with her to Hebrew class, where her friends have been pressuring her to get something pierced and to go out with a boy she doesn't really like. She finds herself telling the dream to Isaac, a boy from the Orthodox tradition, and through his concern and an impassioned class discussion of the book of Job, she finally realizes that "my Judaism *could* mean something. Something practical. Something useful. A way to think about things. To make choices" (*Mind*, 144). We know that a spiritual journey has begun here. Although she cannot yet say that she believes in God, she knows that the truth she has glimpsed inside herself is "maybe, for me, the essence of God. Mystery. And maybe this is the beginning of a very long wrestling match" (*Mind*, 144).

A way to make choices but also a wrestling match. "We are meant to argue with God" (*Mind*, 141), says Isaac, and this may be a new thought to teens who have assumed that faith means accepting ultimate answers without the struggle and experience that makes them personal.[33]

NOTES

1. Pew Research Religion and Public Life Project, Religious Landscape Survey. http://religions.Pewforum.org/reports; adherents.com/religions-by-adherents/html; CIA World Factbook, www.cia.gov/library/publications/world-factbook/geos/html; U.S. Census Bureau, Statistical Abstracts, http://www.census.gov/compendia/statab/2012/tables/12s0075.pdf. All accessed October 12–15, 2014.

2. Pew Research Religion and Public Life Project, Adherents.com, CIA World Factbook, and U.S. Census Bureau.

3. Pew Research Religion and Public Life Project, Accessed October 13, 2014.

4. Mark Twain, as quoted by Hank Pellissier in "Why Is the IQ of Ashkenazi Jews So High? Twenty Possible Explanations." http://immortallife.info/articles/entry/why-is-the-IQ-of-Ashkenazi-Jews-so-high, Accessed October 4, 2014.

5. The Victorians were fond of saying: "How odd of God / to choose the Jews." To which Ogden Nash later added: "But not so odd as those who choose / the Jewish God and spurn the Jews."

6. Chaim Potok, *The Chosen* (New York: Simon & Schuster, 1967).

7. Chaim Potok, *The Promise* (New York: Simon & Schuster, 1969).

8. Parts of this section on *Maus* appeared in "The Young Adult Perplex," *Wilson Library Bulletin* (February 1987): 50–51, and in *Campbell's Scoop: Reflections on Young Adult Literature* (Lanham, MD: Scarecrow Press, 2010), 113–18.

9. Art Spiegelman, *Maus I: A Survivor's Tale: My Father Bleeds History* (New York: Pantheon, 1986); *Maus II: A Survivor's Tale: And Here My Troubles Began* (New York: Pantheon, 1992). Hereafter cited in text as *Maus I* or *Maus II*.

10. Sonia Levitin, *Journey to America* (New York: Aladdin, 1987).

11. Sonia Levitin, *Silver Days* (New York: Atheneum, 1989).

12. Sonia Levitin, *Annie's Promise* (New York: Atheneum, 1993)

13. Sonia Levitin, *Room in the Heart* (New York: Dutton, 2003).

14. Sonia Levitin, *The Cure* (San Diego, CA: Harcourt/Silver Whistle, 1999).

15. http://www.amazon.com/The-Cure-Sonia-Levitin, Accessed October 4, 2014.

16. Sonia Levitin, *Escape from Egypt* (New York: Little, Brown, 1994).

17. amazon.com/Escape-Egypt-Novel-Sonia-Levitinin/dp/product-description/ 03165, Accessed October 2014.

18. Sonia Levitin, *Strange Relations* (New York: Knopf, 2007).

19. http://www.amazon.com/Strange-Relations-Sonia-Levitin/dp/9780375837517/, Accessed October 7, 2014.

20. Sonia Levitin, *The Singing Mountain* (New York: Simon & Schuster, 1998).

21. Una LaMarche, *Like No Other* (New York: Razorbill/Putnam, 2013). Hereafter cited in text as *LNO*.

22. Eishes Chajil and Judy Brown, *Hush* (New York: Walker, 2010).

23. Elana K. Arnold, *Sacred* (New York: Random House, 2012).

24. Elana K. Arnold, *Splendor* (New York: Random House, 2013).

25. Matthue Roth, *Never Mind the Goldbergs* (New York: Scholastic/Push, 2005).

26. Lisa Ann Sandell, *The Weight of the Sky* (New York: Viking, 2006).

27. Dana Reinhardt, *A Brief Chapter in My Impossible Life* (New York: Random House/Wendy Lamb Books, 2006).

28. Gloria D. Miklowitz, *Masada: The Last Fortress* (Grand Rapids, MI: Eerdman's, 1998).

29. Guy D. Stiebel, "Masada," *Encyclopaedia Judaica 13*, 2nd ed. (Detroit: Macmillan Reference, 2007): 593–99.

30. Gloria D. Miklowitz, *Secrets in the House of Delgado* (Grand Rapids, MI: Eerdman's, 2001).

31. Paula J. Freedman, *My Basmati Bat Mitzvah* (New York: Abrams, 2013). Hereafter cited in text as *Basmati*.

32. Carol Matas, "Wrestling with Angels." In Sandy Asher, ed. *With All My Heart, With All My Mind: Thirteen Stories about Growing Up Jewish* (New York: Simon & Schuster, 1999). Hereafter cited in text as *Mind*.

33. Another book that might fit in this chapter, *Intentions* by Deborah Heiligman, was discussed in chapter 1.

Chapter Eight

Other Faiths and Spiritual Practices: Islam, Hinduism, Buddhism, and a Sikh or Two

Why should it matter if young people in the United States have any knowledge of religions other than the two they come in contact with every day, Christianity and Judaism? How can Christians and Jews accept Christianity or Judaism as the way to God, and still give credence to the truth and reality of other religions? The distinguished Biblical scholar and theologian Dr. Marcus Borg answers these questions with characteristic eloquence:

> Religious pluralism is a fact of life in North America, and in the world. To absolutize one's own religion as the only way means that one sees all of the other religious traditions of the world as wrong, and dialogue, genuine dialogue, becomes impossible. Conversion can be the only goal.
>
> I affirm, along with many others, that the major enduring religions of the world are all valid and legitimate. I see them as the responses to the experience of God in the various cultures in which each originated. To be Christian means to find the decisive revelation of God in Jesus. To be Muslim means to find the decisive revelation of God in the Koran. To be Jewish means to find the decisive revelation of God in the Torah, and so forth. I don't think that one of these is better than the other. You could even say they are all divinely given paths to the sacred.[1]

In YA literature, teens can find voices from all of the Big Five faiths, but in varying quantity. As we have seen, Christianity is well represented, Judaism not as much, but still visible. And secular agnosticism is the default position for the majority of authors of YA lit. But what about more exotic religions that have millions of adherents in other parts of the world—Islam, Buddhism, and Hinduism? Are there YA novels that show young people in spiritual search in the context of these faiths? The answer, as is true of so many questions about religion, is yes and no. In the case of Islam, the burning political and cultural issues surrounding the extremist expressions of this faith make its appearance obligatory for both the TV news and YA fiction. However, most YA novels about Muslim teens show them caught in the tides of warring political factions or the ritual practices and customs of the religion, not in the search for a personal relationship to God, or Allah— nor is that search necessarily an expected part of devotion to that belief.

ISLAM

Islam is the second largest religion after Christianity; its adherents make up 23 percent of the world's population.[2] It was founded in 610 CE by Mohammed (570–633 CE) who, unlike Jesus, is considered a prophet but not divine. He is often referred to as "the final prophet," after Adam, Noah, Moses, Abraham, and Jesus. All of these figures appear in the Koran (or Quran), as well as many other stories that are familiar to Jews and Christians through their own holy writings. The Koran is said to have been told to Mohammed by the angel Gabriel and, since the Prophet was illiterate, memorized or written down by the prophet's companions. A second sacred writing is the Sunnah, a gathering from the oral tradition, made up primarily from the sayings and deeds of Mohammed. Muslim sources online maintain that "Islam, a religion of mercy, does not permit terrorism."[3]

And, as we are all too aware from the news stories, Islam is divided into two adversarial factions. These are Sunni (87–90 percent) and Shia (10–13 percent).[4]

Islamic belief is rigorously monotheistic and is founded on the *sha-hadah*, or creed, which must be said by every Muslim: "I testify that there are no deities other than Allah alone and I testify that Mohammed is his messenger." The basic belief is simple: God is one and incomparable and the purpose of existence is to worship him. Muslims are required to pray five times a day, kneeling in the direction of Mecca and reciting designated passages from the Koran. Allah's will is seen as predetermined, although humans have freedom to act, and Muslims, like Christians, expect a Final Judgment, when it will be decided who gets to go to Paradise.[5]

Ethical behavior is based on the Five Pillars of Islam:

Shahadah—Declaring faith in Allah and in his messenger Mohammed

Salat—Praying five times a day

Zakat—Giving to the poor

Sawm—Fasting during the holy month of Ramadan

Hajj—Making a pilgrimage to the holy city of Mecca at least once during one's lifetime[6]

Women's dress in Islam has long been controversial, at least for Western observers of Muslim culture. Observant female Muslims, with interpretation depending on their country and custom, are required to dress modestly and to wear some sort of head covering, or hijab.[7] This requirement varies from the dupatta (a long scarf draped around the head and neck to cover the hair) to the full burka (a long black tent-like garment covering the body and face, leaving only a small screen for the eyes). Women's opportunities for education are limited in some Muslim countries, but not all, and arranged marriages are still expected in many areas. These customs are all factors that show up often in YA fiction because they impact directly on the daily lives of young Muslim women.

Suzanne Fisher Staples

This YA author is an American journalist who traveled widely in the Middle East and South Asia during her time as a reporter. She was for several years the South Asia bureau chief for United Press International, covering stories in Pakistan, Afghanistan, Bangladesh, Sri Lanka, Nepal, and India. In a literary study of Staples's life and work, *Suzanne Fisher Staples: The Setting Is the Story*, Megan Lynn Isaac describes the influence of this period on the writer:

> She . . . met hundreds of ordinary people and learned to relish the everyday details of new places. Although Staples had no idea at the time that she would eventually turn to writing fiction, her years in South Asia helped create the foundation for her books. During this period she

learned some of the languages she would eventually draw upon, made notes about the physical features of the places she visited, and had the opportunity to learn about several cultures in much greater depth than is possible by studying a place from a distance or by visiting it as a tourist.[8]

Later Staples accepted a job as a part-time editor for the foreign desk of the *Washington Post*, but three years later went to work in Pakistan on a project for the U.S. Agency for International Development. Isaac says,

> She returned to Pakistan with her husband to conduct a study of women in rural Pakistan, exploring which activities would be the most productive to improve the lives of families. Eventually she helped develop a project that invited women from small villages to learn to read and trained them to serve as teachers to other members of their communities. The project enriched Staples's life.[9]

It is a mark of her devotion to accuracy in her writing that at this time Staples learned to speak Urdu so that she could communicate more intimately with her interviewees without the intervention of a male interpreter.[10]

When she returned to live in the Washington DC area in 1987, Staples began to use the rich knowledge of other cultures that she had gained in her career as a journalist to generate fiction. Her first novel, *Shabanu: Daughter of the Wind*,[11] was a major success. It won a Newbery Honor, among many other awards. Kirkus Reviews praised its "unforgettable heroine set like a fine jewel in a wonderfully wrought book,"[12] and the *New York Times* called it "a small miracle."[13] In particular, reviewers praised its vivid depiction of the culture and the details of the characters' hard desert life.

Shabanu is a headstrong and independent-minded twelve-year-old girl, a member of a nomadic tribe who live in the Cholistan Desert of Pakistan. Because her family has no son, she has been allowed to work closely with her father in tending the camels that they depend on for transportation and profit, even helping with the delivery of a baby camel whose mother has been killed by a snakebite. Her older sister Phulan is preparing for her arranged marriage, and Shabanu's own wedding will be only a year later. She is looking forward to marrying her cousin Murad, when a murder affects the family's future and forces them to shuffle the plans for the girls' weddings. Phulan will marry

Murad, and Shabanu is to become the fourth wife of an old and wealthy landowner whom she has never met. The marriage will settle a family feud and benefit her community, but Shabanu is not happy with it. Although she was willing to marry her cousin, and she has been raised to obey her father, and then her future husband, she rebels at this new pairing and tries to run away to live with her aunt. When the attempt fails, she gives in to her father and accepts her culture's edicts for her future.

Megan Isaac explores the reaction of American teens to the idea of arranged marriage:

> The freedom to choose a spouse without parental interference, or even without parental advice or approval, is so central to American culture that it can be extraordinarily difficult for young adults to recognize that not only is this practice specific to certain cultures, but it is not even desired or envied by most people in cultures with other traditions. . . . Young readers in the United States also tend to misunderstand the emotional foundation of arranged marriages. . . . In the United States love leads to marriage, while in Shabanu's world marriage leads to love. Although the expectation seems backward to many American readers, it makes perfect sense to millions of people who have experienced the phenomenon themselves.[14]

In response to teen readers' pleas to reveal "what happened to Shabanu," Staples wrote a stand-alone sequel four years later, that again used arranged marriage as a plot device. *Haveli*[15] takes place in a more urban environment, where Shabanu lives as a member of the Punjabi elite with her husband Rahim and his three senior wives. She is now six years older, and the mother of a little girl, Mumtaz. They exist in an atmosphere of constant suspicion, jealousy, and scheming from the other wives. To escape their false accusations and threats, Shabanu takes refuge in the city of Lahore in the haveli, or ancient four-story mansion, of Rahim's widowed sister. There she meets Omar, a young man who has just returned from his studies in the United States to fulfill an arranged marriage with Rahim's daughter. Over time she falls in love with him. The final events of this volatile situation are full of betrayals and violence, but tempered with hope as the story moves to an open-ended conclusion. Shabanu gives up her daughter to her desert family's keeping and goes into hiding in the abandoned upper floor rooms of the haveli.

The third book of the trilogy, *The House of Djinn*,[16] takes place ten years later. Shabanu is nearing thirty, and her daughter Mumtaz is now fifteen, and so becomes the primary protagonist of this YA novel. Staples uses a limited omniscient narrative to go back and forth between the perspectives of these two characters, and also adds a third, Jameel, a teenager who has grown up in San Francisco but has also spent summers with the family in Lahore. A major part of the story involves the relationship between Shabanu, who has come out of hiding to return to the desert and regrets the ten years she was not in contact with her daughter, and Mumtaz, who resents the mother she hardly knows. The setting is more modern, and Western technology is a part of the young people's lives as well as traditional ways.

Mumtaz and Jameel have known each other from babyhood and are close friends, but each secretly has a crush on an unsuitable partner: Mumtaz on her Hindu tennis coach, and Jameel on an American fellow skateboarder, Chloe, who is Jewish. They share talk about their romantic difficulties, but when Baba, the head of the family, dies, it becomes essential for the well-being of the thousands of people who depend on the tribe's holdings that Jameel and Mumtaz marry and that he take over the leadership of the family. At fifteen? Most American teenagers would find such a prospect alarming if not ridiculous. Yet Jameel and Mumtaz eventually accept their roles, even though at first they try to run away, like Shabanu before them.

In this book Staples introduces the belief in mischievous spirits called djinn. Although Staples leaves their existence open to question, several of the characters attribute strange events or sightings to them. These djinn are more than the Western idea of ghosts or devils; they are beings created by Allah to be his messengers, who can marry, have children, and who have free will and are required to worship Allah. They are skilled shapeshifters and can take the form of any animal or human. They are mentioned in the Koran.[17]

In *The House of Djinn*, Baba, Jameel's grandfather, explains the relationship of these creatures to humans:

> The Quran says that God creates a djinni for each one of us. It's the djinni's job to lead us astray, to cause mischief in order that we should learn from the tricks he plays. A djinni can even cause harm—but his purpose is to improve us, sometimes even through temptation. Everyone has a djinni. (*djinn*, 44)

Although belief in djinn is more superstitious than spiritual, Jameel does have a wider understanding of God. When Baba falls sick, his friend Chloe offers to pray for the old man, but asks Jameel if her Jewish prayers are acceptable in this situation. He says, "Muslims and Christians and Jews all pray to the same God" (*djinn*, 97), expressing an ecumenical acceptance that many Americans would be surprised to hear from a Muslim.

Isaac sums up the impact of this concluding book of the Shabanu trilogy. "*The House of Djinn* invites readers to think about [daily life in] a part of the world many people now hear about only in news reports focusing on terrorist camps, border disputes, military conflicts, and diplomatic missions."[18] Staples had been criticized as a Westerner writing about the Middle East, and so for this third book she provides an author's note that briefly lays out the history of Pakistan, its system of government, the languages used by her characters, the city of Lahore, and the custom of arranged marriage. Most important, she takes pains to explain that the situations and people in her books are meant as individual cases, and should not be taken as universal. She emphasizes that "as in most families—both real and fictional—love is a powerful force that draws imperfect people together" (*djinn*, ix).

A fourth book from Staples, *Under the Persimmon Tree*,[19] takes place in post-9/11 Afghanistan, and has a hopeful ending that can only strike current readers as ironic. The story is told through the perspectives of two very different protagonists: Najmah, a young shepherd girl in a village of the Kunduz Province, and Nusrat, an American woman married to Faiz, an Afghan doctor, and living in Peshawar, Pakistan, a major city near the Afghani border. Their two lives are contrasted in alternate but parallel chapters. Nusrat and her husband have come from America for humanitarian reasons: he works at a free medical clinic just across the border, and she runs a school for refugee children. The shepherd girl Najmah's peaceful life in the mountains is disrupted when the Taliban take her father and brother, and an American bomb kills her mother and baby brother. She sets out on the perilous journey to find her father. Meanwhile, Nusrat has not heard from her husband for a long, worrisome time. Eventually the lives of Najmah and Nusrat mesh when the young girl arrives at the American woman's school. They become close friends, but when the news comes that both Najmah's father and Faiz have died, the two women realize that each must return to her own country.

But it is Nusrat's conversion to Islam that is of most interest in our quest for spirituality in YA fiction. What would lead a young American woman living in New York to make such an unorthodox decision? Staples justifies Nusrat's spiritual hunger by linking it to her mourning for her dead sister. She "longed for a poetic and mysterious sense of order that would explain where Margaret had gone" (*Tree*, 134). She searches for a sign from God, and when she touches a copy of the Koran on a neighbor's table she feels a surge of energy. At the same time, she is falling in love with her kind neighbor Faiz, the man she will eventually marry. She studies Arabic so she can read the Koran in the original, consults with a local imam, and changes her name—originally Elaine—to the more Islamic Nusrat. Her parents are puzzled by her conversion, and so is the reader because of the disappointing lack of details on the spiritual thinking that one can only assume led to such a decision. At the end of the book, Staples cops out entirely, as Nusrat tells her in-laws that although "Islam helped her understand what is inexplicable in life, she now understands that Christianity would have offered her the same opportunities if she had allowed it to do so. . . . Nusrat has come to see the practice of faith as more important than its name."[20] Or its content? It seems to me that Staples has missed a golden opportunity here to explain the inner workings of the Muslim faith to American teens.

Throughout the novel, Staples makes no political or ethical judgment about the military actions in Afghanistan. Her purpose, Isaac says, is to insist that "readers consider the ramifications [that] these actions, especially the air strikes, have on the ordinary people of the country. . . . The bombs that drop from the U.S. fighter planes overhead, the land mines planted by the Soviet soldiers a decade earlier, and the bullets fired by the Taliban soldiers are all equally deadly."[21] Yet Isaac maintains that Staples implies peace will be built by the determination of the Afghanis themselves, an assertion that turns bitter in the current age of ISIS.

Islam and Political Upheaval

Other YA novels with Muslim characters and themes focus on the difficulties, especially for women, of living in a place and time of political turmoil. Outstanding among books of this type is Deborah Ellis's Breadwinner trilogy, set in Kabul, Afghanistan.[22] In the first book, *The Breadwinner*, Parvana, only eleven years old, disguises herself as a boy to earn money for her family after her brother is killed and her father is sent to prison. In the second book, *Parvana's Journey*, she leads a group of children to a refugee camp, and in the third, *Mud City*, an older protagonist, Shauzia, fourteen, leaves the refugee camp to find life outside just as hard. The trilogy was praised for its vivid picture of the difficulties girls and women face in contemporary Afghanistan.

More such books set in our politically volatile time take place in the United States or go back and forth between America and the Middle East. *Where I Belong* by Gillian Cross,[23] for instance, opts for additional YA interest by including the London fashion scene. When Mahmoud is kidnapped and held for ransom in the Somalia Desert, his older sister Khadya, a fashion model, must earn his release by her work on the London Fashion Week runway. Two other books concentrate on the furor after 9/11 in America. In Marina Budhos's *Ask Me No Questions*,[24] the father of a family whose U.S. visas have expired tries to flee to Canada but is arrested at the border; the two teenage daughters must carry on at home and in school. And the narrative of *Refugees* by Catherine Stine[25] is an email correspondence from the time right after 9/11 between two runaway foster kids in New York and a boy who is escaping the Taliban at the other side of the world.

The conflict between Palestinians and Israelis has given rise to several YA novels. The eleven-year-old Palestinian protagonist of *A Stone in My Hand* by Cathryn Clinton[26] deals with her father's arrest by Israelis and her brother's involvement with militant extremists. A short story, "The Olive Grove" by Elsa Marston in the collection *Soul Searching*,[27] shows a young Palestinian boy facing down Israeli soldiers who try to cut down his village's olive grove. A moving portrayal of this ancient region's problems comes from poet and Christian Palestinian Naomi Shihab Nye in her autobiographical novel *Habibi*,[28] although the nature of the conflict has changed since this book was published in 1997.

Contemporary Muslim American Teens

On a more light-hearted note, a number of books recently have dealt with the daily problems of Muslim American teens in conflict with Islam's strict rules for young women. Most of these focus on the prohibition of dating or the decision to wear the hijab, and most play it for laughs, like *Bestest. Ramadan. Ever.* by the Kurdish author Medeia Sharif[29]; *Dahling, If You Luv Me, Would You Please, Please Smile* by

Ruhksana Khan[30]; or *Does My Head Look Big in This?* by Randa Abdel-Fattah.[31]

"The only Muslim kid in the school" trope appears in at least two YA novels: *Skunk Girl* by Sheba Karim[32] and *I'm Just Me* by M. G. Higgins.[33] In the latter, a Muslim girl adds the complication of a friendship with a black girl. Interestingly, the Muslim parents are uncomfortable with this, not because the new friend is black, but because she is a Christian. And of course the arranged marriage is a bone of contention between the generations in all these stories. A particularly intense version appears in *Written in the Stars* by Aisha Saeed,[34] as Naila's conservative parents take her from America back to visit their family in Pakistan, supposedly to reinforce her Islamic values. But secretly they plan to deal with her rebellion by marrying her safely off while they are in a country where such arrangements are commonplace.

One of the few contemporary YA novels about Islam with a male protagonist is *Borderline* by Allan Stratton.[35] Again, we have "the only Muslim kid in the school" trope, which means that Sami is bullied mercilessly by his classmates. But things get much more exciting when his father is falsely accused of being part of a terrorist plot and arrested, and Sami sets out to free him by solving the case.

Spiritual Islamic Books

A facet that is mostly missing from all the books that have been mentioned so far is any serious depiction of the inner spiritual striving of Muslim belief. I have been able to find only four novels, and only three of them written for young adults, that examine this aspect of Islam in any depth. This is a distressing scarcity, because, as I said in *VOYA* magazine in my introduction to a list of Islamic titles, "We in the West are dangerously uninformed—or misinformed—about Islam. Our attitudes toward this second largest world religion are shaped by misperceptions and ignorance."[36] And by hysterical reactions to extremist militants, I would now add.

The brilliant and best-selling adult novel, *The Kite Runner* by Khaled Hosseini,[37] goes a long way toward reconciling Western ideas about Islam with universal values. A father and son struggle with Afghanistan's turbulent political situation in "a country in the process of being destroyed." Betrayal and subsequent salvation through forgiveness illuminate the story of a young man who returns to his native village in Afghanistan to atone for the betrayal of a friend, now murdered by the Taliban, by rescuing the man's orphaned son. Although this book was published as adult, it has been widely disseminated to young adults.

Another remarkable book, this one a true YA novel, is Paula Jolin's *In the Name of God*,[38] set in Damascus, Syria, which believably traces the gradual transition of Nadia, seventeen, to sympathy with the extremists, and then willingness to participate as a suicide bomber. A more benign use of Muslim spirituality is pictured in *Overboard* by Elizabeth Fama.[39] Emily, a fourteen-year-old American teenager visiting Sumatra, sneaks away from her parents and boards a crowded ferry to visit her uncle. In a rather uncharacteristicly charitable gesture, she gives her life jacket to a little boy. When the overladen boat capsizes, she is frantic—until the boy appears, wearing the jacket, to hold her up. They float for hours before they are rescued, but during that time the strong, quiet Muslim faith of the boy sustains them both.

HINDUISM AND THE RELIGIONS OF INDIA

Hinduism is the oldest of world religions and the most complex. Its origins are lost in antiquity, and there was no one founder. Religious practices and beliefs of Hinduism have many diverse forms, and could best be described as a wide variety of religious traditions and philosophies that have developed in India over thousands of years. That said, certain characteristics can be found in many versions of this religion, but not necessarily all. "Most Hindus worship one or more deities, believe in reincarnation, value the practice of meditation, and observe festive holidays like Duwali."[40]

Hindus have a multitude of gods and goddesses, but the major deities are the trinity of Brahma, Vishnu, and Shiva, and also Rama, Lakshmi, Kali, the elephant-headed god Ganesha, who clears away obstacles, and the popular and influential god Krishna, who appeared on earth in bodily form, and whose birthday, janmashtami, is widely celebrated. Worship of one or more of these gods takes place through idols or images, and mostly in the home at certain times of day. There is an awareness of a duality between purity and pollution, so symbolic washing before worship is important. In addition, there are many proscribed rituals and celebrations for life cycle events like birth, marriage, and death.[41]

The sacred texts are the Vedas, Upanishads, the Bhagavad Gita, and other epics.[42] The fundamental belief is that the purpose of life is to achieve moksha, or release, of the soul from the cycle of reincarnation by performing good deeds, or karma.[43] The concept of ahimsa, or non-violence, is important for both spiritual and nationalistic reasons. Mahatma Ghandi liberated his country from Britain through the power of this idea and set an example for the nonviolent leadership of black America by Martin Luther King Jr. years later. Many other Hindu concepts and practices have been adopted by the Western world but are often misunderstood. Yoga as a form of exercise, but not a form of worship, is widespread in the United States. The monks in yellow robes who chanted "Hare rama, rama, hare Krishna," accompanied by the tinkling of finger cymbals, were a familiar sight in U.S. cities in the 1960s and 1970s. Another widespread practice adopted by young hippies at this time was the chanting of "ommm" to induce a spiritual mood. Belief in the efficacy of meditation and the concepts of reincarnation and retributive karma have also been Westernized and adopted in some areas of society.

In 1947 the British Indian Empire divided the Indian subcontinent into the Republic of Pakistan and the Republic of India. Muslims were to go to Pakistan, and Hindus to India. This involved much political upheaval, and there was widespread protest and rioting; millions of people were killed or became refugees.[44] Since then Hindus in India are 80 percent of the population, and only 13.4 percent in that country are Muslim,[45] although they make up a majority in Pakistan.

Hinduism in Young Adult Literature

Several YA novels have been set in India, but few of them explore Hindu spirituality. Like the books with an Islamic background, the major emphasis is usually on the difficulty for girls posed by the cultural requirements, the outer trappings, and customs of the religion's practice. Although the discipline of modesty and the head scarf is not so rigidly enforced as in Islam, in these YA books set in India—not surprisingly—it is arranged marriage and the low status of women that make up most of the conflicts in the plots.

And sometimes it is simply the cultural clash of ancient values and contemporary life that is the focus. *Born Confused*[46] and *Bombay Blues*,[47] by Tanuja Desai Hidier, are two cross-cultural comedies that portray the adolescent angst of a young American Hindu girl with the preposterous name of Dimple Lala. The first book takes place in America, where Dimple's conservative parents are attempting to arrange a marriage for her. She rejects her suitor, only to find him more attractive when her girlfriend hits on him. In the second book, Dimple goes with her parents and her boyfriend to a family wedding in Bombay, where she tries to capture the "real India" with her trusty camera, which she calls "chica tikka."

A more serious YA novel, *Keeping Corner* by Kashmira Sheth,[48] gives us a twelve-year-old widow, Leela, whose husband has died from a snake bite. By custom, she must "keep corner" for a year, staying inside the house without ever going out, and giving up pretty clothes and jewelry for a plain brown sari. At first she is devastated, but when her teacher comes to the house to tutor her, she begins to be interested in the newspaper accounts of Ghandi's campaign to free India from British rule. She equates the oppression of her country with her own fate, and finally gets her parents' permission to study in Ghandi's ashram with the goal of helping to free Hindu women.

A third YA novel with the theme of a spunky girl enduring culture clash is *The Secret Keeper* by Mitali Perkins.[49] The time is 1957, during Indira Gandi's regime, and two teenage sisters—Asha, sixteen, and Reet, seventeen—must deal with their mother's depression and the repressive household of their uncle in Calcutta. Their father has gone to America to seek work, and his absence is painful for them. Asha confides her frustrations to her diary—her "secret keeper." In the end she must save her sister from an unwanted marriage by making a major sacrifice.

A more unusual story is *Alpha Goddess* by Amalie Howard,[50] a fantasy in which a girl discovers that she is an incarnation of Lakshmi. Kate Conklin said, in her review for *VOYA* magazine, "The depth of Howard's description of the Hindu deities is a refreshing change. The book addresses some of the feelings that Indian Americans must experience while growing up in towns with little diversity."[51]

Finally, two YA novels that deal with the inner spirituality of Hinduism, and not just cultural differences, are *Climbing the Stairs* by Padma Venkatraman[52] and *Shiva's Fire* by Suzanne Fisher Staples.[53] In the first of these stories, Vidya and her parents—Amma and Appa—and her brother Kitta live happily in Madras, India, during World War II and at the time of Ghandi's crusade for freedom from the British. Appa takes part in a protest march and is beaten so badly by a British soldier that he is left with severe brain damage. He is scorned as "an idiot" by the neighbors, so the family goes north to live with relatives who are strict Brahmins. There Vidya and her mother are treated like slaves. The young girl finds solace by sneaking into her grandfather's library to read, a room that is in the men's part of the house. Her brother Kitta enlists in the British Army, which is doubly controversial for the family, both because of British oppression and Brahmin dedication to nonviolence. Vidya goes to the army camp to tell him goodbye, and on the way is horrified to see the poverty in the city. At last she falls in love with a handsome and intelligent young man, Raman, who is living in the same house. However, he needs to be enlightened about equality for women. They get engaged, but then go off to college in different countries. The characters discuss Hindu philosophy and celebrate many Hindu festivals in this richly wrought book.

Shiva's Fire expresses another spiritual aspect of Hindu culture, the classical Indian dance form of bharata natyam. This demanding art evolved from the temple dances of South India many centuries ago. It declined, but was revived in a modern form in the nineteenth and early twentieth centuries. The dance form has many expert performers today in India and can be seen on the Internet in online videos of performances, competitions, and even lessons. Bharata natyam is deeply spiritual, with many layers of symbolism and drama. [54]

As a dancer myself, I cannot resist the temptation to describe at least the outward basics of this exotic form from what I have observed of it online. Bharata natyam begins with the feet turned out, in what is known in ballet as first position. The movements of the body stem from deep knee bends, or plies, and there are spectacular extensions of the legs. The dancer must master two types of moves: the adavi, or steps, and the mudras, or hand gestures. The feet stamp the floor in intricate rhythms, strongly enough to make a loud explosive "thwap." Unlike Western dance, in which the toe is pointed down, bharata natyam footwork often leads with the heel, and the toes are pointed upward. The hand gestures are coordinated with the rhythms of the feet and have many expressive meanings. For instance, the mudra called araala can signify a violent wind or poison, while the shikara mudra can represent the goddesses Lakshmi and Saraswati, or milking cows, or holding flowers while making love, and several other equally explicit symbolisms. Added to these movements, the dancer's face, and especially the eyes, are used expressively to tell the story in proscribed ways. [55]

But most important is the spiritual dimension of the dance as an offering to Shiva. In Staples's novel, a young girl named Parvati (consort of Shiva) has mystical connections, starting from the day of her birth, when a cyclone hits her village and her father, the Maharaja's elephant keeper, is killed. As she grows up, these magical links grow more obvious and alienate her from the suspicious villagers. At six she dances in the cooking fire and is unhurt, and animals, including a cobra, communicate with her. As she grows into her teens she shows such ability in dance that a master teacher comes to the village to invite her to study in his school of classical dance in the city of Madras. At this point in her life, Parvati must make the first of many choices to follow her dharma, or destiny, rather than her human desires. To go to Madras would mean to leave her beloved mother, whom she then might never see again. Nevertheless, she goes to the dance academy and begins her study to master the intricacies of bharata natyam. Within a couple of years, instead of the usual twelve needed for physical and spiritual mastery, she is ready to dance her first public performance, by which both she and her teacher will be judged. She performs so extraordinarily well that she is invited to return to her home area to live at the Maharaja's palace and dance at his birthday celebration.

But soon she must again make a difficult decision—should she accept her religious and societal responsibilities as a gifted dancer or follow her heart to be with the Maharaja's son Rama, who loves her, even though they are incompatible because of caste and class? Staples leaves the outcome of Parvati's story open, but Megan Isaac finds hope for her in the dance: "Parvati feels a world of possibilities spring up from her feet and flow from her hands. As she dances with Shiva she can drum a whole new world into creation—even, perhaps, a world with Rama."[56] Amazon reviewer Jennifer Hubert found inspiration in Staples's novel for contemporary young women in their own life choices: "Parvati's story will inspire readers to set high goals and settle for nothing less than their true heart's desire. An instant classic."[57]

A richly sensual verse novel that draws the same message from the spiritual aspects of bharata natyam is the aptly named *A Time to Dance*, by Padma Venkatraman.[58] Veda, like Staples's Parvati, is a child prodigy in dance, until an accident robs her of her lower right leg. Devastated, she no longer knows who she is without her ability to dance. Her grandmother encourages her with warm love and Hindu wisdom, and when an American specialist devises a prosthetic for Veda that may allow her to dance, she returns to her dream and again takes up classes, this time with a new teacher, a young man who helps her understand the spirituality inherent in her passion to dance.

BUDDHISM

This fourth major world religion can be more easily characterized by what it isn't than what it is. Buddhism has no deity, no prayer in the sense of supplication, no clergy other than monks, no membership requirements, and no one body of sacred scripture. In essence, it might be considered not a religion at all, but a way of life.[59] It was founded somewhere between the fourth and sixth centuries BCE by Siddhartha Gautama, a wealthy young man, who at the age of thirty-five sat down under a Bodhi tree and vowed not to rise until he found enlightenment, or understanding of life. He eventually achieved this goal, and shared his insights with his followers in the Four Noble Truths for living:

1. Existence is suffering.
2. Suffering is caused by craving and attachment.
3. It is possible to achieve the end of suffering, or nirvana—
4. through the Eightfold Path, which consists of right views, right resolve, right speech, right action, right livelihood, right effort, right mindfulness, and right concentration, or meditation.[60]

Added to these precepts is the Middle Way of moderation and five moral principles: to refrain from taking life, stealing, acting unchastely, speaking falsely, and using intoxicants. However, an individual must achieve his own salvation from the cycle of life and rebirth by meditation and the development of mindfulness. There are many divisions and sects of Buddhism and an estimated 360 million adherents. The practice has spread from its origins in India throughout all of Asia, and, in a much lesser degree, to Europe and the United States.

Nevertheless, in spite of its appeal to popular culture, Buddhism has appeared in YA fiction in only four books. The first is the iconic classic *Siddhartha* by Herman Hesse,[61] a book which was almost an article of faith itself among young people in the 1960s and has been reprinted in many new editions since. It traces a young man's spiritual journey from a life of wealth as a Brahmin to realization of the sufferings of life and eventual awakening, or nirvana.

A later, but regretfully out of print, book is *Tulku* by Peter Dickinson.[62] During the Boxer Rebellion in China, the thirteen-year-old son of a missionary escapes from the slaughter by fleeing to Tibet with an English botanist. There they are given sanctuary in a Buddhist monastery, where their lives are transformed by relating to the monks. Another book with the same setting is *Rebel: A Tibetan Odyssey* by Cheryl Whitesel,[63] which is set at the turn of the last century and traces the life of a young boy unwillingly living in a monastery. A more recent title, and a more recognizably YA novel, is *Buddha Boy* by Kathe Koja.[64] A strange new kid arrives at school, and the other kids nickname him "Buddha Boy" for his calm silence. A boy who befriends him is rewarded by learning about Buddhist beliefs, like Hungry Ghosts and the influence of karma.

To make up for this scarcity of Buddhist-oriented YA fiction, we need to mention several nonfiction titles aimed at explaining Buddhism for American teens. See, for instance, *Buddha in Your Backpack: Everyday Buddhism for Teens* by Franz Metcalf[65] or *Wide Awake: A Buddhist Guide for Teens* by Diane Winston.[66]

AND A SIKH OR TWO

Many Americans have the misunderstanding that Sikhism, the fifth largest world religion, is a subset of Islam or Hinduism.[67] This idea is far from the truth. Their monotheistic beliefs and guiding principles are strikingly different from other Eastern and Middle Eastern religions— and many are congenial to modern Western thought. Sikhs believe in the absolute equality of every human being—men or women notwithstanding. Astonishingly, God is regarded as both mother and father, and all religions are valid in their ability to approach him/her. In addition, Sikhism rejects the trappings of extremism: superstition, rituals, fasts, asceticism, and self-mortification. They have no priests, but like the early Christians, every Sikh house of worship, or gurdwara, serves a free community meal daily to the hungry, regardless of their ethnicity or religion.[68]

The youngest of the major world religions, Sikhism was founded five hundred years ago in the northern Indian subcontinent by Guru Nanak (1469–1539). After his death, he was followed by a succession of ten other gurus, each of whom helped to develop the faith and accumulate the scriptures, of which the primary writing is the Guru Granth Sahib—known familiarly as the GGS. Sikh men are identified by the wearing of the turban, which is required garb for males, and by their uncut hair and beards.[69] Originally as a move to eliminate the caste system, all Sikh men have the last name Singh (lion), and women Taur (lioness).[70]

Sikhs have a reputation as fierce soldiers, and under the Raj, they earned that description in two wars against the British invaders. In 1947, at the time of the partition of India, they fought a losing but bloody battle for a separate state of their own. In the eighties, political unrest and fighting led to the assassination of Prime Minister Indira Gandi by her Sikh guards, and in the four days of rioting that followed, many thousands of Sikhs were killed.[71]

There are currently more than thirty million Sikhs in the world. In the Indian subcontinent they are centered in the Punjab, but there are Sikh communities in Europe, Canada, and the Western United States.[72]

Inexplicably, this interesting faith has engendered only two YA novels. The first of these, *Karma* by Cathy Ostlere,[73] is a verse novel that tells the story in diary format of Maya, a girl with a Hindu mother and a Sikh father. She has been raised in Canada, but when her mother commits suicide, Maya and her father travel to take her ashes to India for burial. They arrive in Delhi on the fateful date of October 31, 1984, the day of Indira Gandi's assassination and the beginning of massive anti-Sikh riots. Somehow Maya and her father are separated in the turmoil, and she witnesses a terrible sight—a Sikh man being burned alive. Alone in a violent foreign country, Maya must depend on the help of a mysterious boy, Sandeep, who rescues her from the angry crowds and helps her look for her father. The novel shapes a horrifying time in recent history into an engrossing narrative, sweetened by the good karma of a love story.

Shine, Coconut Moon by Neesha Meminger[74] presents another American-Sikh teen girl, but this one doesn't know that's what she is until her estranged uncle shows up on the doorstep—wearing a turban. Samara's mother has kept her away from her strict Sikh family, and Sam has never identified with them. This uncle wants to heal their relationship and tell her about her Indian heritage. She is eager to learn, but the time is just after 9/11, and the atmosphere in America is full of hate. When boys attack her uncle with cries of "Go home, Osama!" she realizes the dangers of ignorance and the need for her to accept and reconcile with her newly found Sikh identity.

And finally, a book that sets an example of the possibilities of spiritual themes by showing teens struggling to find God in the context of a variety of faiths. In *I Believe in Water*, Marilyn Singer[75] has brought together twelve outstanding YA authors—Jacqueline Woodson, M. E. Kerr, Naomi Shihab Nye, Joyce Carol Thomas, and others— each to write about a teen going through a spiritual crisis. Nancy

Springer contributes a story about "The Boy Who Called God She"; Virginia Euwer Wolff gives us the voices of three girls—Catholic, Buddhist, and Muslim—each asking for Divine guidance about whether to end an unwanted pregnancy. In "Forty-Nine Days," Kyoko Mori shows a Christian girl gaining new understanding of her own faith through a visit with her Buddhist Japanese grandmother. Jacqueline Woodson sets her story in the mind of a young Jehovah's Witness, and Joyce Carol Thomas examines the cringe-worthy religious practice of "Handling Snakes." A reluctantly Jewish girl gets more comfortable with her heritage in Marilyn Singer's "Fabulous Shoes." And a boy stands up to some anti-Semitic waitresses in Gregory Maguire's "Chatterbox" by lying that his grandmother died in the concentration camps.

Another group that has often been the target of hate and misunderstanding is the Church of Jesus Christ of Latter-day Saints (LDS), or Mormons, a homegrown American religion. There is no scarcity in YA literature of books by Mormon authors, although they are often not recognized as such. To understand LDS values and to learn about the YA fiction they have inspired, I have asked the award-winning YA novelist Chris Crowe to wind up this book on spirituality with a chapter about Mormons and Mormonism in YA literature.

NOTES

1. Marcus Borg, "Questions of Faith and Doubt: How Can Christians Accept Christianity as the Way to God, and Still Give Credence to the Truth and Reality of Other Religions?" http://www.explorefaith.org/questions/credence.html, Accessed January 17, 2015.

2. pewresearch.org/fact-tank/2013, Accessed January 26, 2015.

3. "A Brief Illustrated Guide to Understanding Islam." http://www.islamguide.com/frm-ch-2-4 htm, Accessed January 26, 2015.

4. pewforum.org/2011/01/27/future-of-the-global-muslim-population-sunni-and-shia/, Accessed January 26, 2015.

5. http://www.religionfacts.com/islam/practices, Accessed January 26, 2015.

6. "Guide to Understanding Islam."

7. http://www.islamicbulletin.org/newsletters/issue_24/beliefs.aspx, Accessed January 26, 2015.

8. Megan Lynn Isaac, *Suzanne Fisher Staples: The Setting Is the Story*. Scarecrow Studies in Young Adult Literature, No. 37 (Lanham, MD: Scarecrow Press, 2010), 35.

9. Isaac, *Suzanne Fisher Staples*, 7.

10. Isaac, *Suzanne Fisher Staples*, 8.

11. Suzanne Fisher Staples, *Shabanu: Daughter of the Wind* (New York: Knopf, 1989).

12. http://www.amazon.com/Shabanu-Daughter-Suzanne-Fisher-Staples/dp/0028189178/ref, Accessed November 1, 2014.

13. amazon/Shabanu.

14. Isaac, *Suzanne Fisher Staples*, 38, 40.

15. Suzanne Fisher Staples, *Haveli* (New York: Knopf, 1993).

16. Suzanne Fisher Staples, *The House of Djinn* (New York: Farrar, Straus and Giroux, 2008). Hereafter cited in the text as *djinn*.

17. http://www.djinnuniverse.com/a-short-course-on-the-djinn.

18. Isaac, *Suzanne Fisher Staples*, 67.

19. Suzanne Fisher Staples, *Under the Persimmon Tree* (New York: Farrar, Straus and Giroux, 2005). Hereafter cited in the text as *Tree*.

20. Isaac, *Suzanne Fisher Staples*, 151.

21. Isaac, *Suzanne Fisher Staples*, 143.

22. Deborah Ellis, *The Breadwinner; Parvana's Journey; Mud City* (Toronto, Canada: Groundwood Books, 2001).

23. Gillian Cross, *Where I Belong* (New York: Holiday House, 2011).

24. Marina Tamar Budhos, *Ask Me No Questions* (New York: Atheneum, 2006).

25. Catherine Stine, *Refugees* (New York: Delacorte, 2005).

26. Cathryn Clinton, *A Stone in My Hand* (Somerville, MA: Candlewick, 2002).

27. Elsa Marston, "The Olive Grove," in *Soul Searching: Thirteen Stories about Faith and Belief*, ed. Lisa Rowe Faustino (New York: Simon & Schuster, 2002).

28. Naomi Shihab Nye, *Habibi* (New York: Simon & Schuster, 1997).

29. Medeia Sharif, *Bestest. Ramadan. Ever.* (Woodbury, MN: Flux, 2011).

30. Ruhksana Khan, *Dahling, If You Luv Me, Would You Please, Please Smile* (Markham, Ontario, Canada: Fitzhenry & Whiteside/Stoddart Kids, 1999).

31. Randa Abdel-Fattah, *Does My Head Look Big in This?* (New York: Orchard, 2007).

32. Sheba Karim, *Skunk Girl* (New York: Farrar, Straus and Giroux, 2009).

33. M. G. Higgins, *I'm Just Me* (Costa Mesa, CA: Saddleback, 2014).

34. Aisha Saed, *Written in the Stars* (New York: Penguin, 2015).

35. Allan Stratton, *Borderline* (New York: HarperTeen, 2010).

36. *Voice of Youth Advocates (VOYA)* magazine, Dec. 2005.

37. Khaled Hosseini, *The Kite Runner* (New York: Penguin, 2003).

38. Paula Jolin, *In the Name of God* (New York: Macmillan, 2007).

39. Elizabeth Fama, *Overboard* (Peru, IL: Cricket, 2002).

40. http://www.religionfacts.com/hinduism/index.htm, Accessed January 26, 2015.

41. Hinduism.about.com/od/godsgoddesses/tp/, Accessed January 27, 2015.

42. Patheos.com/Library/Hinduism.htm, Accessed January 26, 2015.

43. http://www.religionfacts.com/hinduism/index.htm.

44. http://asianhistory.about.com/od/India/t/partitionofindiafaq.htm, Accessed January 27, 2015.

45. https://www.cia.gov/library/world-factbook/geos/in.html, Accessed January 27, 2015.

46. Tanuja Desai Hidier, *Born Confused* (New York: Scholastic, 2002).

47. Tanuja Desai Hidier, *Bombay Blues* (New York: Scholastic, 2014).

48. Kashmira Sheth, *Keeping Corner* (New York: Disney-Hyperion, 2009).

49. Mitali Perkins, *The Secret Keeper* (New York: Delacorte, 2009).

50. Amalie Howard, *Alpha Goddess* (New York: Sky Pony Books, 2014).

51. Conklin, Kate, *Voice of Youth Advocates (VOYA)*, October 2014, 83.

52. Padma Venkatraman, *Climbing the Stairs* (New York: Putnam, 2008).

53. Suzanne Fisher Staples, *Shiva's Fire* (New York: Farrar, Straus and Giroux. 2000).

54. http://onlinebharatanatyam.com.

55. www.youtube.com/watch?v=Sgil.OzFQh14.

56. Isaac, *Suzanne Fisher Staples*, 138–39.

57. Hubert, Jennifer, "Editorial Reviews," http://www.amazon.com/Shivas-Fire-Su-zanne-Fisher-Staples, Accessed November 21, 2014.
58. Padma Venkatraman, *A Time to Dance* (New York: Penguin, 2014).
59. http://www.buddhanet.net/nutshell03.htm, Accessed November 21, 2014.
60. www.infoplease.com/encyclopedia/society/buddhism-basic-beliefs-prac-tices.htm, www.bbc.co.uk/religion/religions/Buddhism.htm, www.uri.org/kids/world_budd_basi.htm, Accessed November 21, 2014.
61. Herman Hesse, *Siddhartha* (Boston: Shambhala, 2002).
62. Peter Dickinson, *Tulku* (Gloucester, MA: Peter Smith Publisher, 1995).
63. Cheryl Whitesel, *Rebel: A Tibetan Odyssey* (New York: HarperCollins, 2000).
64. Kathe Koja, *Buddha Boy* (New York: St. Martin's, 2003).
65. Franz Metcalf, *Buddha in Your Backpack: Everyday Buddhism for Teens* (n.p.: Seastone, 2002).
66. Diane Winston, *Wide Awake: A Buddhist Guide for Teens* (New York: Penguin, 2003).
67. "Most Americans Are Clueless about Sikhs," http:/www.religionnews.com/2015/01/26/americans-clueless-sikhs/, Accessed January 27, 2015.
68. www.sikhs.org, Accessed January 27, 2015.
69. Sikhismguide.org, Accessed January 27, 2015.
70. Sikhiwiki.org, Accessed January 27, 2015.
71. Sikhiwiki.org.index.php/1984_massacre_of_Sikhis, Accessed January 27, 2015.
72. www.sikhs.org, Accessed January 27, 2015.
73. Cathy Ostlere, *Karma* (New York: Penguin, 2011).
74. Neesha Meminger, *Shine, Coconut Moon* (New York: Simon & Schuster, 2009).
75. Marilyn Singer, ed. *I Believe in Water: Twelve Brushes with Religion* (New York: HarperCollins, 2000).

Chapter Nine

Mormon Themes in YA Literature

Chris Crowe

It is no longer a surprise to discover a popular YA novel written by a Mormon, and if readers hadn't known Stephenie Meyer was a Mormon, the media coverage of the explosive success of her Twilight series made it clear that Meyer and a good many other popular YA authors were members of the Church of Jesus Christ of Latter-day Saints. In 2009, a *Boston Globe* article titled, "Faith and Good Works: Mormon Writers Find Their Niche in Wholesome Young Adult Genre," provided a brief overview of current Mormon authors along with speculation about why so many of them seemed to have found a home in popular YA literature.[1] Four years later, an article in the *New York Times*, "Mormons Offer Cautionary Lesson on Sunny Outlook vs. Literary Greatness," covered similar ground, helping to confirm that despite their relatively small presence in the U.S. population in the twenty-first century, Mormons are very well represented in YA publishing.[2]

According to the 2012 Religious Landscape Survey, only 2 percent of the U.S. population are members of the Church of Jesus Christ of Latter-day Saints (more commonly known as the Mormon church).[3] The religion, founded in the United States in 1830, has always been a minority among the larger and more prominent Christian religions, but in the last fifty years the faith has seen steady growth in America and around the world. In the mid-to-late twentieth century, Mormons began to make their marks in popular culture: business tycoons, J. Willard Marriott and George W. Romney; singers Donnie and Marie Osmond; professional athletes, Steve Young in football, Johnny Miller in golf,

Danny Ainge in basketball, and Dale Murphy in baseball; and best-selling authors Anne Perry, Orson Scott Card, and Stephen R. Covey all enjoyed a certain degree of fame for their various accomplishments. In the twenty-first century, the Mormon population in the United States continued to grow, but the visibility of the faith made far greater gains in cultural prominence. Underdog Rulon Gardner defeated the traditional Russian favorite in Greco Roman wrestling to win an Olympic gold medal in 2000. Four years later, brainiac Ken Jennings went on a record winning streak on the popular TV game show, *Jeopardy.* Shannon Hale's novel, *Princess Academy*, received a Newbery Honor Award in 2005, the same year that Stephenie Meyer's blockbuster novel *Twilight* first appeared. A year or so later, political commentator and radio personality Glenn Beck began his rise to media celebrity, and in 2008, David Archuleta sang and charmed his way to runner-up on the hit TV show *American Idol.* The *Book of Mormon*, a Tony Award–winning musical, debuted on Broadway in 2011, and in the presidential election the next year, the Republican Party nominated Mormon church member Mitt Romney as its candidate, while fellow Mormons Harry Reid and Orrin Hatch occupied senior positions in the U.S. Senate.

It hasn't always been the case, but in recent years, one of the most successful public arenas for Mormons has been YA literature. Mormon writers for young readers had their first notable splash of success in 1957 when Virginia Sorenson's novel, *Miracles on Maple Hill*, edged out *Old Yeller* to win the Newbery Medal. Sorenson remains the only LDS to win the coveted literary award, but in the decades since her success, Mormon YA novelists have grown in number and quality. In 1971, Beatrice Sparks published *Go Ask Alice*, the first of her popular "anonymous diaries," and in 1972 R. R. Knudson published *Zanballer*, a groundbreaking, pre–Title IX novel that featured a girl as an athlete. Orson Scott Card broke into the mainstream in 1985 with *Ender's Game*, a science fiction novel that has found an eager and enthusiastic YA audience for the last three decades. Since then, many other Mormon authors have entered the national market: A. E. Cannon, Dean Hughes, Martine Leavitt, Kimberley Griffiths Little, Louise Plummer, Janette Rallison, and Carol Lynch Williams to name only a few. These novelists have maintained a steady presence in YA literature and helped set the stage for the next, and even more successful, generation of Mormon writers for young readers.

In the last decade, it hasn't been unusual to find a Mormon author listed in the *New York Times* best-seller list: Julie Berry, Ally Condie, James Dashner, Becca Fitzpatrick, Shannon Hale, Stephenie Meyer, Brandon Mull, Jennifer Nielsen, Aprilynne Pike, Brandon Sanderson, Kiersten White, and other Mormon authors have been regulars on that prestigious list.

While they share the same faith and religious culture as their twentieth century predecessors, what distinguishes the work of these contemporary writers from an earlier generation is audience. Of course, a good many Mormons still write novels for fellow believers, but more Mormons than ever before are writing for the mainstream YA market, and to a careful reader, their Mormon values are apparent in nearly all of their books.

So what counts for Mormon values?

Though some outsiders might disagree with their claim, Mormons consider themselves Christians, people who value and do their best to follow the teachings of Jesus. They tend to be a politically and socially conservative people who embrace traditional values: honesty, hard work, family. As with many other faith traditions, Mormonism places great importance on youth: teenage men and women have many opportunities for leadership and service in their congregations and communities, and they are taught that they have great potential. That tradition may come from the fact that the church's founder, Joseph Smith, had his own encounter with the divine, an experience that led him to leave his parents' religion when he was only fourteen. One of the church's primary religious texts, *The Book of Mormon*, includes stories of young men who, like David and Moses in the Old Testament, were great heroes, and Mormon families use those stories to teach their children of their own potential for greatness.

In reflecting on how his Mormon childhood shaped him as a writer, Orson Scott Card explained that the young heroes in his novels are based on the stories he had read as a boy and on the self-confidence his religion had inspired in him:

> Part of my turning to childhood for the beginnings of my books comes from my Mormon upbringing, however. As a child, I considered myself the equal of any adult because the Mormon church taught me to see myself that way. I was the age of Samuel or of Mormon or of Nephi or of Joseph Smith. God took them seriously and set them doing His work in the real world. Didn't I have the same duty to serve God's purposes, no matter what my age? When I spoke in church, it wasn't about little

Scott Card and whether he would do well or not—it was about salvation
and trying to produce a talk that might help others get a little closer to it.
Likewise, when I write about children in my books, they are not children of a dream childhood in which there are no consequences and
nothing much matters. What my children do will change the world; their
actions reverberate, and the world trembles with their footfalls. And yet
to all those around them they remain children. This is the secret I understood as a child and have not forgotten since then: what children do is
real, not just (in the patronizing phrase) "real to them," but real, period. . . . I learned young that God thinks children are people and can do
His real work in the real world, often better than adults. This shows up
in my writing; this is what ultimately makes me a writer of young adult
fiction whether I ever meant to be one.[4]

It's no surprise, then, that Ender Wiggins, the protagonist in Card's
novel *Ender's Game*, is called upon to save the world.

In addition to seeing great potential in young people, Mormons
embrace many other traditional values. In the 1990s, the church issued
a policy statement titled, "The Family: A Proclamation to the World,"
that reinforced many of its basic principles, including that "the family
is central to the Creator's plan for the eternal destiny of His children."[5]
Mormons tend to have large families and to place great emphasis on the
importance of family relationships now and in the life to come; Mormons believe that family relationships can continue in heaven. They
recognize that not all families look the same, but they teach the importance of loving parents, respectful children, and the strength that comes
from family unity. The church and its families also teach members to
be good people as summed up in the last of the church's thirteen Articles of Faith:

We believe in being honest, true, chaste, benevolent, virtuous, and in
doing good to all men; indeed, we may say that we follow the admoni-
tion of Paul—We believe all things, we hope all things, we have en-
dured many things, and hope to be able to endure all things. If there is
anything virtuous, lovely, or of good report or praiseworthy, we seek
after these things.[6]

It's no surprise, then, that Shannon Hale would tell a *New York Times*
reporter, "I think Mormons tend to have hope and believe in goodness
and triumph"or that a *Boston Globe* reporter would conclude that "because Mormonism is a very child-centered culture and many Mormon
families are large, Mormons are particularly attuned to young audi-

ences."[7] And because Mormons in general seek after things that are "virtuous, lovely, or of good report or praiseworthy," YA literature, as opposed to adult literature, is a space where their stories can comfortably coexist with their religious values.

In addition to striving to live good lives, members of the Mormon church are encouraged to be students of their religion and of secular learning, with an emphasis on secular learning that reinforces basic moral values. A verse from one book of Mormon Scripture reminds members to "seek ye diligently and teach one another words of wisdom; yea, seek ye out of the best books words of wisdom; seek learning, even by study and also by faith."[8] To some, this means to read only church books, including the proliferating number of a wide variety of books written exclusively for Mormon readers. But other Mormons see a broader mandate, a call to study and read religious books, of course, but also to read outside the faith, to appreciate "best books" on all sorts of topics, by all sorts of writers. Students, especially English majors, at the Mormon church's Brigham Young University (BYU) study traditional/canonical and contemporary literature, including YA literature. In fact, in 1962, BYU's English department was among the first in the nation to offer a course in adolescent literature, a course that remains popular today and that has inspired many students to go on to careers as YA authors.

Combining their Mormon values with their writing hasn't been difficult for most Mormon YA authors and that may partially explain why so many Mormon writers are drawn to the field. In addition to teaching its members to refrain from coffee, tea, alcohol, and illegal drugs, the church expects its families to teach their children to dress modestly, to avoid profanity, and to remain chaste until after marriage. In addition to reinforcing those principles, an official church publication for youth urges young people to avoid any entertainment that is "vulgar, immoral, violent, or pornographic."[9] As people striving to live the principles taught by their church, Mormon writers have found that YA and middle-grade fiction allows them more freedom than adult fiction would. Julie Berry told the *Boston Globe*, "It's true that there are aspects of contemporary adult literature that I'm less comfortable with, and a romance that doesn't end in sex would seem ridiculous to a contemporary American audience. Young Adult literature is one of the last places where you can tell a wonderful story without having to be sexual."[10]

Despite standards that some people would consider repressive, Mormons generally are a happy people who are optimistic about the future.

A recent church president often reminded members that "things work out" even when circumstances or personal challenges may be overwhelming. "Mormons tend to have hope and believe in goodness and triumph," explained Shannon Hale, "and those portrayals can ring false in [an adult] literary world."[11] Scholars of contemporary YA literature recognize the trend toward bleak or edgy stories, but most of even the bleakest YA novels conclude with a glimmer of optimism. As author Richard Peck has often said, YA novels must "end at a beginning." YA authors and their readers understand that adolescence is a middle ground, a trying and sometimes scary middle ground to be sure, but it is a phase of life that will pass. Peck's guideline reflects real teen experience, and the faith that challenges will pass, that in time, life will get better. This resonates not only with many teen readers but also with the faith traditions of Mormons and their church.

In addition to accounting for Mormon writers' predilection for YA literature in general, the church's history and beliefs may also explain why so many Mormon authors choose to write fantasy. Some conservative religions reject fantasy for various reasons, including its use of witches, wizards, and magic, but Mormons, despite beliefs and principles that align in many ways with conservative, evangelical religions, have embraced, not rejected fantasy. Mormon writers Jessica Day George, Shannon Hale, Tracy Hickman, Brandon Mull, Jennifer Nielsen, Brandon Sanderson, and Dave Wolverton (who also writes under the name of David Farland) are among some of the best-known authors of contemporary fantasy. Sanderson is perhaps one of the most successful not only because of his prolific storytelling but also for his work in completing Robert Jordan's epic fantasy series The Wheel of Time. Another appealing aspect of fantasy for Mormon writers may be its traditional plot format that clearly defines good and evil. Mormons believe in moral absolutism, that in most cases its members can discern right from wrong, that the purpose of the mortal experience is to be confronted with choices which will help them learn right from wrong. But there are additional reasons why Mormon writers are attracted to the fantasy genre. Shannon Hale says, "There's never been any fear of fantasy or science fiction among Mormons [because we] believe a lot of things that are pretty fantastic—we believe in miracles and angels and ancient prophets and rediscovered Scripture—so maybe it's almost natural for us to dive into these other stories."[12] Julie Berry connects those influences to a childhood where her family read Scriptures daily. "I've been spoon-fed a diet of biblical literature that had fed my imagination. Scripture is the ultimate fantastic literature. Everything else is milquetoast compared to the parting of the Red Sea."[13]

A final Mormon principle is central to all of their writing and also partially explains why Mormons are attracted to particular novels. Perhaps the most central, most basic of all Mormon beliefs is that of moral agency, the ability to choose right from wrong. Mormons believe that this principle has been in place since the Creation as evidenced in the story of Adam and Eve in the Garden of Eden. Eve had a choice to accept or reject the temptation to partake of the forbidden fruit, and it was her choice to violate God's commandment, a choice that led to a mortal life filled with trials and tribulations, but also filled with family and faith, a life of making choices, learning from those choices, and being the better for it. Mormons recognize that all choices have consequences, just as Eve's primordial choice did, and those consequences are a necessary part of life. Young Mormons are taught—and most strive—to make wise choices, to rely on faith to help them when they are weak, and to resolve to be better when they have made a poor choice. Mormons acknowledge the essential role of faith in their lives, but because they also have the power to choose, they believe that their choices and actions are incredibly important. In fact, they are often taught this verse from the book of Matthew in the New Testament: "Wherefore by their fruits ye shall know them" (Matthew 7:20). Mormons believe that their actions, combined with their faith, are what make them true followers of Jesus.

Most Mormons acknowledge that their history (one that includes a self-proclaimed prophet, rediscovered Scriptures, and a few decades of polygamy) and their principles (abstaining from coffee, tea, alcohol, and illegal drugs; dressing modestly; abstaining from premarital sex; going on full-time missions) make them a peculiar people in today's world. This was also the case in the nineteenth century when the church was in its infancy. This strange new religion received more than its share of ridicule and persecution, including harshly negative and inaccurate portrayals in newspapers and literature. Many nineteenth-century writers used Mormons in popular fiction as literary devices, archetypal villains, or objects of derision, and regardless of the role Mormon characters played, they served to represent "what a good American was not."[14] Nineteenth-century American humorists Artemus Ward and Mark Twain in their books *Artemus Ward (His Travels) among the Mormons* (1865) and *Roughing It* (1872) used the popular stereotypes of Mormons as vehicles for humor. One example from *Roughing It* serves best to show how they achieved humor at Mormons' expense. Twain had planned, he said, to write an expose of polygamy, but changed his mind after he saw Mormon women in Salt Lake City:

> [My heart] warmed toward these poor, ungainly, and pathetically home- ly creatures, and as I turned to hide the generous moisture in my eyes, I said, "No—the man that marries one of them has done an act of Chris- tian charity which entitles him to the kindly applause of mankind, not their censure—and the man that marries sixty of them has done a deed of openhanded generosity so sublime that the nations should stand un- covered in his presence and worship in silence." [15]

In the fiction of the 1800s, Mormons appeared as villains perhaps more often than as objects of humor. Zane Grey, Jack London, and Robert Louis Stevenson at one time or another used a stereotypical Mormon, usually some sort of deranged and/or violent polygamist, as a negative character. One novel in particular, Arthur Conan Doyle's *A Study in Scarlet* (1887) showed Mormons in such a negative light that it drew criticism from Mormons, of course, but also from other critics who considered Doyle's Mormon characters and their actions unfairly and stereotypically negative.

BOOKS ABOUT MORMONS BY NON-MORMONS

It's not too surprising that this trend continues today. As pointed out in chapter 1, clergy and churches, especially those that are conservative and evangelical, often do not come out well in YA literature. Though Mormons are far better understood and accepted today than they were in the nineteenth century, they are still sometimes harshly stereotyped in contemporary YA books. Most often, Mormon characters are flat, minor characters who serve a small part in the overall plot, and some- times their affiliation with the Mormon church is vague or distant, as in the self-righteous preacher from the Red Brick Church in Chris Crutch- er's *The Sledding Hill* (2005) or in the creepy 'prophet' in Carol Lynch Williams's *The Chosen One* (2009). But sometimes, the nineteenth- century tradition of using negative stereotypes of Mormons as a central plot device emerges in contemporary YA literature. One example is Ellen Hopkins's *Burned* (2006), a novel called "literary group character assassination" by Jewish YA novelist Jeff Gottesfeld who critiqued the book for its harshly negative portrayal of Mormons and the Mormon

fair ≠ positive

church.[16] The novel's protagonist, seventeen-year-old Pattyn Von Stratten, is one of seven children in a Mormon family ruled by a drunken, domineering, abusive, and hypocritical father. In *Burned*, says Gottesfeld, "the reader finds the church unrelentingly bashed."[17] Pattyn's father uses church doctrine to justify his abuse; the bishop of Pattyn's congregation and the members themselves know about but ignore the vicious abuse taking place in Pattyn's home; and, says Gottesfeld, "there is the clear implication that higher-ups must be complicit and that the faith is at the root of all this evil."[18]

But *Burned* is an exception to the norm these days. Mormon characters rarely figure into YA novels, but when they do, they are usually given fair, positive representation. *Jungle Dogs* (1998) has one such example. The main character, sixth grader Boy Regis, has a paper route that requires him to confront his great fear, feral dogs, on a daily basis. Boy's greater challenge, though, is to discover his own identity as he grows up in his small Hawaiian town. His father is strong but distant, his older brother Damon belongs to a gang, and both men appear to be poor role models for Boy. Early in the novel, he meets an unlikely mentor, an old man named Buzzy, whom Boy sees each morning on the beach. Buzzy loves the ocean and his handmade canoe that he takes out into the surf most mornings, and the old man takes Boy under his wing. Later in the novel when Boy is assigned to write a personal essay about someone he most admires, he cannot think of anyone, so he asks Buzzy who his heroes are. Buzzy tells Boy the story of his older brother Mike, who converted to Mormonism when he was in tenth grade. "He's the one I would say was the one I look up to. And you know why? Because he ain't afraid to be himself."[19] Then Buzzy explains that when Mike told their parents he wanted to be baptized into the Mormon church, his father angrily told him he'd have to leave the house if he did. Rather than argue, Mike explained, "Papa, I love this family. You and Mama mean everything to me. But I found something else, too. Something that makes me feel good inside, something that makes me happy. I have to do it, Papa. I was hoping you'd be there."[20] His father and mother refused the invitation to Mike's baptism, so Mike extended the offer to Buzzy who, fearing his father's wrath, declined. Buzzy concluded the story by telling Boy, "So you see, Mike had the guts. Me? I was a coward. Inside, I wanted to see him get baptized, because that's what he wanted. . . . My brother has class, Boy. Class."[21] Buzzy's secondhand account of a Mormon shows Mormons in general to be good people with "class."

Susan Campbell Bartoletti's *The Boy Who Dared: A Novel Based on the True Story of a Hitler Youth* (2008) is the story of Helmuth Hübener, a Mormon teenager in Germany during Hitler's rise to power. In this moving historical novel, Bartoletti shows how Helmuth's Mormon faith sustained him through boyhood and later through his arrest by the Gestapo for spreading anti-Nazi propaganda, and the ensuing brutal interrogation, imprisonment, and execution. She also shows how Helmuth's beliefs led to trouble. For example, Helmuth rejects the enforced acceptance of Nazism, citing the Mormon church's Eleventh Article of Faith about how all people are entitled to worship how, where, or what they want. Later, when seeds of resistance are beginning to sprout in Helmuth, he's conflicted because he "knows he's supposed to honor his country and his leaders. . . . That's what the Mormons' Twelfth Article of Faith tells him."[22] When Brother Worbs, an older man from Helmuth's congregation, tells Helmuth about his time in a concentration camp, Helmuth condemns the Nazis. Rather than accepting Helmuth's reaction, Brother Worbs nobly reminds the boy of the Christian principles their church teaches: "We must pray for those who hate and persecute us. . . . You cannot repay evil with evil. . . . God loves us all. He does not love us more than he loves our enemies."[23] Finally, when Helmuth is contemplating his execution, he does what a good Mormon boy should do: he prays and recalls Scriptural passages as a source of comfort. Throughout the novel, Bartoletti presents Helmuth as a faithful Mormon and a heroic young man.

BOOKS WITH MORMON THEMES BY NON-MORMONS

Many YA books by non-Mormons represent Mormon values even if they don't have Mormon characters. At first glance, Pete Hautman's National Book Award winner, *Godless* (2004), has nothing to do with Mormon values, but the inspiration for the novel comes from Mormon history. On his website, Hautman recalls reading the account of Mormon church founder Joseph Smith, "just another 14-year-old kid who was vaguely dissatisfied with the faith of his fathers when God called young him as his prophet. . . . Reading his story I thought, wow—what an incredible coming-of-age story that is!"[24] Teenager Jason Bock, the novel's protagonist, becomes disenchanted with Catholicism and, as a lark, invents his own religion that worships water towers. The elements of Hautman's story don't align with church history, but some of the experiences Jason has, especially persecution and self-doubt because of his new "religion," are things Mormon readers can relate to. A more recent YA book with Mormon values, R. J. Palacio's surprise best seller, *Wonder* (2012), places its main character, Auggie Pullman in the midst of a warm, unified, loving family, a support system that helps him endure his first entry into the painful real world of middle school. Though religion does not play a role in Auggie's story, his family does, and it reflects the family values so highly prized by Mormons.

A much lauded nonfiction book with Mormon themes is coincidentally about a famous contemporary of Joseph Smith's, a scientist whose radical ideas also drew praise and scorn from all corners. *Charles and Emma: The Darwins' Leap of Faith* (2009) recasts Charles Darwin as a loving, patient family man who rejected the faith of his fathers to pursue his own truth. A devoted father, Darwin was, in many ways, the very ideal of a Mormon father, a man with a large, unified family. Mormon readers will appreciate that, but they will really connect with the Darwins' marriage and hope of eternal togetherness. In a letter to Charles, churchgoing Emma expressed her fears to her agnostic husband: "I would be most unhappy if I thought we did not belong to each other forever."[25] A letter from Emma's Aunt Jessie reflecting on the loss of her own husband expresses a hope similar to Emma's: "If I could but have . . . firm faith that he has only passed from the visible to the invisible world, and already lives and is waiting for me, oh what happiness that would be."[26] Both of these women express doctrine that Mormons believe in: the afterlife and eternal families.

J. K. Rowling's Harry Potter books have been praised and vilified by people of faith, but the series has much that resonates with Mormon readers. As mentioned earlier, most Mormons have no difficulty accepting fantastic stories, so there's little in the Harry Potter books to alienate them; instead, there are Mormon values at the very core of the series. Even though he's a child, Harry has greatness in him, and he's able to make his own choices and learn from the consequences. The boundaries between good and evil are clearly drawn, and the good people in the series generally possess virtues Mormons and other people of faith value: loyalty, self-sacrifice, hard work, education, and the like. But one aspect of the novel represents a precious Mormon principle, the same one Emma Darwin and her aunt shared in their letters: love so powerful that it creates family ties that go beyond the grave. Rowling makes it clear that Harry yearns for his parents and that his parents still care for him from beyond the veil. By the end of the series, it's implied that the precious connection between parents and child will be a lasting one for the Potter family, and that when Harry's time on earth is finished, his parents will be there to greet him in the "great beyond." Mormon theology promises such eternal family connections to those who earnestly seek them, and that broad sense of yearning for family may be one quality that helped the series reach such popularity among Mormon readers.

Marcelo in the Real World (2009) by Francisco Stork is the story of seventeen-year-old Marcelo, a young man of deep faith who is afflicted by what his father calls a "cognitive disorder," a form of Asperger's syndrome. The summer before his final year of high school, Marcelo is forced to enter the real world by working in his father's law office, and there he observes many of the unsavory aspects of the real world: lechery, dishonesty, drunkenness. These encounters send the naïve and literal young man reeling. To survive the summer, and to learn from it, Marcelo relies on prayers, lessons from Scripture and from his Rabbi mentor, and his rock-solid faith in God. In many ways, this novel serves as an archetype for young Mormon readers who leave the sheltered comfort and safety of their homes, sometimes burdened with idealism and naïveté, to enter the real world of high school, college, or career. They have been taught by their families and their church that they must be in the world but not of the world, and their best chances for surviving the real world depend on faith, prayer, and their adherence to the principles of behavior they've been taught.

The Giver (1993), Lois Lowry's Newbery-winning dystopian novel, is perhaps the best example of a YA novel written by a non-Mormon that's based on essential Mormon values, in this case what Mormons call moral agency, the ability to choose. Jonas, the eleven-year-old protagonist, lives in a perfect, safe, and controlled society, and he seems to have an idyllic childhood. That all changes when he turns twelve and attends the formal Ceremony of Twelve where he learns that his designated career is to be the Receiver of Memories. He meets his mentor, a wise old man who would become the Giver of Memories to Jonas. From him, Jonas learns the history of humanity, the joys and pains of human existence; he also learns how his society evolved into the tightly controlled world he grew up in. This new knowledge gives him the ability to see not only color for the first time but also the inherent flaws in his utopian society. His conversations with the Giver help him understand how those in power decided that the only way to keep humanity from destroying itself was to eliminate choice. As he grows in knowledge, Jonas realizes that freedom of choice can be dangerous—but also wonderful:

> "If everything's the same, then there aren't any choices! I want to wake up in the morning and *decide* things! . . ."
> "It's the choosing that's important, isn't it?" The Giver asked him.
> Jonas nods and talks about Gabriel, the newchild his family has taken, wondering if Gabriel could replace Sameness with choice. The Giver replies, "He might make wrong choices."
> "Oh, I see what you mean. It wouldn't matter for a newchild's toy. But later it *does* matter, doesn't it. We don't dare to let people make choices of their own."
> "Not safe?" The Giver suggested.
> "Definitely not safe," Jonas said with certainty. "What if they were allowed to choose their own mate? And chose *wrong*?"
> "Or what if," he went on, almost laughing at the absurdity, "they chose their own *jobs*?"
> "Frightening, isn't it?" The Giver said. [27]

The plot accelerates as Jonas gains more knowledge of history and as his brother, the newchild Gabriel, comes closer to being released, euthanized, because he has not developed according to society's strict standards. Armed with knowledge and a powerful desire to rescue his baby brother from death, Jonas makes a monumental choice that permanently changes his life—and the lives of everyone in his community.

In Mormon theology, the freedom to choose was the basis for the war in heaven that's mentioned in chapter twelve of the book of Revelation in the New Testament. Mormons believe that this war resulted from the necessity of all preexistent spirits to choose a plan for mortality. Satan's plan guaranteed that everyone would return to heaven, but that could only be accomplished if they gave up the freedom of choice. Jesus' plan allowed people the freedom of choice but also the freedom to suffer—and learn from—the consequences resulting from bad choices. To a Mormon reader, *The Giver* wonderfully represents the tension surrounding the argument for free will and the consequences that ensue when moral agency is restricted or prohibited. Yes, the ability to choose can lead to pain and suffering, but it also offers sublime opportunities to learn and grow from experience. In that way, *The Giver* is a powerful parable about a core tenet in the Mormon religion.

BOOKS WITH MORMON THEMES BY MORMONS

Mormons have, of course, also written YA novels that contain Mormon values. Because of its phenomenal success, Stephenie Meyer's *Twilight* and the three novels that followed it have received the most scrutiny from readers and critics. Many articles have been written examining Meyer's Mormonism in the novel, with particular attention paid to Bella's chaste, Mormon-standard love affair with the vampire Edward. This chapter won't add anything new to the discussion of Mormon content in the Twilight series.

The first of Mormon author Brandon Mull's fantasy series, *Fablehaven* (2006), introduces thirteen-year-old Kendra Sorenson and her younger brother, Seth, to their grandparents' curious old home and extensive gardens in Connecticut. The siblings soon discover that the estate is actually a preserve for magical creatures and that their grandparents are the caretakers. In such an environment, Seth has plenty of opportunities for trouble, and he rarely misses an opportunity to get tangled up in something as he and his sister become involved in protecting the preserve—and saving the world in the process. As Card pointed out earlier in this chapter, Mormons believe in the potential of young people, and this novel places Kendra and Seth in a position of importance and power. Despite overwhelming odds, the sister and brother use their wit, courage, and faith in one another and in their family to save the day by the time the book is finished. Other Mormon themes in this story include the importance of family, including extended family, and the power of love to sustain people in trying times.

James Dashner's *The Maze Runner* (2009) launched a popular franchise that included successful film adaptations. This thrilling novel has a fair amount of violence, enough that some readers might be surprised to learn that Dashner is a Mormon. The novel begins when Thomas, its protagonist, climbs out of a freight elevator and into a place known as the Glade that is populated by other teenage boys. None of the boys have any memory of how they got there or of their lives before they arrived at the Glade. The space outside the Glade is a massive maze, haunted by night by terrifying and deadly mechanical creatures the boys call Grievers. Knowing their lives are at risk, the boys struggle desperately to solve the maze and find a way to escape to the outside. Mormon values appear in this novel by showing the negative consequences young people suffer when they live without a family. The boys have neither a father nor a mother to turn to for advice or comfort, and without any family organization, they live chaotic, dangerous lives. When they do collaborate as siblings, they begin to discover solutions to their problems.

Ally Condie wrote a few novels for a Mormon press before her national best seller, *Matched*, was published in 2010. This novel, the first in a trilogy, builds on the popularity of YA dystopian novels that preceded it: *The Giver*, *Hunger Games*, and *The Maze Runner*, but it successfully creates its own spin on a dystopian plot. Condie credits the idea for the novel from a question asked by her husband, a professor of economics at BYU. In a discussion about agency and free will, he wondered, "What if someone wrote the perfect algorithm for lining people up, and the government used it to decide who you married, when you married, etc.?"[28] Condie immediately went to work on the story of Cassia Reyes who, along with every other seventeen-year-old in her Society, learns whom the government has assigned as her perfect Match. The Society controls Matches to guarantee successful marriages and healthy offspring, but it's only one of many aspects of life controlled by the government. Food, art, literature, careers are tightly managed by the Society, and all homes have a port, a two-way TV like something out of *1984*, that allows the government to monitor them. As Cassia gains experience, she begins to recognize the fetters that have shackled her and her family since birth, and that knowledge sows the seeds of rebellion that will lead her to fight for freedom. As in *The Giver*, the Mormon notion of free agency is central to the conflict of this novel: Cassia yearns for real choice, real freedom, and realizes that she cannot be happy without it. As the story moves forward, she also gains a greater appreciation of family, love, and trust—and of the importance of having access to "the best books."

The dominant Mormon theme in Tess Hilmo's delightful debut novel, *With a Name Like Love* (2011), is the importance of family, friends, and trust. Ollie Love is the oldest of itinerant preacher Reverend Everlasting Love's five daughters, and the summer of 1957 finds them in a new, and yet another temporary, location: Binder, Arkansas. The family's strong conservative Christian values resonate with Mormon readers, but when Ollie befriends the local white trash kid, Jimmy Koppel, she learns that not everyone's family is as safe and secure as hers is. Jimmy's mother is in jail, accused of murdering her husband, and although everyone in town is convinced of her guilt, Ollie believes she's innocent. As she tries to get to the bottom of the mystery of Jimmy's father's murder, she and her family become a target of animosity from the sleepy little town that had already resented the presence of her family. As her personal crisis escalates, Ollie learns that she can rely on the love and good nature of her family to carry her through the storm.

A Mormon author might be the last person one would expect to write a novel about a crack-addicted teen prostitute, so Martine Leavitt's heart-wrenching novel in verse, *My Book of Life by Angel* (2012), is a surprising one to be included in a discussion of Mormon values in YA literature. Loosely based on the murders of more than thirty Vancouver prostitutes in the 1990s and early 2000s, the novel opens with sixteen-year-old Angel worrying about the disappearance of a fellow prostitute and benevolent mentor, Serena. The reader then learns Angel's backstory, how she was picked up and sweet-talked by Call, a pimp who gets her addicted to crack cocaine and pressures her into turning tricks in downtown Vancouver to maintain her supply of "candy." Angel's situation seems hopeless, but the loss of her friend motivates her to kick her drug habit and find a way to return home to her family. While enduring the agony of withdrawal and Call's abuse, Angel longs for the life she left behind, but Call refuses to release her, threatening to keep her captive until she returns to work—or dies. She's prepared to die, then, but everything changes when Call brings home eleven-year-old Melli, a new girl he plans to initiate into the business. Angel will do anything she can to save the innocent child from the hell of prostitution and drug abuse, and she eventually sacrifices her life and freedom for Melli's sake.

Leavitt said she wrote *My Book of Life by Angel* in verse because she realized poetry "was a way for me to tell the truth about something without rubbing my nose in the gory details."[29] The lyrical beauty of her verse stands in stark contrast to the darkness of Angel's life. Leavitt found other ways to infuse her Mormon values into this bleak tale. One of Angel's regular customers is an English professor who makes her read to him from Milton's *Paradise Lost*, a poetic text filled with religious and Christian metaphor and allusion, stuff that helps Angel find her voice. The novel also shows the terrible risk teenagers take when they stray from traditional Mormon values by using illegal drugs and by losing the trust—real or perceived—of their family. When Angel finds herself in such a situation, she clings to spirituality to soften the harsh world she inhabits, something a Mormon might be expected to do in a perilous circumstance. According to Leavitt, this plot point comes from Leavitt's own religious values but also from the encounters she had with Vancouver prostitutes while researching the novel: "These women have so little to hang onto that many of them are deeply spiritual."[30] A final Mormon value in this novel is the importance of agency. As in the novels discussed previously, *My Book of Life by Angel* presents the dramatic consequences that come with the loss of free agency—in this case Angel's addition to crack and her enslavement by Call—and in the nobility of love, trust, and honesty.

BOOKS ABOUT MORMONS BY MORMONS

Every year, scores of YA novels about Mormons written by Mormons are published, but their circulation is limited to the robust but relatively closed market dominated by Deseret Book and a handful of other publishers who market books exclusively to Mormon readers. Mormon themes and standards permeate these novels, and church members expect the books to conform to and reinforce standard Mormon values. The success of these books depends on meeting those expectations.

YA novels about Mormons written by Mormons for a national audience are rare, perhaps for the very same reasons that novels about any religious group are so scarce. The remainder of this chapter will review a notable group of these books.

Louise Plummer's *A Dance for Three* (2000) is the story of Hannah Ziebarth, a sweet, naïve Mormon girl who, despite her own weaknesses, provides emotional stability for her depressed, widowed mother. Hannah has never quite recovered from her father's death, and instead of looking to her church and religion for comfort, she turns to Milo, her charismatic, manipulative boyfriend, who takes advantage of her naïveté and her hunger for love. When Hannah discovers she's pregnant, she's thrilled because she believes that this will be her chance to start her own happy, intact family: mother, father, and baby. When she breaks the news to Milo, however, he punches her and calls her a whore, and this sudden and surprising turn around sends Hannah spiraling into a deep and debilitating depression. Her depression is aggravated by her guilt in knowing that she transgressed the Mormon law of chastity. Despite her fears that her Mormon bishop will condemn her for her sin, she reveals her situation to him—and she is surprised and overwhelmed by his reaction. Rather than judging her, he offers understanding, hope, and help. Hannah is ultimately responsible for recovering from her losses, but she could not have done it without the support of her bishop.

Mormons are proud of their American pioneer heritage, and many families have ancestors who crossed the plains in the middle of the nineteenth century to escape religious persecution and to establish their own community in Salt Lake City, Utah. *Charlotte's Rose* (2002) is based on a family story A. E. Cannon heard while growing up in Utah. In the novel, Welsh immigrant, twelve-year-old Charlotte, tells the story of crossing the Atlantic with her widowed father to join other Mormon converts on the trek to Utah. Charlotte's journey is complicated when a mother dies in childbirth leaving an infant that will need to be cared for over the long, difficult journey. Overly confident in her own abilities, Charlotte agrees to carry the baby girl she names Rose, the rest of the way to Utah. The novel is filled with references to Mormon history and doctrine, material entirely familiar to Mormon readers, but new to most others. Cannon doesn't hold back on such details, managing to integrate them into her story without seeming to preach or push. Her novel received praise from *Publisher's Weekly* on that point: "While offering some insight into Mormon doctrine, Cannon also proposes personal motivations for her Welsh characters' embrace of a new religion. Charlotte herself blossoms through her sacrifice, and her maturation will likely endear her to readers."[31]

Another YA novel dealing with Mormon history is Kimberley Heuston's *The Shakeress* (2002). Set a couple decades earlier than *Charlotte's Rose*, this novel tells the story of Naomi Hull, a young woman who, at the age of twelve, became responsible for her family. After a house fire kills Naomi's parents and her infant brother, Naomi and her three surviving siblings are taken in by an aunt and uncle who don't welcome the additional mouths to feed. When Naomi learns of her aunt's plans to put her out to work in a local mill, she and her siblings escape to a nearby Shaker community. Naomi's faith and skills as a healer thrive with the Shakers, but as the years pass, she feels that something's missing in her life. She comes to believe that the love of Joseph Fairbanks may be the answer, but an encounter with missionaries from the newly formed Mormon church changes her outlook on life and religion.

Heuston shows Naomi dealing with her spiritual struggle through dedicated faith and prayer. Ultimately, God doesn't provide an easy answer for Naomi, but the new path she decides to take leads her to a spiritual peace and joy that she hadn't previously known. Such a blatant faith-story didn't faze reviewers. The *New York Times* praised the novel and its courageous heroine: "As an independent, self-reliant teenage girl, Naomi provides a model for any quickly maturing questioner, even those who don't share her questions. Her quest is recognizable and welcoming. Tolerance for God-related musing and God-inspired ending are, however, necessary equipment for this journey."[32] Another reviewer cited Naomi's faith-story as key to the novel's success: "What is noteworthy about this story is the intensity with which it treats spiritual questions; the place of prayer; the path to faith; the meaning and mystery of the divine."[33] Few mainstream novels have ever taken on Mormonism in such a head-on, honest, and accurate fashion.

Kristen D. Randle's contemporary realistic novel, *Slumming* (2003), deals with Mormonism much more subtly. Narrated in turn by three high school seniors, good friends and fellow Mormons Nikki, Sam, and Alicia, the novel opens with the three friends agreeing to take on a sort of *Pygmalion* project: to reach out, befriend, and uplift a marginalized classmate. Nikki chooses a brainy nerd; Sam selects the mysterious Goth girl; Alicia targets the school's most dangerous bad boy, but this good-hearted project results in serious consequences for all three teens that none of them could have imagined. Mormonism is not central to the story, but Randle doesn't hide the fact that all three characters adhere to Mormon standards or that, in times of crisis, they turn to family or prayer for answers just as all Mormon teenagers are encouraged to do. Early in the novel, Sam professes his faith. "This has to be very clear: I believe in God. This is true. It is my honest belief. And I believe that Christ is more than just a religious story; I believe he was a real person who walked the earth two thousand years ago, and that somehow, after they crucified him, he came alive again, and by doing that, changed everything."[34] Much later in the novel, after Sam knows he must report the horrifying abuse his "project" has been enduring at the hands of her father, the decision overwhelms him. Through prayer, he finds strength to do the right thing: "I spent the whole night praying about it. I know I have to do this. I know it's right. But my hands are still shaking."[35] Throughout the novel, Randle presents Sam and his two friends as most Mormons like to think of themselves: basically good, but decidedly human, people striving to live good Christian lives, people who believe that faith matters, that God is real, that prayer works.

Emily Wing Smith's debut novel, *The Way He Lived* (2008), also relies on multiple narrators, but this novel is much more directly about Mormons and Mormon culture. The narrators all live in Haven, a quiet, predominantly Mormon community in Utah. The community values are common, obvious, and Mormon. The narrators allude to Mormon standards and culture throughout the novel, especially as they question why their friend Joel may have given away his water and died of exposure on a poorly planned Boy Scout campout. It's whispered that Joel may have been gay and that his guilt or the pressure to conform to Mormon standards may have led to his suicide. Joel's death causes each of the six narrators to begin to see their world differently, to recognize hypocrisy and judgment, and to question their faith and religion. Each character copes in a different manner, but each ultimately comes to terms with Joel's death in his own way, a way that reaffirms their faith in Mormonism. That kind of optimistic, faith-promoting conclusion reflects Mormons' inherent faith in young people and confidence that, even in dire circumstances, things work out.

NOTES

1. Paulson, Michael. "Faith and Good Works: Mormon Writers Find Their Niche in Wholesome Young Adult Genre." *Boston Globe*, March 1, 2009. Online.
2. Mark Oppenheimer, "Mormons Offer Cautionary Lesson on Sunny Outlook vs. Literary Greatness." *New York Times*, November 8, 2103. Online.
3. "U.S. Religious Landscape Survey." *Pew Research*. n.d. Web. Accessed November 3, 2014.
4. Jesse S. Crisler and Chris Crowe, eds. *"How I Came to Write": LDS Authors for Young Adults* (Provo, UT: Center for the Study of Christian Values in Literature, 2007), 43–44.
5. "The Family: A Proclamation to the World." The Church of Jesus Christ of Latter-day Saints. n.d. Web. Accessed November 3, 2014.
6. "The Articles of Faith." *LDS Scriptures*. The Church of Jesus Christ of Latter-day Saints. n.d. Web. Accessed November 3, 2014.
7. Paulson, "Faith and Good Works."
8. "Doctrine and Covenants, Section 88, verse 118." *LDS Scriptures*. The Church of Jesus Christ of Latter-day Saints. n.d. Web. Accessed November 3, 2014.
9. "Entertainment and Media." *For the Strength of Youth*. The Church of Jesus Christ of Latter-day Saints. n.d. Web. Accessed November 3, 2014.
10. Paulson, "Faith and Good Works."
11. Oppenheimer, "Mormons Offer Cautionary Lesson."
12. Oppenheimer, "Mormons Offer Cautionary Lesson."
13. Paulson, "Faith and Good Works."
14. Richard H. Cracroft, "Distorting Polygamy for Fun and Profit: Artemus Ward and Mark Twain among the Mormons." *BYU Studies* 14, no. 2 (1974): 272.
15. Mark Twain, *Roughing It* (New York: HarperBrothers, 1959), 101.
16. Jeff Gottesfeld, "My View: LDS Faith Unfairly 'Burned' in Novel." *Deseret News*, May 16, 2006. Online.
17. Gottesfeld, "My View: LDS Faith Unfairly 'Burned' in Novel."
18. Gottesfeld, "My View: LDS Faith Unfairly 'Burned' in Novel."
19. Graham Salisbury, *Jungle Dogs* (New York: Delacorte, 1998), 147.
20. Salisbury, *Jungle Dogs*, 148–49.

21. Salisbury, *Jungle Dogs*, 149–50.
22. Susan Campbell Bartoletti, *The Boy Who Dared: A Novel Based on the True Story of a Hitler Youth* (New York: Scholastic, 2008), 35.
23. Bartoletti, *The Boy Who Dared*, 134.
24. Pete Hautman, "A Few Thoughts about *Godless*, in No Particular Order . . ." Pete Hautman, n.d. Web. November 14, 2014.
25. Deborah Heiligman, *Charles and Emma: The Darwins' Leap of Faith*. (New York: Holt, 2009), 100.
26. Heiligman, *Charles and Emma*, 115.
27. Lois Lowry, *The Giver* (New York: Dell, 1994), 97–98.
28. Ally Condie, "What Is Your Inspiration for Writing *Matched*?" Ally Condie, July 7, 2012. Web. Accessed November 14, 2014.
29. Rick Margolis, "Touched by an Angel: Martine Leavitt's 'My Book of Life by Angel' Is a Harrowing Tale of Redemption." *School Library Journal* 58, no. 1 (October 2012): 22.
30. Margolis, "Touched by an Angel," 22.
31. Review of *Charlotte's Rose*, by A. E. Cannon. *Publisher's Weekly*. Online.
32. Simon Rodberg, "Children's Books; Answered Prayers." *New York Times*, May 19, 2002. Web.
33. Review of *The Shakeress. Kirkus Reviews*. April 1, 2002. Web.
34. Kristen D. Randle, *Slumming* (New York: HarperTeen, 2003), 21.
35. Randle, *Slumming*, 163.

BIBLIOGRAPHY

"The Articles of Faith." *LDS Scriptures*. The Church of Jesus Christ of Latter-day Saints. n.d. Web. Accessed November 3, 2014.

Bartoletti, Susan Campbell. *The Boy Who Dared: A Novel Based on the True Story of a Hitler Youth*. New York: Scholastic, 2008.

Cracroft, Richard H. "Distorting Polygamy for Fun and Profit: Artemus Ward and Mark Twain among the Mormons." *BYU Studies* 14, no. 2 (1974): 272–88.

Crisler, Jesse S., and Chris Crowe, eds. *"How I Came to Write": LDS Authors for Young Adults*. Provo, UT: Center for the Study of Christian Values in Literature, 2007.

"Doctrine and Covenants." *LDS Scriptures*. The Church of Jesus Christ of Latter-day Saints. n.d. Web. Accessed November 3, 2014.

"Entertainment and Media." *For the Strength of Youth*. The Church of Jesus Christ of Latter-day Saints. n.d. Web. Accessed November 3, 2014.

"The Family: A Proclamation to the World." The Church of Jesus Christ of Latter-day Saints. n.d. Web. Accessed November 3, 2014.

Gottesfeld, Jeff. "My View: LDS Faith Unfairly 'Burned' in Novel." *Deseret News*, May 16, 2006. Online.

Heiligman, Deborah. *Charles and Emma: The Darwins' Leap of Faith*. New York: Holt, 2009.

Hautman, Pete. "A Few Thoughts about *Godless*, in No Particular Order . . ." Pete Hautman, n.d. Web. Accessed November 14, 2014.

Lowry, Lois. *The Giver*. New York: Dell, 1994.

Margolis, Rick. "Touched by an Angel: Martine Leavitt's 'My Book of Life by Angel' Is a Harrowing Tale of Redemption." *School Library Journal* 58, no. 1 (October 2012): 22.

Oppenheimer, Mark. "Mormons Offer Cautionary Lesson on Sunny Outlook vs. Literary Greatness." *New York Times*, November 8, 2013. Online.

Paulson, Michael. "Faith and Good Works: Mormon Writers Find Their Niche in Wholesome Young Adult Genre." *Boston Globe*, March 1, 2009. Online.

Randle, Kristen D. *Slumming*. New York: HarperTeen, 2003.

Review of *Charlotte's Rose*, by A. E. Cannon. *Publisher's Weekly*. Online.

Review of *The Shakeress*. *Kirkus Reviews*, April 1, 2002. Web.

Rodberg, Simon. "Children's Books; Answered Prayers." *New York Times*, May 19, 2002. Web.

Salisbury, Graham. *Jungle Dogs*. New York: Delacorte, 1998.

Twain, Mark. *Roughing It*. New York: HarperBrothers, 1959.

"U.S. Religious Landscape Survey." *Pew Research*. n.d. Web. Accessed November 3, 2014.

TITLES MENTIONED IN THIS CHAPTER

Bartoletti, Susan Campbell. *The Boy Who Dared: A Novel Based on the True Story of a Hitler Youth*. New York: Scholastic, 2008.

Cannon, A. E. *Charlotte's Rose*. New York: Delacorte, 2002.

Card, Orson Scott. *Ender's Game*. New York: Tor, 1985.

Condie, Ally. *Matched*. New York: Dutton, 2010.

Crutcher, Chris. *The Sledding Hill*. New York: Greenwillow, 2005.

Dashner, James. *The Maze Runner*. New York; Delacorte, 2009.

Gipson, Fred. *Old Yeller*. New York: Harper, 1956.

Hale, Shannon. *Princess Academy*. New York: Bloomsbury, 2005.

Hautman, Pete. *Godless*. New York: Simon & Schuster, 2004.

Heiligman, Deborah. *Charles and Emma: The Darwins' Leap of Faith*. New York: Holt, 2009.

Heuston, Kimberley. *The Shakeress*. Ashville, NC: Front Street, 2002.

Hilmo, Tess. *With a Name Like Love*. New York: Farrar, Strauss and Giroux, 2011.

Hopkins, Ellen. *Burned*. New York: Margaret K. McElderry, 2007.

Knudson, R. R. *Zanballer*. New York: Delacorte, 1972.

Leavitt, Martine. *My Book of Life by Angel*. New York: Farrar, Strauss and Giroux, 2012.

Lowry, Lois. *The Giver*. New York: Dell, 1994.

Meyer, Stephenie. *Twilight*. New York: Little, Brown, 2005.

Mull, Brandon. *Fablehaven*. Salt Lake City: Shadow Mountain, 2006.

Palacio, R. J. *Wonder*. New York: Knopf, 2012.

Plummer, Louise. *A Dance for Three*. New York: Delacorte, 2000.

Randle, Kristen D. *Slumming*. New York: HarperTeen, 2003.

Salisbury, Graham. *Jungle Dogs*. New York: Delacorte, 1998.

Sorenson, Virginia. *Miracles on Maple Hill*. New York: Harcourt, 1956.

Sparks, Beatrice. *Go Ask Alice*. New York: Prentice Hall, 1971.

Smith, Emily Wing. *The Way He Lived*. Woodbury, MN: Flux, 2008.

Stork, Francisco X. *Marcelo in the Real World*. New York: Scholastic, 2009.

Williams, Carol Lynch. *The Chosen One*. New York: St. Martin's, 2009.

Afterword

And so we come back to the eternal YA question: Who am I, and what am I going to do about it? This book has tried to show that the corollary—Is anybody in charge around here?—follows from the first two. Finding an identity is only the beginning point for finding God. But regarding the self as the ultimate authority is the dominion of childhood, precluding growth toward maturity. So let us welcome a truth that is characteristic of all YA fiction: to end a story with the protagonist settling for a closed set of spiritual beliefs is a betrayal of the covenant between author and young reader. To be faithful to that covenant, which requires hopefulness, the book must end with the young person still growing, albeit with new energy and direction, still seeking answers for the Godsearch.

Appendix

Godsearch: Issues of Faith in YA Fiction

SECULAR YA FICTION WITH SPIRITUAL THEMES, CHARACTERS, OR QUESTIONS, 1967–2015

For a number of years I have kept this ongoing list, and from the tens of thousands of novels and short story collections published for teens during the forty-eight years of the genre's history (and the forty-five years of my own history with it), I have been able to discover only these few hundred titles that qualify for this bibliography—and a number of these are included because of just one scene or one character. Notice that there is a second section of this bibliography that lists books with negative portrayals of church and clergy.

NOVELS

Abdel-Fartha, Randa. *Does My Head Look Big in This?* New York: Scholastic, 2007.
Almond, David. *The Fire-Eaters*. New York: Delacorte, 2003.
———. *Skellig*. New York: Delacorte, 1999.
———. *The True Tale of the Monster Billy Dean Telt by Hisself.* Somerville, MA: Candlewick, 2014.
Amateau, Gigi. *Claiming Georgia Tate*. Somerville, MA: Candlewick, 2005.
Arnold, Elana K. *Sacred*. New York: Random House, 2012.
———. *Splendor*. New York: Random House, 2013.
Asher, Jay. *Thirteen Reasons Why*. New York: Penguin, 2007.
Bardi, Abby. *The Book of Fred*. New York: Simon & Schuster, 2001.

Bartoletti, Susan Campbell. *The Boy Who Dared: A Novel Based on the True Story of a Hitler Youth.* New York: Scholastic, 2008.

Betts, A. J. *Zac and Mia.* New York: Houghton Mifflin, 2014.

Blume, Judy. *Are You There, God? It's Me, Margaret.* Seattle, WA: Bradbury, 1970.

Bradley, Kimberly Brubaker. *Leap of Faith.* New York: Dial, 2007.

Brooks, Bruce. *Asylum for Nightface.* New York: HarperCollins, 1996.

Brown, Devin. *Not Exactly Normal.* Grand Rapids, MI: Eerdman's, 2006.

Budhos, Marina Tamar. *Ask Me No Questions.* New York: Atheneum, 2006.

Cannon, A. E. *Charlotte's Rose.* New York: Delacorte, 2002.

Carson, Rae. *The Crown of Embers.* New York: Greenwillow, 2012.

———. *The Girl of Fire and Thorns.* New York: Greenwillow, 2011.

Chajil, Eishes, and Judy Brown. *Hush.* New York: Walker, 2010.

Chambers, Aidan. *NIK: Now I Know.* New York: HarperCollins, 1987.

Clinton, Cathryn. *The Calling.* Somerville, MA: Candlewick, 2001.

Connelly, Neil O. *St. Michael's Scales.* New York: Scholastic, 2002.

Cooney, Caroline B. *A Friend at Midnight.* New York: Delacorte, 2006.

———. *The Ransom of Mercy Carter.* New York: Delacorte, 2001.

———. *What Child Is This?* New York, Delacorte, 1997.

Cormier, Robert. *Heroes.* New York: Delacorte, 1998.

———. *Other Bells for Us to Ring.* New York: Delacorte, 1990.

Cross, Gillian. *Where I Belong.* New York: Holiday House, 2011.

Crumb, Robert. *The Book of Genesis.* New York: W. W. Norton, 2009.

Crutcher, Chris. *Deadline.* New York: Greenwillow, 2007.

———. *The Sledding Hill.* New York: Greenwillow, 2005.

Downham, Jenny. *Before I Die.* New York: Random House, 2007.

Epstine, Robin. *God Is in the Pancakes.* New York: Dial, 2010.

Erskine, Kathryn. *Quaking.* New York: Penguin, 2007.

Fama, Elizabeth. *Overboard.* Chicago: Cricket, 2002.

Fletcher, Susan. *Alphabet of Dreams.* New York: Simon & Schuster, 2006.

Freedman, Paula J. *My Basmati Bat Mitzvah.* New York: Abrams, 2013.

Galloway, Gregory. *The 39 Deaths of Adam Strand.* New York: Dutton, 2013.

Going, K. L. *Saint Iggy.* New York: Harcourt, 2006.

Green, John. *The Fault in Our Stars.* New York: Dutton, 2012.

———. *Looking for Alaska.* New York: Penguin, 2005.

Grimes, Nikki. *Dark Sons.* New York: Hyperion, 2005.

Hartnett, Sonya. *Surrender.* Cambridge, MA: Candlewick, 2005.

Hautman, Pete. *Eden West.* Somerville, MA: Candlewick, 2015.

———. *Godless.* New York: Simon & Schuster, 2004.

———. *Invisible.* New York: Simon & Schuster, 2005.

Hayes, Rosemary. *Mixing It.* London: Frances Lincoln, 2007.

Heiligman, Deborah. *Intentions.* New York: Knopf, 2012.

Heuston, Kimberley. *The Shakeress.* Brooklyn: Handprint Books, 2002.

Heynen, Jim. *Cosmos Coyote and William the Nice.* New York: Henry Holt, 2000.

Hickman, Janet. *Susannah.* New York: Greenwillow, 1998.

Hilmo, Tess. *With a Name Like Love.* New York: Farrar, Straus and Giroux, 2011.

Jenkins, A. M. *Repossessed.* New York: HarperTeen, 2007.

Johnson, Varian. *Saving Maddie.* New York: Delacorte, 2010.

Jolin, Paula. *In the Name of God.* New York: Macmillan, 2007.

Karim, Sheba. *Skunk Girl.* New York: Farrar, Straus and Giroux, 2009.

Koertge, Ron. *Coaltown Jesus.* Somerville, MA: Candlewick, 2013.

Koja, Kathe. *Buddha Boy.* New York: St. Martin's, 2003.

Krisher, Trudy. *Fallout.* New York: Holiday House, 2006.

Laird, Elizabeth. *A Little Piece of Ground.* Chicago: Haymarket Books, 2006.

LaMarche, Una. *Like No Other*. New York: Penguin, 2014.
L'Engle, Madeleine. *A Ring of Endless Light*. (1980). New York: Macmillan, 2008.
Lester, Julius. *Pharaoh's Daughter*. New York: Harcourt, 2000.
Levithan, David. *Wide Awake*. New York: Knopf, 2006.
Levitin, Sonia. *Annie's Promise*. New York: Atheneum, 1993.
———. *The Cure*. New York: Silver Whistle/Harcourt, 1999.
———. *Escape from Egypt*. New York: Little, Brown, 1994.
———. *Silver Days*. New York: Atheneum, 1989.
———. *The Singing Mountain*. New York: Simon & Schuster, 1998.
———. *Strange Relations*. New York: Knopf, 2007.
Linko, Gina. *Indigo*. New York: Random House, 2013.
Littman, Sarah Darer. *Confessions of a Closet Catholic*. New York: Puffin, 2006.
Lucier, Makiia. *A Death-Struck Year*. New York: Houghton Mifflin, 2014.
Martel, Yann. *Life of Pi*. New York: Houghton Mifflin, 2002.
McCaughrean, Geraldine. *Not the End of the World*. New York: HarperTeen, 2005.
———. *The White Darkness*. New York: Harper Tempest, 2007.
McVoy, Terra. *Pure*. New York: Simon & Schuster, 2009.
Meminger, Neesah. *Shine, Coconut Moon*. New York: Simon & Schuster, 2009.
Miklowitz, Gloria D. *Masada: The Last Fortress*. Grand Rapids, MI: Eerdmans, 1998.
———. *Secrets in the House of Delgado*. Grand Rapids, MI: Eerdmans, 2001.
Moore, Christopher. *Lamb: The Gospel According to Biff, Christ's Childhood Pal*. New York: HarperCollins, 2002.
Morpugo, Michael. *The War of Jenkins' Ear*. New York: Philomel, 1996.
Napoli, Donna Jo. *Song of the Magdalene*. New York: Scholastic, 1996.
———. *Storm*. New York: Simon & Schuster, 2014.
Nelson, R. A. *Days of Little Texas*. New York: Knopf, 2009.
Ness, Patrick. *A Monster Calls*. Somerville, MA: Candlewick, 2011.
Nolan, Han. *Send Me Down a Miracle*. New York, Harcourt, 1996.
———. *When We Were Saints*. New York: Harcourt, 2003.
Ostlere, Cathy. *Karma*. New York: Penguin, 2011.
Parry, Roseanne. *Heart of a Shepherd*. New York: Random, 2010.
Paterson, Katherine. *Jacob Have I Loved*. New York: HarperTeen, 1980.
Paulsen, Gary. *The Tent*. New York: Harcourt, 1995.
Pinkwater, Daniel. *The Neddiad: How Neddie Took the Train, Went to Hollywood, and Saved Civilization*. New York: Houghton Mifflin, 2007.
Plummer, Louise. *A Dance for Three*. New York: Delacorte, 2000.
Potok, Chaim. *The Chosen*. New York: Simon & Schuster, 1967.
———. *The Promise*. New York: Simon & Schuster, 1969.
Pratchett, Terry. *Dodger*. New York: Harper, 2013.
Provoost, Anne. *In the Shadow of the Ark*, trans. John Nieuwenhuizen. New York: Scholastic, 2004.
Quarles, Heather. *A Door Near Here*. New York: Delacorte, 1998.
Quick, Matthew. *Sorta Like a Rock Star*. New York: Little, Brown, 2010.
Randle, Kirsten D. *Slumming*. New York: HarperTeen, 2003.
Reinhardt, Dana. *A Brief Chapter in My Impossible Life*. New York: Random House, 2006.
Reisz, Kristopher. *The Drowned Forest*. Woodbury, MN: Flux/Llewellyn, 2014.
Robert, Naima B. *Boy vs. Girl*. London: Frances Lincoln, 2011.
———. *From Somalia with Love*. London: Frances Lincoln, 2009.
Rosoff, Meg. *There Is No Dog*. New York: Putnam, 2012.
Roth, Matthue. *Never Mind the Goldbergs*. New York: Scholastic/Push, 2005.
Rowling, J. K. *Harry Potter and the Deathly Hallows*. New York: Scholastic, 2007.
Sanchez, Alex. *The God Box*. New York: Simon & Schuster, 2007.

Sandell, Lisa Ann. *The Weight of the Sky*. New York: Viking, 2006
Sharif, Medeia. *Bestest. Ramadan. Ever*. Woodbury, MN: Flux/Llewelyn, 2011.
Sheinkin, Steve. *The Adventures of Rabbi Harvey: A Graphic Novel of Jewish Wisdom and Wit in the Wild West*. Woodstock, VT: Jewish Lights, 2006.
Smith, Emily Wing. *The Way He Lived*. Woodbury, MN: Flux, 2008.
Smith-Ready, Jeri. *This Side of Salvation*. New York: Simon Pulse, 2014.
Spiegelman, Art. *Maus I: A Survivor's Tale: My Father Bleeds History*. New York: Pantheon, 1986.
———. *Maus II: A Survivor's Tale: And Here My Troubles Began*. New York: Pantheon, 1992.
Staples, Suzanne Fisher. *Haveli*. New York: Knopf, 1993.
———. *The House of Djinn*. New York: Farrar, 2008
———. *Shabanu: Daughter of the Wind*. New York: Random House, 1991.
———. *Shiva's Fire*. New York: HarperCollins, 2001.
———. *Under the Persimmon Tree*. New York: Farrar, Straus and Giroux, 2005.
Stork, Francisco X. *Irises*. New York: Scholastic, 2012.
———. *Marcelo in the Real World*. New York: Scholastic, 2009.
Taylor, G. P. *Shadowmancer*. New York: Putnam, 2004.
Venkatraman, Padma. *Climbing the Stairs*. Penguin, 2008.
———. *A Time to Dance*. New York: Penguin, 2014.
Weaver, Will. *Full Service*. New York: Farrar, Straus and Giroux, 2005.
Whaley, John Corey. *Where Things Come Back*. New York: Atheneum, 2011.
Whitcomb, Laurie. *The Fetch*. New York: Houghton Mifflin, 2009.
Whitesel, Cheryl. *Rebel: A Tibetan Odyssey*. New York: HarperCollins, 2000.
Williams, Carol Lynch. *The Chosen One*. New York: St. Martin's, 2009.
Wolff, Virginia Euwer. *This Full House*. New York: HarperTeen, 2009.
Yolen, Jane. *The Gift of Sarah Barker*. New York: Viking, 1981.
Zarr, Sara. *Once Was Lost*. New York: Little, Brown, 2009.
Zusak, Markus. *The Book Thief*. New York: Knopf, 2006.

NOVELS WITH NEGATIVE PORTRAYALS OF GOD, CLERGY, OR CHURCH

(but not necessarily unspiritual themes)
Note: Some titles may appear in both this and the previous list.

Agell, Charlotte. *Shift*. New York: Henry Holt, 2008.
Aidinoff, Elsie. *The Garden*. New York: HarperCollins, 2004.
Barkley, Brad, and Heather Hepler. *Scrambled Eggs at Midnight*. New York: Dutton, 2006.
Beale, Fleur. *I Am Not Esther*. New York: Hyperion, 2002.
Bennett, James. *Faith Wish*. New York: Holiday House, 2003.
Bliss, Bryan. *No Parking at the Ends Times*. New York, Greenwillow, 2015.
Brande, Robin. *Evolution, Me and Other Freaks of Nature*. New York: Knopf, 2007
Brooks, Bruce. *Asylum for Nightface*. New York: HarperCollins, 2001.
Chibbaro, Julie. *Redemption*. New York: Atheneum, 2005.
Connelly, Neil. *The Miracle Stealer*. New York: Scholastic, 2012.
Cormier, Robert. *The Chocolate War*. New York: Pantheon, 1974.
Coy, John. *Box Out*. New York: Scholastic, 2008.
Coyle, Katie. *Vivian Apple at the End of the World*. New York: Houghton Mifflin, 2015.

Crew, Linda. *Brides of Eden: A True Story Imagined*. New York: HarperCollins, 2001.
Crutcher, Chris. *The Sledding Hill*. New York: Greenwillow, 2005.
Danforth, Emily M. *The Miseducation of Cameron Post*. New York: Baker and Bray, 2012.
Downham, Jenny. *Before I Die*. New York: Random House, 2007.
Freitas, Donna. *This Gorgeous Game*. New York: Farrar, Straus and Giroux, 2010.
Greene, Bette. *The Drowning of Stephan Jones*. New York: Delacorte, 1991.
Hartzler, Aaron. *Rapture Practice*. New York: Little, Brown, 2013.
Heiligman, Deborah. *Intentions*. New York: Knopf, 2012.
Hemphill, Helen. *Long Gone Daddy*. Honesdale, PA: Boyds Mills, 2006, 2014.
Heynen, Jim. *Cosmos Coyote and William the Nice*. New York: Henry Holt, 2000.
Hrdlitschka, Shelley. *Sister Wife*. Custer, WA: Orca, 2008.
Jacobson, Jennifer Richard. *Stained*. New York: Atheneum, 2005.
Jaden, Denise. *Losing Faith*. New York: Simon Pulse, 2010.
Johnson, LouAnne. *Muchacho*. New York: Knopf, 2009.
Jolin, Paula. *In the Name of God*. New York: Macmillan, 2007.
Kerney, Kelly. *Born Again*. New York: Houghton Mifflin Harcourt, 2006.
Lasky, Kathryn. *Memoirs of a Bookbat*. New York: Harcourt, 1994.
Levithan, David. *Wide Awake*. New York: Knopf, 2006.
Lurie, April. *The Less-Dead*. New York: Delacorte, 2010.
Lynch, Chris. *Sins of the Fathers*. New York: HarperTempest, 2006.
Nolan, Han. *Send Me Down a Miracle*. New York: Harcourt, 1996.
Paulsen, Gary. *The Tent*. New York: Harcourt, 1995.
Pullman, Philip. *The Amber Spyglass* (His Dark Materials, Book III). New York: Knopf, 2000.
Reynolds, Sheri. *The Rapture of Canaan*. New York: Putnam, 1996.
Rylant, Cynthia. *A Fine White Dust*. Seattle, WA: Bradbury, 1986.
———. *The Heavenly Village*. New York: Scholastic, 1999.
Sanchez, Alex. *The God Box*. New York: Simon & Schuster, 2007.
Smith-Ready, Jeri. *This Side of Salvation*. New York: Simon Pulse, 2014.
Waite, Judy. *Forbidden*. New York: Atheneum, 2006.
Walker, Melissa. *Small Town Sinners*. New York: Bloomsbury, 2011.
Weinheimer, Beckie. *Converting Kate*. New York: Viking, 2007.
Williams, Carol Lynch. *The Chosen One*. New York: St. Martin's, 2009.
Wittlinger, Ellen. *Blind Faith*. New York: Simon Pulse, 2007.
Yolen, Jane, and Bruce Coville. *Armageddon Summer*. New York: Harcourt, 1999.
Zarr, Sara. *Once Was Lost*. New York: Little, Brown, 2009.

SHORT STORIES

Asher, Sandy, ed. *With All My Heart, With All My Mind: Thirteen Stories about Growing Up Jewish*. New York: Simon & Schuster, 1999.
Cart, Michael. "Starry, Starry Night." In *Tomorrowland: Stories of the Future*. New York: Scholastic, 1999.
Faustino, Lisa Rowe, ed. *Soul Searching: Thirteen Stories about Faith and Belief*. New York: Simon & Schuster, 2002.
Giblin, James Cross. "Night of the Plague." In *Tomorrowland: Stories of the Future*. New York: Scholastic, 1999.
Lanagan, Margo. "Under Hell, Over Heaven." In *Red Spikes*. New York: Knopf, 2007
———. "Ferryman." In *Yellowcake*. New York: Knopf, 2013.
———. "Into the Clouds on High." In *Yellowcake*. New York: Knopf, 2013.

Noyes, Deborah, ed. *The Restless Dead: Ten Original Stories of the Supernatural.* Somerville, MA: Candlewick, 2007.

Ritter, John H. "Baseball in Iraq." In *Dreams and Visions: Fourteen Flights of Fantasy,* ed. M. Jerry Weiss and Helen S. Weiss. New York: Starscape/Tom Dougherty Associates, 2006.

Singer, Marilyn, ed. *I Believe in Water: Twelve Brushes with Religion.* New York: HarperCollins, 2000.

POETRY

Nye, Naomi Shihab. *19 Varieties of Gazelle: Poems of the Middle East.* New York: Greenwillow, 2002.

Vecchione, Patrice, ed. *Faith and Doubt: An Anthology of Poems.* New York: Henry Holt, 2007.

Index

About the Authors

Patty Campbell is an active Christian and a member of the Episcopal Church. She has been a librarian, critic, author, teacher, speaker, and literary agent in the field of YA literature for forty-five years. During the formative time of the genre, she was the Assistant Coordinator of Young Adult Services for the Los Angeles Public Library system. Her critical writing has appeared in the *New York Times Book Review* and in many other professional and literary journals. From 1993 to 2007 she wrote "The Sand in the Oyster," a sometimes serious column on controversial issues in YA lit, for the *Horn Book Magazine*. She is also the series editor of Studies in Young Adult Literature, published by Rowman & Littlefield.

Campbell is the author of nine books, the most recent being *Robert Cormier: Daring to Disturb the Universe* (2006), *War Is . . . Soldiers, Survivors, and Storytellers Talk about War* (2008), and *Campbell's Scoop: Reflections on Young Adult Literature* (Scarecrow, 2010). She has served on the board of directors of both the Young Adult Library Services Association of the American Library Association and the Assembly on Adolescent Literature of the National Council of Teachers of English (NCTE). In 2005 she was the president of the latter organization. She has also been a member or chair of many committees and task forces for these associations. In 1989 she received ALA's Grolier Award for distinguished service to young adults and books; in 2001 NCTE chose her the winner of their ALAN Award, and in 2010 she was the recipient of Greenwood's Young Adult Achievement Award.

Campbell lives on an avocado ranch in Fallbrook, California, with her husband, David Shore; a lovable Labrador retriever; and a headstrong black cat.

Chris Crowe is an active member of the Church of Jesus Christ of Latter-day Saints. He has been a teacher and a writer for more than thirty years. After earning a bachelor's in English from Brigham Young University, he taught English at his high school alma mater for ten years while simultaneously attending graduate school at Arizona State University. Shortly after receiving his doctorate in English education, he accepted a teaching position at Himeji Dokkyo University in Japan. From there he moved to BYU–Hawaii for four years, and then to BYU in Utah, where he has been a professor in the English department since 1993.

Crowe is the author of fiction and nonfiction for YAs and of professional articles and books about YA literature. His YA books include *Mississippi Trial, 1955*; *Getting Away with Murder: The True Story of the Emmett Till Case*; *Up Close: Thurgood Marshall*; and most recently, *Death Coming Up the Hill*. His professional books include *Presenting Mildred D. Taylor*; *Teaching the Selected Works of Mildred D. Taylor*; and *More Than a Game: Sports Literature for Young Adults*. In addition to his books, he has published a handful of poems, eleven short stories, thirteen chapters in academic books, more than eighty academic articles, and sixty magazine articles. He served as president of ALAN in 2001–2002 and received the Ted Hipple Service Award from ALAN in 2010. Crowe, a father of four and grandfather of six, lives in Provo, Utah, with his wife, Elizabeth.

CPSIA information can be obtained at www.ICGtesting.com
Printed in the USA
BVOW04*1732150615

404329BV00001B/1/P